THE SPACESHIP NEXT DOOR

ALSO BY GENE DOUCETTE

The Frequency of Aliens

Unfiction

Fixer

Immortal

Hellenic Immortal

Immortal at the Edge of the World

Immortal and the Island of Impossible Things

Eve

Immortal at Sea (volume 1)

Hard-Boiled Immortal (volume 2)

Immortal and the Madman (volume 3)

Yuletide Immortal (volume 4)

Regency Immortal (volume 5)

For information about permission to reproduce selections from this book,
write to trade.permissions@hmhco.com or to Permissions,
Houghton Mifflin Harcourt Publishing Company, 3 Park Avenue,
19th Floor, New York, New York 10016.

hmhco.com

Library of Congress Cataloging-in-Publication Data
Names: Doucette, Gene, 1968- author.
Title: The spaceship next door / Gene Doucette.
Description: Boston ; New York : Mariner Books, 2018. |
"A John Joseph Adams Book." | Summary: Three years after a spaceship landed
in Sorrow Falls, Massachusetts, a government operative comes to investigate
and finds that Annie Collins, sixteen, might have the answers he seeks.
Identifiers: LCCN 2018017521 (print) | LCCN 2018023314 (ebook) |
ISBN 978-1-328-56754-3 (ebook) | ISBN 978-1-328-56746-8 (paperback)
Subjects: | CYAC: Space ships—Fiction. | Science fiction. | BISAC: FICTION /
Science Fiction / General.
Classification: LCC PZ7.1.D68 (ebook) | LCC PZ7.1.D68 Sp 2018 (print) |
DDC [Fic]—dc23
LC record available at https://lccn.loc.gov/2018017521

Printed in the United States of America
DOC 10 9 8 7 6 5 4 3 2 1

THE SPACESHIP NEXT DOOR

GENE DOUCETTE

A JOHN JOSEPH ADAMS BOOK
MARINER BOOKS
HOUGHTON MIFFLIN HARCOURT
BOSTON   NEW YORK
2018

CONTENTS

THE SPACESHIP NEXT DOOR

1
THE FAULT IN OUR STARSHIP

*T*he spaceship landed on a cool night in August, in a field that wasn't being used for anything in particular.

Like most remarkable things, nobody realized it was remarkable as it happened. The ship lit up the sky above Sorrow Falls when entering the atmosphere, but that was only slightly unusual in the way a meteor could be slightly unusual.

Later, eyewitness accounts would describe the evening as becoming "as bright as daytime" in that moment, but this was a profound exaggeration. The truth was, while the object flashed brightly, an observer had to already be looking skyward to see it. If one were instead looking at the road, or the television, or the ceiling, the craft would have gone unnoticed as it traveled toward that field on the edge of town.

It was also nearing midnight, on a Tuesday.

Prior to the arrival of the spaceship, Sorrow Falls was a prototypical rural mill town, which is to say there was nothing unusual or spectacular about it. Most residents were either mill employees or farmers. Nearing midnight, on a Tuesday in August, just about everybody was sleeping.

It's possible the sonic boom woke up one or two people, but as was the case with the supposed eyewitnesses startled by the profound brightness that didn't happen, the *boom* was unlikely to have

2 · GENE DOUCETTE

awoken anyone. The sound made by the object was more like a *pop*. To those who did hear it, the volume was approximately equivalent to that of a Jake-braking eighteen-wheeler two blocks away.

In other words, had the spaceship arrived at the surface of the earth as the meteor it resembled initially, the number of people who claimed to have seen its passage across the sky would have dwindled significantly.

It wasn't a meteor, though, and it didn't behave like one. Not entirely.

Meteors didn't slow down and turn. Meteors didn't have landing lights. And in all of history there had never been a recorded instance of a meteor hovering. These exceptions to the standard trajectory of a falling object were what convinced the handful of true witnesses that this was indeed a remarkable thing.

Someone called the police. (Two hundred and seventeen people in the town claim to have made the call; nobody knows who actually did.) At the time, the Sorrow Falls local police force consisted of twenty-two officers — two of whom were on maternity leave — and seven official squad cars. Three of those cars were dispatched to locate the object.

They couldn't find it.

In fairness to those officers, they were told to locate a brightly glowing object that had landed from space, which wasn't a particularly accurate description once the ship touched down and turned its lights off. Also, they had every reason to believe there was no such object and somebody had been drinking.

That left the job of first contact to a man named Billy Pederson. This was entirely due to a combination of luck and an unkind work schedule, as Billy happened to be the first person to drive down the road nearest to the unused field — or if not the first person, the first one to look to his right at the correct moment — and spot the object through an opening in the trees.

He would say later he knew what was there was *not of this world*, but that wasn't the truth. The truth (as he would admit in private to anyone who asked provided they didn't work for a media outlet) was that his first thought was *where did this house come from and how did it go up overnight?*

The spaceship didn't look like a house, but Billy's initial perception was understandable only because most rational people tend to go to "interstellar spacecraft" *last*, after exhausting other options.

It also wasn't large enough to be a proper house. A pool house, perhaps, or a large shed.

It was a matte black vehicle resting on four squat legs, with a curved surface and with no apparent door. The sides were a warren of tubes and vents and dark round holes that looked either like a place for spotlights or — if you were in the midst of a nightmare and looking at this craft — eyeballs.

It was arguably saucer-like, and no doubt looked round from beneath or above, but from the side it looked like a tall, black, birthday cake, or an unusually thick and wide cap on a steam pipe.

The ship sat in a ring of blackened grass. Again, what Billy did next depended upon who was asking. To the many, many interviewers he sat with after the morning of first contact, he would say that he reached the edge of the landing ring (as it was soon called) and understood somehow that going any further would be dangerous, so he stopped and called the sheriff.

That wasn't really true. He actually did step past the burnt grass ring, and got within about five or six feet of the ship before deciding he didn't really feel like getting any closer.

When asked to elaborate on this, he couldn't.

"I dunno, I just sort of lost interest," he said. "Didn't seem important anymore."

He did call the sheriff, though. Thus, the first confirmed sighting of an alien spaceship on the planet was recorded in the police logs at 6:42 a.m., August 14, as a case of possible trespassing.

⋮

The police came, and someone remembered the meteor hunt from the night before and connected it to the strange object in the field, and then more police came. Then the fire department, a couple of state police troopers, and an ambulance for some reason, and soon the tiny road—at the time it was called Tunney Way—was so overrun with vehicles nobody could get past.

Sometime around 10:00 a.m., the sheriff got his hands on a bullhorn and started asking if *the occupants of the ship could please come out with your hands up*. This sparked a minor debate as to the likelihood that anyone inside the spaceship (a) understood English, and (b) had hands. The debate and the question were both moot, though, as nobody inside the craft responded in any obvious way. It didn't open, or make a noise, or flash a light, or otherwise react to the query.

Another debate ensued, regarding the legitimate alienness of the ship and the potential that this was only an elaborate hoax. The fire chief pointed out that the craft could easily be something constructed out of cardboard and foam, and surely if that were the case it would be light enough to be moved to the field in one evening, perhaps specifically on an evening when a meteor had also been spotted. The report could have even been a part of the hoax: perhaps there was no meteor either.

This theory gained enough traction that by 11:30, the sheriff decided to postpone the call he'd been planning to make to the National Guard and just walk up to the ship and see what was what.

He and two of his deputies did just that, retracing the same steps Billy had taken and getting just about as far, until all three of them decided this was actually a bad idea—suffering, some said, from a sudden and inexplicable lack of fortitude—and they should try something else.

They stepped back. And when it was pointed out that by not getting any closer they failed to resolve the question of whether or not the object was a large prank, the sheriff took out his gun, dropped to a knee, and fired two rounds at the center of the ship.

A spectacular thing—the first *real* spectacular thing—happened.

The bullets ceased to exist. They reached a certain point in the air beyond the skin of the ship's hull, flashed brightly, and then were gone, much like a mosquito in a bug zapper. Their disappearance was accompanied by a deep THUD, like a thousand pianos hitting a low C at the same time. It wasn't so much heard as felt, deep in the belly near the umbilical.

It was enough to convince the sheriff not to fire a third round.

He got to his feet and turned to the nearest deputy.

"Somebody get me the president," he said.

Of all the embellishments surrounding the events of the morning of first contact, one thing remained true: he actually did say that.

⋮

Calling the president of the United States was not something the sheriff's department of a small Massachusetts mill town could just do, it turned out. There were steps to take, and jurisdictions to consider, and people to convince.

Convincing people was a big hurdle. It didn't much matter how sane and level-headed any one person in this chain of reportage was, the person on the other end of each link was going to begin with, *no really, why are you calling?* and there wasn't much anyone could do about that.

Compounding the problem was that as far as anybody was concerned, alien spaceships didn't simply land at the edge of little towns in the Connecticut River valley, and if they did, they didn't land *only* there. Admittedly, that opinion was colored by Hollywood movies and science fiction books, but actual military history and tactics further informed those stories. If the ship was the vanguard of an invasion, it was in the wrong place. If it was part of a fleet, there would have been other ships. If it was lost, it would have moved, or asked for directions. If it was disabled—it didn't look disabled, but how would anybody know?—somebody would have asked for help or a wrench. Or something.

In other words, once past the whole spaceship thing, the hardest part about getting the right people to believe that this remarkable event had happened in Sorrow Falls was that the spaceship hadn't *done* anything.

It just sat there. Sure, it could make bullets disappear, but someone had to shoot the gun. That wasn't so much a thing it did, as it was a thing it did in response to someone else doing a thing. It was not in any real sense — after landing — a proactive spaceship.

Still, the president was eventually notified. It happened about two weeks after the ship landed and approximately six hours before the media was to go live with the story. By the time of the media announcement, the army had already cordoned off the field and taken over about a third of the town. (In fairness, this was not a lot of space in terms of pure acreage, and the land they claimed was fallow farmland, and the army was, on the whole, extremely polite about the entire thing.)

That evening, the president held a press conference confirming that the planet had been visited by aliens, and Sorrow Falls became the most-talked-about place in the world.

That was three years ago.

2

ON A PALE BIKE

There were about seventeen different ways to get to Main Street from Annie's front door by bicycle. Annie had tried all of them, and liked to brag about it under circumstances in which such bragging was appropriate, which wasn't all that often. She never listed out what the seventeen or so routes actually were, and also never bothered to count them, so the number was likely closer to ten or eleven.

It was still a large number, but that number became less impressive when broken down mile-by-mile. The problem was there were only five ways to get within a half-mile of Main Street before the warren of side streets and petty tributaries complicated the process of reaching the central drag. Two of those ways were over bridges on either side of Main that would have been impossible for her to use without having begun on the wrong side of the Connecticut River. Two others came from the northern and northwestern side of the valley. She could have counted one of those as a valid route if she first went an extra fifteen miles out of her way, looping northward via some minor highway before turning back south in an entirely impractical detour. She hadn't ever done this, but thought about trying it someday, maybe when she was older and in possession of a bike that was more forgiving on steep hills.

That left one practical road leading into town. She could jump off that road at any number of places and cut through side streets before intersecting with Main, and that was where most of the variance she ascribed to her route came from.

She had two ways to get to this one practical road—it was called Patience Road, named after one of the original settlers, not the virtue one had to have to drive on it—but she always ended up taking the same one. The first option was to go left from her front door, uphill, until hooking up with Liberty Way. Liberty took her through the farmlands belonging to about six extremely private families whose names she didn't know but whose cows she was intimately familiar with. It looped down below the farmland, flattened out into a dirt road that was impassible in rain (at least on a bike) and that connected with the lower end of Patience. It was the longer route of the two in terms of miles traveled, but the shorter on the clock.

The second route began as a right turn from her front door and down the hill to connect with a road that used to be called Tunney back when it was one-and-a-half car lengths wide. It was four cars wide now, newly paved, and a dead straight shot to Patience (which had also been widened since, although not as much). Three years ago it was nearly as fast a route as Liberty, but now it had traffic lights, and traffic.

And now it was called Spaceship Road.

Annie had witnessed every last iteration of this road, because as much as she knew the Liberty route would ultimately be more efficient, she preferred the path down Spaceship Road, so she took it almost every day.

She preferred it because it was more scenic. Liberty had cows and pastures, which was nice and all, but Spaceship Road had a little bit of everything. It had become a legitimate major thoroughfare, of sorts. The problem with it as compared to most large roads was that it didn't actually *go* anywhere special. It went *past* something amazing, but the spaceship and the surrounding territory weren't officially a destination for anyone who didn't wear an army uniform. There was no tourist center or lookout point or souvenir shop around the ship, because the government's approach was to treat it as an unexploded bomb that might or might not be nuclear.

The road had been widened and paved for exactly two reasons: one was to get large, heavily armored vehicles to the spot quickly to defend the nation and the world against an impending alien attack that was exceedingly tardy; and two, so all the campers had a place to park.

Traffic in front of Spaceship Base One—this is what the army called it, despite the notable absence of a second ship to occupy a theoretical Base Two—was a constant tangle of slow-going rubberneckers trying to catch a glimpse of the alien vehicle on a road cut down to one-and-a-half lanes (roughly the width of the original Tunney Way) because of the unofficial trailer park taking up the rest of the street across from the fence. It was fair to say that in the event of a daytime extraterrestrial attack, humanity's initial defenders would be a cross section of self-appointed alien experts, mill employees heading to or from work, a farmer or two, and whatever army soldiers had the misfortune of being on gate duty that day. That would be about it, because there was no way the big guns stored in the semi-permanent base two miles up the hill would ever make it through traffic.

Also available to defend the world—for about ten minutes each morning and ten minutes every evening—was Annie Collins, atop a pale yellow cyclocross bicycle.

⋮

"Annie!" greeted Mr. Shoeman from the top of his RV, with a friendly smile and a wave. "C'mere!"

He gestured her over from the other side of the road. Heading downhill toward Main put her and her bike on the side of the army's fifteen-foot-tall chain link fence and the inbound traffic, which wasn't moving much. (In the same way Annie had alternative routes down, so did every car stuck on the road. They drove past anyway.) It was an easy enough matter to steer the bike between cars along here, since the cars were traveling slower than she was. The civilian trailers were camped out across the street, on the shoulderless side of the road and at least partway onto farmland that used to be owned by old Mike Pequot, up until the state claimed part of it to build the road. Now it was mostly owned by summer mosquitos and rented by alien watchers, protesters, and the occasional Jesus freak.

She hopped off the bike and walked it between the immobile cars.

"Any news?" she asked.

Art Shoeman was of the alien watcher variety, which was actually the only kind of squatter still around consistently. Protesters tended to turn up only for a few hours every day, and the religious zealots mostly confined themselves to the end of Main Street, where they could command more eyeballs.

Mr. Shoeman was in cargo shorts and a Polo shirt with old stains from at least two different meals on it. Scruffy and suffering from what he insisted was premature balding ("I'm not as old as I look!"), he had the same kind of non-threatening vibe as a schoolteacher or a priest. Never mind that one of the first things her mother told her when she started to blossom was to be careful around schoolteachers and priests. Such was the world.

"Dobbs thinks it moved," he said.

"No kidding!"

Dobbs, a younger, chubbier, slightly weirder version of Art Shoeman, poked his head over the side of the trailer. "Swear to God," he said.

"I'm coming up."

Dobbs vanished, as Annie leaned her bike against the side of the trailer and headed up the ladder. Dobbs had a tendency to sit in his lawn chair on the roof in boxers and not much else, for basically the whole summer. As a tubby thirty-year-old with a perpetual sunburn, there was a lot to be said for him keeping his shirt on, and about a year ago—approximately when Annie started to display the more outward effects of puberty—he arrived at the same conclusion. So as she climbed up, he was undoubtedly grabbing a shirt and making himself slightly more presentable.

It was a little weird, because she could see him from the road every morning. It was like he only cared how he looked if he knew he was being looked at.

Standing on top of the camper was like discovering a new layer to the world: camper rooftop city. Each roof was a singular collection of makeshift furniture—a preponderance of folding chairs and card tables—and gonzo electrical equipment, telescopes or binoculars, antenna arrays, and laptop computers. About half of it was equipment invented by the inhabitants of the rooftop city, to test one theory or another regarding the spaceship. In the unlikely event any of them had a verifiable claim to make, they would first have to prove that the device they used did what they thought it did. The last detail was probably insurmountable.

Like Mika and Morrie, two roofs over. They'd taken an old Geiger counter, attached it to something they promised would amplify its range—somehow—and adjusted it (again *somehow*) to detect auras. If they ever made a discovery, they would have to prove the thing did what they said, and then they would have to prove auras were real.

Annie was pretty sure the last part was going to be tough. Already, at sixteen, she had a mature appreciation of the degree to which adults could delude themselves about things. She'd also learned not to take a whole lot of what she heard on Spaceship Road all that seriously.

Mika and Morrie were just one example. There were dozens of others, all doing what they could to study an object that was perhaps a quarter of a mile away and only partly visible through the tree line for most of the summer. (In the fall and winter, when the trees had fewer leaves, it was easy to see.)

Mr. Shoeman's roof was kind of homey in its way. He had a green Astroturf carpet that smelled only a little like mildew, a few comfortable chairs, and a cooler with a surprisingly robust variety of beverages. And snacks. Lots of snacks. The alien trailer park collective was fueled primarily by pizza delivery and salty snacks, although on weekends in the summer they liked to have a big cookout, combining the forces of all the trailer neighbors. It was festive. Sometimes a few of the soldiers even came.

"So it moved?" Annie said, once she gained the high ground. Dobbs was (of course) now wearing a shirt, and standing in front of an array of electronic equipment that looked a lot like what happens when Radio Shack has a yard sale. There were three cameras slaved to a laptop, something that may have been a seismometer at one time, and a fourth camera with a telephoto lens mounted on a small tripod. The entire collection was on top of a table with tiny springs beneath it and under a roof made up of plastic sheets. The springs were supposed to be shock absorbers to keep local events such as a sixteen-year-old climbing up the ladder from causing a tremble in the equipment. The roof and plastic were to protect the equipment when it rained.

"Maybe as much as two inches!" Dobbs said.

"No kidding!"

"Here, I'll show you. Hang on."

Dobbs started tapping away on the computer he used to collect information from the other computers.

"Pretty exciting, huh?" Mr. Shoeman said. He was on the other side of the roof tweaking one of the solar panels.

Power was always an issue. The campers weren't near any sources of electricity and to refill their gas tanks they had to move, which at least half of them hadn't done in two years. They made do with a combination of reusable generators, gas trading, and makeshift solar paneling. In perspective, it was funny, only because these were people at risk of running out of power and food and—in the winter—heat, while only a few miles from an ample supply of all of those things. The aliens would have made everyone's lives a whole lot easier if they'd only landed across from a hotel.

"Sure. Two inches?"

"It's not nothing."

"No."

Pretty close to it, though, she thought.

She looked across the road. Mr. Shoeman's trailer was in a prime location. Whenever newspeople showed up, they were guaranteed to take at least one photo from the spot where Annie was standing. The trees framed the ship almost perfectly, and nearly all of it was in view.

They weren't close. Sure, in the event the spaceship one day rose up and began attacking the citizens of Planet Earth, they were entirely *too* close, but putting aside that potential outcome, they weren't meaningfully nearby. Certainly, they were not close enough to make a potential two-inch movement—in a thing that hadn't budged since it landed three years ago—more likely than a measurement error in Dobbs's equipment. Assuming Dobbs was measuring what he thought he was.

"Here, here, here," Dobbs said excitedly. "Look!"

He turned the laptop around so she could see the screen. It showed a graph with a notable spike. The graph had no context.

"Two inches caused that?" she asked.

"The Y-axis . . . yeah, it's in millimeters."

"Oh, really cool," she said, mustering a little enthusiasm. "What do you think it means?"

Mr. Shoeman laughed. "Who knows? We have so much more to do first. We have to wait and see if it does it again, and then we'll see about any patterns and *then* maybe something. We're publishing our results in a few days. Could be somebody caught the same thing, or something different at the same time. We'll know soon."

Publishing our results meant *telling everyone else about it at the weekend barbecue.* These were enthusiasts, not scientists. All the actual scientists were either working with the government (and tacitly not sharing their findings if they had any) or had already gone home.

"That's really exiting, guys," she said with a little smile. "You'll let me know, right?"

"Of course!" Mr. Shoeman clapped her on the shoulder while Dobbs mostly blushed. "Maybe soon the whole world will know!"

"Fingers crossed!" Annie said.

⋮

It was difficult to muster up the kind of enthusiasm they were looking for from her. Not so long ago, every burp, tweet, and shrug ostensibly discovered by the members of the trailer park collective was a landmark event. Annie would hear about it and tell her friends and her mom, often out of breath and wide-eyed with the anticipation of a thing to come.

The thing never came, though, because the ship never moved.

There were only two things that could be easily verified from the distance of the roof city: the ship still existed; it was warm enough that snow melted off it.

The second thing was extremely interesting, but it seemed like most times the people in the campers focused on the first thing, since that was why they were there in the first place. An alien spacecraft had landed in Massachusetts, and this was something to bear witness to.

The problem appeared to be that nobody knew what to do after having borne witness, aside from continuing to do so routinely.

When the ship first landed Annie couldn't get enough of the entire experience. Excited people showed up every day with weird equipment and wild theories and none of them cared who they told about it: a reporter from NBC or an inquisitive thirteen-year-old girl, it was all the same to most of them. *Listen to us*, they said, over and over, as often as possible to as many people as would stop to hear.

There was a breathlessness to the whole thing, as surely any minute something would happen, and the world lost its collective mind just thinking about the possibilities. It was crazy and intoxicating, and Annie loved the whole thing.

She also believed a lot of what she was told. At thirteen, the idea that adults could be thoroughly and completely wrong-headed about anything was just a growing notion. So if Derinda Lake wanted to tell her the aliens had burrowed from underneath the ship and walked among them, Annie was inclined to believe her, even if it contradicted Carter Kent's calm assertion that the machine was clearly an unmanned probe presaging the arrival of a space fleet. Likewise, Loonie Larry and his zombie theory didn't fit the first two theories — or any other sane theory — but she was willing to take him seriously too, for a little while.

Dobbs and Mr. Shoeman didn't have a strong theory, or not one they were willing to share. They were more interested in collecting evidence first and then developing a conclusion.

That was all fine, except there was no evidence to collect, and every day that passed without real evidence was a day that made Mr. Shoeman and Dobbs seem that much more desperate, and more like everyone else out there in the camper rooftop city. They were all as friendly as ever, and she still liked talking to them, but she was approaching a point where her interactions were more out of pity than interest. One day she was going to grow up and leave Sorrow Falls. The only way any of them — Dobbs and Mr. Shoeman or, really, anyone else in the campers — were going anywhere was if the ship did something, and Annie was growing convinced that this would never happen.

⋮

Annie climbed down from the ladder, hoping the display of modest enthusiasm she'd given was sufficient. It was unfortunate that once the camera crews and print reporters stopped coming around on a weekly basis, the only people who would still listen were people like Annie, which meant in a weird way that they needed her affirmation.

Or something.

It was a dynamic she didn't really understand. Mr. Shoeman was retired, his wife had died a decade earlier, and if he had children and grandchildren, he didn't talk about them. (His relationship to Dobbs was a complete mystery. They weren't related by blood and that was all she knew.) It was possible he had adopted her in his own way.

She already had a grandfather. Her mom's dad. He died when she was seven, and she only remembered seeing him one time. He spent ten minutes trying to make her laugh and impressing her by making it look like his thumb was detachable. The smile on his face when he performed this trick was a little like what Art Shoeman did when he had something new to tell Annie. She didn't quite know how to tell him she knew his thumb wasn't really coming off, especially when he seemed to believe it was.

She walked the bike back across the street through the slow-moving traffic of perpetual rubberneckers.

"Morning, Annie," one of the soldiers said with a smile and a wave.

"Morning, Corporal," she said back, wheeling the bike over to him.

His name was Sam Corning. He was a twenty-four-year-old six-foot-four square-jawed soldier with baby blue eyes and a smile that never went away even when he stopped smiling.

Annie was going to run away with him one day, to live on a ranch in the hills of Virginia, and make babies and fresh vegetables. That he didn't know any of this had surprisingly little impact on her plans.

"You can call me Sam, you know that."

"What, out here in the open? People will talk."

Annie learned to flirt by watching old black-and-white movies. She couldn't tell yet if she was any good at it.

He laughed. "It's Corporal if you need rescuing or something, otherwise Sam is just fine. We've been through this."

Sam Corning was the only soldier she'd met from the base that didn't like to be reminded he happened to be a soldier. Annie was pretty sure that meant something, but didn't know what.

"How's things? Quiet?"

"As always. Saw a bug earlier; pretty sure I never saw one like it before. Probably not an alien."

"Probably not."

"Killed it anyway, just in case."

"With the gun?"

Sam had an M16A2 on his shoulder, a Beretta M9 handgun on his hip, and a Bowie knife on his belt. She knew this not because of any particular fascination with guns — she had no love for them—but because he'd given her a walkthrough of his weaponry in a prior conversation.

"I used my boot. Anything exciting going on over there?"

He nodded toward Dobbs.

"I'm afraid that's classified, Corporal Corning. How about here?"

"Equally classified. Although rumor has it someone will be going through the gate in another hour or two. My orders are to let them in and close the gate behind them."

"Truly, this is a challenging job."

"You want me on that wall. You need me on that wall."

Annie laughed. She quoted *A Few Good Men* to him one time and he never quite got over it.

"So who is it?"

"Classified."

"The president? THE PRESIDENT IS COMING?"

"No, stop shouting."

She turned to the trailers. "HEY, EVERYONE!"

"Stop!"

"So who's coming?" she asked, turning back. "Spill."

"Some journalist. Doing a retrospective. *Time* magazine or . . . one of them, I forget."

"Oooh, that's more exciting than the president."

"Really? To whom?"

"Pretty much everyone."

By the third year of the spaceship occupation, everyone in town had either met the president or met someone whose job it was to keep them from meeting the president, at least two or three times. Sorrow Falls also had seen its share of members of Congress and visiting heads of state, plus a variety of religious dignitaries. It was an understatement to say the community was jaded when it came to famous people.

On the other hand, a journalist was someone who would stop and talk to the trailer city collective. That was much more important than any president.

"Well, keep it to yourself anyway," Sam said. "No idea if people are even supposed to know."

"A retrospective, huh?"

"I think so. Probably just talk to the usuals. Billy Pederson and everyone."

"Right."

There were about a dozen people from Sorrow Falls who were legitimately famous. Billy was one of them, but there was also the sheriff and his deputies, the fire chief, the guy who drove the ambulance that day, the owners of the land adjacent to the ship, and one or two other people who had come about their fame honestly, which is to say they happened to be in the right place at the right time and this could be verified independently. A dozen other people were famous for the opposite reason: they claimed to be somewhere they weren't, or do something they hadn't done. They achieved a temporary fame, which devolved into a public shaming. Annie knew a couple of them, and didn't find them to be all that regretful. Fame was the be-all and end-all for some folks.

What the famous people of Sorrow Falls had in common was direct interaction with the alien spacecraft. The early days before the army came in with their military cordon and their giant fence, and daily bomber runs over the no-fly zone above, and helicopter flyby's, and so on, were tumultuous. A lot of people had an opportunity to see the ship up close. Those that did eventually became famous for it, even if they had nothing to say.

"Probably looking for some story nobody's told yet," Sam said. "As you do. Pretty much no stories left, though, huh? Not until it does something."

"Yeah, probably not," she said. "But he's getting a close-up of the ship, huh?"

"So I'm told."

"That's a *little* unusual, right? When was the last time that happened?"

Sam shrugged. "I guess. I don't think about it much. Maybe he was just the first to ask in a while."

"Maybe. Well, I gotta run, but thanks for the info. Now I know what I'm doing with my day."

Sam laughed. "You're going to track down the one reporter in Sorrow Falls in the next two hours?"

"Oh, I won't need two hours. C'mon, Sam, who do you think you're talking to?"

"Fine, well, when you do find him, keep my name out of it."

She kicked her leg over the bike and pointed it toward town. "Don't worry, Soldier. I always protect my informants."

3
ALERT THE MEDIA

*T*he reporter was a skinny white guy with the kind of glasses people who lived in cities tended to wear: they had almost no frames to them and looked too small to render the entire world on the other side of the eyeballs crisp for the owner of those eyeballs.

He appeared to have made a conscious effort to look rugged, countrified, or otherwise non-*other* to the locals of Sorrow Falls, but couldn't entirely pull it off. One reason for this was pretty simple: nobody in town dressed like he was dressed. People from the city didn't understand that people living outside of the city didn't really have a different style, or if they did it wasn't a style you could arrive at by mimicking the fashion choices from a pickup truck commercial.

He had a red flannel shirt and jeans—the jeans were unquestionably brand-new, but he did make an effort to buy the kind that came pre-distressed—and tan leather hiking boots.

Annie had spent her entire life in Sorrow Falls, and the only people she'd ever seen dressed this way were the ones coming from outside of town and trying to fit in. It said "farmer" to a certain group of people who had never farmed.

He was in good company. The president dressed this way when he visited too. So had the French ambassador, although in his case he probably thought all Americans dressed like this: he wore a cowboy hat with it. Annie had to think for a while before she could come up with a visiting dignitary who hadn't worn the outfit. The only two that came to mind were the vice president (a woman, who also had decent fashion sense) and the Dalai Lama.

The reporter was sitting alone in a booth in the back of Joanne's Diner, typing at a modest pace on a laptop that would have been a spiral notebook only a few years earlier. He checked his watch every couple of minutes, and looked up every time the bell above the door announced someone's entry or exit.

"How long's he been here?" Annie asked Beth. Beth was four years older than Annie, and a member of the diner's ownership family, the Welds. She was also the closest thing Annie had to an older sister, largely because the Welds were in the habit of adopting locals who helped out in the diner, and *everyone* was in the habit of adopting Annie. It was a popular local tradition.

The only sign to ever grace the diner was one that said D I N E R on it, but everyone called it Joanne's. This was sort of funny for anybody familiar with the Welds, because nobody in the family was, or had ever been, named Joanne. It was true that for about fifteen years in the late middle period of the twentieth century, the diner employed a waitress who called herself Joan, and it was also true that Joan was a very popular lady in the way some ladies could be at times (Annie took this to mean she had large breasts, but Beth had a much more salacious interpretation), and so it was very possible "the Diner" became "Joan's Diner" and later—because that *s* and *d* in the makeshift title were awkward when shoved together like that—it became "Joanne's Diner" before finally becoming "Joanne's." It was equally possible there was another explanation, for which no adequate historical record existed. What remained true was that there was no Joanne in the establishment, and it did not appear there ever had been.

It was a local tradition, therefore, to tell intrepid reporters who had just arrived that they absolutely must (a) eat at Joanne's, and (b) ask to speak to Joanne, as she had all the best information.

It was an entertaining prank, and also served the important

purpose of notifying locals when someone contributing to the official record was in the vicinity. For while there was no Joanne, her diner was the closest thing to an information hub the town had.

"About an hour. Don't know who he's waiting on."

"His escort, probably," Annie said. "He's going to see the ship."

Beth flexed an eyebrow. "How do you know that?"

Annie shrugged, which wasn't an answer, but it also sort of was. Annie knew people and people told her things. It was just how things were. If anyone in town knew that, it was Beth.

"Well, if that's true he must be more important than he looks," Beth said.

"Maybe. What do important people look like? I can never tell."

Annie put down the half-full buss pan she was ostensibly transporting to the back of the diner. There was an industrial-sized dishwashing machine in back made by a company called Hobart that everyone just called Bart. Bart was always hungry and always complaining and occasionally—more often than not of late—needed a visit from a specialist, because Bart was getting old. There were a not inconsequential number of customers who believed there was a human named Bart in the back, who was perhaps chained there and not permitted to leave.

The breakfast rushes came in shifts, and this was a moment between those shifts, so Annie had already fed Bart.

She grabbed a coffee urn and headed to the back of the diner, winking at Beth as she went.

"Refill?" she asked, to the journo.

"No thanks," he said, not looking up. She thought he looked younger up close, like just-out-of-college young. That didn't make a lot of sense contextualized with his opportunity to see the ship up close, though. She expected a more seasoned individual.

Annie sat down on the opposite side of the booth and waited for him to notice.

It took a lot longer than it should have.

"Hello?" he said, confused.

"Hi."

He saw the coffee urn and successfully associated it with the person he had just spoken to, rather than concluding she materialized in the seat somehow, which would have been cooler but far less likely.

"I really don't want more coffee. I've had enough for now, thanks."

"Oh, I know. You're a reporter."

He looked past her and down the length of the diner, perhaps in anticipation of discovering someone capable of explaining Annie.

"You couldn't possibly be Joanne."

"No, Joanne isn't here."

"So I was told." His eyes went back to the laptop, which was the kind of thing people did when they wanted to signal in a less rude sort of way that the conversation they were having was over. It actually *was* rude, but it was a socially permissible rude. It had the effect of making the person they were dismissing seem like *they* were the rude ones.

Annie didn't have a real sense of shame, though, so it didn't work. This could have been why people told her things.

"She doesn't actually exist," Annie said.

"Joanne of Joanne's Diner doesn't exist?" he said, not looking up. He did stop typing, though.

"Now you have it."

"Who are you?"

"I'm Annie. Annie Collins."

"How old are you?"

"Sixteen."

"And you work here?"

"Just part time. I don't wait tables, though, mostly I just pick up and feed Bart, answer the phone sometimes. Less during the school year."

"Well, that's fascinating."

She decided he was older than the college-age impression he first gave off. The way to tell was by looking at people's necks. He was at least thirty.

"I work in the library too. Have you seen the library yet? It's down at the south end of Main. We have municipal buildings on each end and right in the middle. It's very *feng shui*. Probably not what the founders were thinking, but still."

"I'm nearly positive *feng shui* has nothing to say about city planning."

He had one of those voices that made him *sound* smart. Clean elocution, crisp word-choice. Someone people might respect but simultaneously dislike. She decided he probably wasn't really a journalist.

"I agree, but most people around here don't know that. Or what *feng shui* is, and if they did they probably wouldn't know it's mostly crap."

"Is it?"

"I think it's probably something invented by an interior decorator to charge more per hour."

He looked up from the screen, which was a great triumph for Annie.

"How old are you again?"

"Sixteen."

"And you're Annie."

"That's good."

"Annie, maybe you can tell me why you're sitting here?"

"Because you're a reporter."

"According to whom?"

"Joanne."

"I've never met Joanne. And you said a minute ago she wasn't real."

"I did, but that doesn't mean Joanne didn't tell me you were a reporter."

"Are you in a special needs class of some kind, Annie?"

"What's your name?"

"Ed Somerville."

"Ed short for Edward?"

"Edgar."

"I can see why you're rolling with Ed. What time are you supposed to see the ship?"

He coughed, looking in five directions in two seconds, and

closed his laptop. She hoped he remembered to hit *save* on whatever he had going on there.

"Who *are* you?" he asked.

"Annie Collins."

"Sixteen-year-old Annie Collins."

"You keep saying it like you expect me to get it wrong. Don't I look sixteen?"

"You probably do. It's a tough age to pin down in some people."

"Well, I am. Ask anyone. Most folks know me around here."

"Why is that?"

"I dunno. I'm that kind of girl, I guess. Not in a bad way. Probably not in a bad way."

"I really don't understand what's going on."

"Well, we haven't had a reporter around in a while. What's your angle?"

"My angle?"

He was definitely not a reporter.

"You answer questions with questions a lot, that's a terrible habit. Your angle, for the piece you're here to write. I assume write and not telecast because I don't see any cameras and, I mean . . . well, you don't look like on-air talent."

"Thanks?" His expression suggested he thought maybe he was losing his mind.

"So is it: *Sleepy spaceship town returns to normal,* or *Local community embraces alien fanatics,* or what?"

"I don't have an angle yet."

"Of course you do. Oh! I bet it's one of those big long-form pieces, right? The *Atlantic Monthly* or something like that?"

"Something like that, yes."

"Those always sell well. But that isn't it either, is it? You're just agreeing with me so I'll stop guessing."

"Why do I have to have an angle?"

"Because if you don't have an angle, you're not here for a puff piece at all, you're here for some other reason. And *that* would mean something happened to report about, and we all know that can't be true because there hasn't been anything new about the ship since the day it landed. And if there *was* something new, well . . . I can think of a lot of people who would want to know all about that."

He stared at her for a few beats.

"You're sixteen."

"Haven't turned seventeen since the last time you asked."

"It's possible a sixteen-year-old is attempting to blackmail me right now, so I wanted to re-establish that."

"I understand."

"So I'm clear: you think I'm a reporter, and that I'm going to be getting a close-up of the only thing in this town anyone cares to see, and that I'm doing this because something's happened involving that very thing. And you'd like me to know if I don't . . . do something for you? You'll tell everybody this. Do I have that correct?"

"I would never say blackmail, that's a terrible word. I'm an innocent young woman."

"Right. And what is the thing you would like for me to do?"

"I am offering my services," she said. She more or less decided on this the second she said it.

"Come again?"

"Not *those* services, dude. God."

"What kind of services?"

"As I said, everyone in town knows me and I know everyone. A reporter such as yourself would benefit from having a person such as myself around."

"For information?"

"For all sorts of things. Everyone here's been interviewed a dozen times. If you want to get *good* answers instead of the *usual* answers, you need someone there to call bullcrap on them when they say it."

"I think I can detect my own . . . bullcrap . . . just fine, thanks."

"Oh, yeah? Maybe you can ask Joanne when she gets here."

"You'd like to be my tour guide."

"Sure, you can call it that. I prefer translator. Like in *The Killing Fields.*"

"Northern Massachusetts is a poor substitute for Cambodia."

"But you see my point."

"I do," he said. "Except you're bluffing."

"I am?"

"Oh yes."

The front door chime rang, and as was the case every other time this happened, Ed looked at the door. In this instance, though, he saw someone he was expecting. Annie turned around to see a man she didn't recognize. He was in civilian clothes, but he had the sort of crispness she'd seen many times before in members of the army.

"Huh, looks like they changed the press liaison," she said.

"Never mind him," Ed said, as he collected his laptop and his bill and stood.

"Last chance."

"It's an interesting offer, Annie Collins. But I don't need a translator."

"And you think I'm bluffing."

"I know you are. I know the type."

"What type is that?"

"The type who likes secrets but not gossip. But it's a pleasure to meet you, and I thank you for the offer."

He shook her hand, as if this had been a job interview — which it sort of had been — and headed to the front register to handle his bill. A minute later he was out the door and climbing into a black SUV.

"So?" Beth asked, when Annie returned the coffee urn to the counter. "What's his story?"

"Not sure yet," Annie said. "But he's definitely not a reporter. Which makes him a whole lot more interesting."

4

THE LITTLE THINGS

as that Annie Collins you were sitting with?"

This was the first thing Brigadier General Morris had to say to Ed, as soon as they were in the back of the car, at which point Ed began to wonder if he was losing his mind or if everyone else in this town had lost theirs and he was only catching up.

"That's what she said her name was. Do you know her?"

"I know *of* her. We've never been introduced. You didn't tell her anything, did you?"

Ed's security clearance was actually higher than the general's, so he wasn't sure what to make of the question. Surely the man understood that *not* revealing classified information to a sixteen-year-old on his first morning in town was an expectation for someone with his permissions.

"Of course I didn't."

"No offense intended, son. She has a knack, that one."

"Does she."

"You spent any time in a war zone, Mr. Somerville?"

The general had a gosh-howdy sort of cadence, but it hid a shrewdness.

"Some might say I'm doing that right now, General."

He laughed. "Sure, and you might be one of those people. I've read your papers. I mean a live ammo war zone. Well, I'll tell you. Every occupied village, town, and neighborhood has an Annie Collins. If you want to succeed at whatever it is you're planning, you want to find that person."

"To . . . to shoot them?"

"No, no, they're too important. Besides, if you shoot 'em someone'll take their place. No, to get them on your side. My point, we know all about Annie Collins. We leave her be, and maybe someday we'll need her help for something. So what did she know?"

Ed remained convinced either he or everyone around him was going mad.

"She knew I was going to see the ship."

The army man nodded slowly.

"I guess that's okay."

"I didn't tell her that."

"Never said you did, son."

The SUV was taking them down Main, a double-wide road with the kind of retail variety that only came from organic growth over time. It had the sort of homey, old-next-to-new-next-to-old series of façades that most open-air shopping malls had been trying to replicate for years without success.

Maybe the most interesting thing about how the spaceship impacted the local economy and industry of Sorrow Falls was that it had had almost none. One of the most consequential events in history happened right up the road, and that event brought in a lot of money, yet more than half of the real estate of Sorrow Falls Main Street looked the same, and by all accounts *was* the same. Lots of owner-occupied shops (residences above the storefront were very popular in these parts) with the only difference being most of these owners now had a big vacation house to head off to when they wanted.

The sudden influx of cash to the local economy did have consequences, though, most obviously in the half of Main that flipped: it now had a Denny's and a McDonald's and a Marriott and a lot of other things that made no sense in most mill town communities. Likewise, a fair number of the original witnesses didn't even live in town anymore, thanks to the money they made telling their stories and the dearth of large estates in the immediate vicinity. If Ed wanted to interview the sheriff from that night, he'd have to travel to Nantucket, for example.

But Sorrow Falls still felt and looked an awful lot like the Sorrow Falls of old, according to just about everyone. It was Ed's first time in town, but he'd been studying the place from afar for three years.

In this, he was almost completely alone. The others focused on the ship, and he did too, but he considered the town a part of the whole. Even now, seeing in person how normal it all was, he was sure there was something *wrong* somehow with this town.

It would have made for an interesting story angle, if he were actually a reporter.

I have to get better at pretending to be one, he thought.

If there was one thing he learned from his exchange with Annie, it was that Sorrow Falls had a lot of media-savvy people, and those people knew how real reporters acted, which was more than Ed could say. He was definitely going to have to work on his cover if he was going to get any answers.

⋮

A lot more had changed outside the town line than inside. The first time Ed really appreciated this was when he drove into town, because crossing the river to Main felt like entering a different Disney World kingdom—which only reinforced the notion that the homey-ness of Sorrow Falls was being maintained artificially somehow. In contrast, the bordering towns saw franchising as the only way to capitalize economically on the random good fortune of their neighbor, and so the number of hotels and motels and chain restaurants and souvenir shops and so on increased almost exponentially the farther one got from downtown Sorrow Falls.

Of course, beyond *that* was the rest of the world, which suffered a global nervous breakdown shortly after the president's instantly famous "We Are Not Alone" speech, and had calmed down only a little bit since.

The first outward manifestation of collective insanity was the spate of mass suicides. These quickly became so routine that they stopped being newsworthy after a few months. It turned out there were an awful lot of people who—individually and in groups—decided the world was either ending or already had, and wanted to beat the rush to the afterworld. There was also a significant increase in religiously motivated terrorist acts. Ed never really understood the connection to those and the ship, but nobody else seemed to either. And of course there were riots, which happened all over the place, with the bigger ones in such disparate locales as New Delhi, Perth, and Cincinnati.

A lot had been written about that year, some of it good, most of it pop psychology of the worst sort. All the analyses worked with the same thesis: the modern psyche was more fragile than anyone imagined, and all it took to reveal that was an alien ship that didn't even do anything. Mostly, they proved only that the best history was the kind written long after the fact.

Three years later, there was still a higher-than-average suicide rate internationally, and one or two religions continued to cope poorly—*do aliens have souls* was becoming a large enough topic of dispute to cause a philosophical schism in Christianity, and was the basis of two new major cults—but overall there was no longer the sense that the entire planet was resting on the edge of a cliff.

Ed thought that was probably healthy. He also thought it was a little soon to stop worrying about the ship.

⋮

Main Street *did* sort of sit on the edge of a cliff, if one looked at it from a purely geographic perspective. The SUV—in a slow crawl down the street thanks in part to a traffic light every fifty feet—came to just past the halfway point, where the southern edge of the gigantic Hollis Paper Mill could be seen on the left.

Viewing the mill from Main meant looking directly at the top floor of the building and the base of one of five smokestacks. This was because everything on the Eastern side of Main was built on a steep downhill, which was part of the Connecticut River valley. The drop was more than seventy-five feet before it hit water.

The mill was built to jut out over the river, supported by great wooden pylons that looked structurally suspect in every picture Ed saw of the place. He expected to read one day about the building being swallowed up whole by the rushing water, with follow-up stories declaring aliens had destroyed the mill, and not gravity and fluid dynamics.

Falling into the river would be bad for a lot of reasons, as the building wouldn't last very long. About a half mile from the mill, downstream, was a waterfall that was also called Sorrow Falls. (According to one version of the town's history, the town was named after the waterfall. The other version involved the word "falls" as a verb, and was more interesting.) Ed wasn't sure exactly how steep that drop was, but it was steep enough to wreck a canoe.

There were four blocks of neighborhood between Main and the mill. Not so long ago, each one of those blocks held low-rent row housing for employees of both the mill and the local retail shops. Since the ship landed many of those buildings had either been taken down and replaced by prettier versions of the same thing or renovated with the same approximate goal in mind: capitalize on a burgeoning local interest. This ended up being wishful thinking. About half of the world expected the ship to destroy all life on earth at any given second, and nobody possessed of that opinion was interested in moving closer to said object. The other half of the world was mostly curious, but the number of that half who could see themselves living next to it turned out to be smaller than the number of available condos in town. As a consequence, the property values dropped—or more precisely failed to rise—and soon the owners of those buildings were renting the spaces to the same families they'd been trying to evict, and for about the same monthly charge.

Basically, everyone ended up with a Jacuzzi and marble kitchen counters thanks to the spaceship and some unwise speculation.

"Here's all we have on the second anomaly," General Morris said. In his hand was a tightly packed manila folder. "I'm told you haven't seen it yet. We've got an office set aside for you at the base, so you don't leave this lying."

Morris was speaking of the hotel room Ed rented, because a reporter wouldn't stay at the army base. Reporters also didn't have classified folders lying around for maids to find.

"Thank you, I'll look at it later," Ed said. He slid the packet into his messenger bag. "I'd like to see it for myself first."

They reached an army checkpoint. This was another reason traffic on Main moved at a perpetual slow crawl: there were checkpoints every half mile from the northern bridge into town on the far end of Main, up Patience and onto Spaceship Road, all the way to the base. At no time had they been anything other than open and allowing traffic to pass unobstructed through town. (Except, of course, for passage through the fence to see the ship, and passage onto the army base.) However, they were ominous-looking, tollbooth-like structures staffed by armed soldiers whose existence demanded that cars slow for them.

The checkpoints were reminders of the extremely peculiar legal nature of the town of Sorrow Falls as compared to every other American municipality in the history of the country.

In a decision that was no less controversial after nearly three years, Congress—with the backing and signature of the president—suspended the Posse Comitatus Act as it applied specifically to the town surrounding the spaceship. The groundwork for the modification was actually laid a few years earlier in response to concerns about large-scale terrorist acts on domestic soil. Essentially, "acts of invasion from a non-terrestrial source" were lumped in with terrorism, which in turn shaped the nature of the government's response: from that point forward it was assumed that the aliens were hostile. A not-insignificant number of people took issue with that assumption, and for every year in which nothing continued to happen, their voices got louder.

Ed wasn't one of those voices. His first official recommendation as an employee of the federal government was the complete evacuation of the area, and this remained—in his opinion—the correct choice, albeit the least politically savvy one.

The local suspension of Posse Comitatus only legalized something that had already happened in Sorrow Falls, more or less the minute enough people were convinced that this thing was real: the army rolling into town and taking over.

In hindsight, this went pretty well, which is to say it could have gone disastrously wrong and it didn't. There were protests—some from residents, many more from local non-residents, and many more still from non-local non-residents a great distance away and expressed only on Internet pages—but the overall sentiment, from local law enforcement up to the town council and the governor of the state, was: *here, you deal with this, we don't know how to.*

The potential for an adversarial relationship was, essentially, mitigated by the presence of a common enemy. And since the enemy was silent and apparently peaceful, the result was sort of the best of all possible worlds. The locals and the soldiers both agreed to act like members of the human race together.

It helped that the army didn't bow to what ended up being significant pressure to take more extreme actions. Few realized that in the first few months all it would have taken was a stray rock thrown at the head of someone drawing a government salary for the entire town to end up evacuated. (An evacuation that would have followed a plan drafted by Ed, since he was the one who wanted to do it in the first place.) The rock never got thrown, though, and the military was able to push back and avoid the P.R. nightmare that would come from seizing twenty square miles of public and private land and displacing an entire community.

In the end, the army claimed only two plots: a half-acre perimeter around the ship (which was on public soil), and three acres a mile up the road. This was purchased rather than claimed, from landowners who otherwise would never have made anything like the kind of money the government was throwing around.

So everyone got along really well, and pretended to ignore the fact that the United States Army was the actual law in this prototypically sleepy Massachusetts town. The town council still functioned as one would expect in a democratically structured civic arrangement, and private property was still treated as private property by all the people making gobs of money off owning land there, but the reality was that if the army decided to disband the council, seize all the businesses on Main Street, and lock up everyone, legally they could do it.

They just hadn't.

Past the checkpoint, the SUV reached the end of Main: east would have taken them to another bridge over the Connecticut River, while west sent them uphill and toward the ship. This was the effective termination point of "downtown" Sorrow Falls, a Y junction that was a favorite for protesters. Every car reaching that point had to commit to a slow turn in one direction or another, which gave them plenty of time to read a poorly spelled sign or two.

Ed was pretty sure the protesters were mostly from out of state, and mostly positive he didn't understand what made them do this sort of thing. The signs represented a startling array of opinions: aliens are bad and must be nuked; aliens are good and must be loved; the army is bad and the government is lying; the ship is a hoax; and Jesus died for our sins.

Morris noted Ed's attention.

"I hear it used to be a whole lot worse," he said. "More bodies, more anarchy. These folks are really pretty polite. Even the ones who think a man in a uniform is . . . well, pick your nightmare scenario. We're either incompetent actors or masterful orchestrators of a super conspiracy hoax."

"And in league with Satan, according to that last one."

"Oh yes. Well, that's true, of course."

Ed laughed.

"You've only been here a few months, isn't that right, General?"

"Four months. Long enough to get my bearings, figure out who's who, not much else. Then all this happened."

All this was why Ed was there.

"Do you like it?"

"Sure. High-profile assignment with nobody shooting at me?

Other than the winters—which I hear can get bad—it's about the perfect assignment. I don't even need to learn a new language or adjust to a weird cuisine."

"As long as nothing changes about the ship."

"You mean nothing else. Well, sure. But front row for the end of the world's a pretty good show too."

⋮

It was another twenty minutes of driving to get from the edge of Main to the ship. About half of that twenty was spent in the slow crawl directly before the ship.

Ed had to lean over the general to get a decent look at the campers on the right.

"There used to be more of them," Ed said.

"There was more of everybody. That whole field used to be three-deep and looking like a hippie festival. I've seen pictures, it looked like the only thing missing was a stage."

From Ed's perspective, there *was* a stage. It was the obsidian-black object on the other side of the fence. There would have been no fence in the first couple of months, nothing but armed men to keep someone from rushing the stage while the band was still setting up. It was a miracle nobody was shot trying to do that.

"Mostly all we have left over there is the crackpots," Morris said. "Real nice, for the most part."

When the band doesn't play music, people go home, Ed thought. *Except for the ones expecting to hear the most important song in history.*

The car cut a left turn through the inbound traffic, and after a show of identification, the gate was opened. Ed snuck a look over his shoulder at the trailer people, noting the excitement of activity his arrival signaled.

"Not many people go through here, I take it."

"Not many. We make do with passive detectors set within the perimeter and mostly keep out otherwise. I've only been inside once myself, before today. Nobody wants to catch the space flu."

Ed laughed.

"Is that what they're calling it?"

"I like it better than space cancer," Morris said. "I've lost folks to cancer. Doesn't seem right to use that word. But soldiers aren't an imaginative bunch."

"I guess being succinct is more important than being accurate."

They stopped the car and climbed out. Ed looked through the fence, and saw the bustle of activity atop the trailer roof system had only gotten worse. Binoculars and telescopes were being pointed at him, and now none of the people over there were likely to have an unguarded conversation with Edgar Somerville, reporter.

But he was facing the wrong direction. The most extraordinary object in history was only about thirty paces away.

"So here we are," Morris said.

"It's smaller than I thought it would be."

"I think everybody says that."

Everybody hasn't been studying it for three years, he thought.

"How many people can that even really hold?"

"People? Maybe one or two. But aliens? Depends on how big they are, doesn't it?"

The ship was completely enclosed by the perimeter fence, which Ed began to follow. The grass was springy with patches of mud from a recent rain. Every effort to avoid the mud involved taking a step closer to the ship, which he was reluctant to do.

Morris trailed behind. The driver of the car stayed in the car, and looked entirely content to remain there.

"It's not radioactive?" he asked. He knew perfectly well that it was not, but asked anyway.

"Nope. One of the sensors will tell us if one day it changes its mind and, I don't know, develops a case of radiation. Not sure how it would work. But we've got stuff checking for it. You know how that goes."

"I do, yes."

There were dozens of electronic gadgets in the field around the ship, powered by solar panels and battery packs. They transmitted information wirelessly to a receiver in a tiny black box on the other side of the fence. From there the information was sent via secure landline to the base, and from there it was shared with a small collection of scientists around the world on a heavily encrypted site that was an example of the finest application of online security in the history of computing.

According to the publicly distributed quarterly reports from the committee responsible for monitoring these sensors, there was nothing happening. This was, in fact, the entirety of the last five reports: *Nothing to report.* It was perhaps the most to-the-point document ever submitted by a government-sponsored committee in the history of government-sponsored committees, and so nobody believed it.

A whole lot of people thought the scientists were hiding something important, and not just the people who made it their life's work to stand outside the compound and point equipment at the anomaly from the roof of a camper. For example, there were people who knew about the space flu, or whatever they wanted to call it. It had no official name because it hadn't been officially acknowledged. It hadn't been acknowledged because nobody could detect it, measure it, and define its scope. Because of *that,* as far as hard science was concerned, it didn't exist, or it existed but was purely psychosomatic. Nobody was lying about that, they just couldn't prove it was real, basically.

Despite the lack of scientific rigor, Ed was well aware that the army chose not to station any men inside the perimeter fence out of concern for what might happen to them if they remained in close proximity for long periods. Army-speak on the subject was remarkably similar to the language employed when discussing radioactivity: *length of exposure* and *long-term impacts* and so on. Rumor was, this was the real reason they'd built a base so far from the landing site.

"Hold up," Morris said. Ed had managed to make it all the way around to the back of the craft, staying within arm's reach of the fence the entire time. He felt no effect from the perhaps-nonexistent space flu, but didn't know if that meant everything or nothing.

Morris stepped past him, looked left and right, and up.

"Yeah, about here. This is where we think the incursion must have begun."

"How can you tell?"

He shrugged, and pointed to the sensors. "Ask the fellas jacked into those things."

"There would have been a lot of foot traffic to sort through."

"Oh, I agree." He pointed to the land on the other side of the fence. "Three years back, there were more trees. We cleared a lot of 'em out to put up the fence and clean up sightlines for the guards. Maybe it was a terrain assessment, I don't know."

"Not much to tell about it now."

"No, we can't get anything from the site, we know that. Just saying, this is where they probably came up to it. Useful information or not, that's up to you."

Ed stopped at the point Morris identified, turned and faced the ship.

It was a known thing that the ship looked more or less the same from every angle. It had four landing feet, and six distinct spotlight-sized indents, so obviously there were differences of perspective when looking at them, but the vehicle's torso had little in the way of distinguishing features. If there was a hatch, nobody knew where it was.

"We gotta get closer," Morris said.

He pulled out a thing that looked like a flashlight but that was actually a slightly modified flashlight.

"Do we really?"

"No we do not. We have pictures in that folder I gave you. But you said yourself you want to go in this order, and look at the anomaly with your own eyes, so here we are. I can't even promise we'll see it, but we can try."

"But . . ."

"Just walk with me, son. It's not so bad."

They took ten paces toward the ship. With each step, Ed found himself interrogating every stray thought as if it didn't belong. He'd heard so many stories from the people who'd come close to the craft regarding what, *exactly* what, they were thinking in those moments. He knew approximately what to expect. He didn't know what it would feel like, though.

It turned out when one expected one's mind to begin to wander inappropriately, one's mind began to wander inappropriately. It was exactly the kind of self-fulfilling prophecy which made arguments that the effect was real sound so nutty.

"Breathe normal," Morris said. "We aren't close enough yet."

"You've done this before?"

"Sure. First thing I did when I got here was try and touch it."

"*Really?*"

Morris laughed. "Yeah. I'm not the only one who's tried over the years. My predecessor tried at least once a month."

"There isn't anything in the reports about it."

"Nope. We keep it to ourselves."

"But the sensors . . ."

"They have their little brown-outs from time to time. Lightning storms'll knock out half of them just from atmospheric charge. It's not monitored a hundred percent reliably, I'm saying. One of us wants to give it a go, we know where the switch is, nobody's the wiser."

"They might be aware now, don't they have audio equipment out here?"

"You know as well as I do, the system's designed to filter out human noise. Plus the ship sucks up sound."

"I'm just a little surprised to hear you're all disobeying orders."

"Funny thing, nobody's issued a command not to touch the ship. I've checked. They just figure we won't. And hey, nobody's done it. It'd be a much bigger deal otherwise."

Ed wondered if Morris was either exaggerating the frequency by which this was attempted or, if not that, understating the impact a successful incursion would have. It was a little like checking the safety on a gun by holding it to your head and pulling the trigger. The safety never failed, but if it did the consequences wouldn't offset the importance of proving it faulty.

Or not. They didn't know the consequence of touching the ship because, supposedly, nobody ever had. The very fact that nobody seemed capable of doing this meant great import was attached to the performance of this act, which was where the gun-safety analogy became important. It could also explain why even military men who should know better were lining up to give it a try.

They got closer, and Ed began to think about what he had for breakfast, grew concerned that this wasn't him thinking this at all, then took a deep breath and tried lowering his heart rate.

All in my head, he told himself.

"We usually do the infrared scans at night, by drone," Morris said. "We're doing this manually during the day, so like I said I can't promise we'll see anything."

"How close does the drone get?"

"About ten feet. They get any closer and they'll malfunction. We crashed a few on purpose to see what that malfunction would look like. It's pretty awesome."

"Is that something you do once a month too?"

"No, the drones are too expensive. But if you want to watch, we have video footage of it. It's not the bug zap, though. You gotta fire a high-impact projectile to experience that. The drones lose altitude, flip around, and crash. Like their on-board instruments got hacked."

"A virus."

"You'd think. But we broke down one of the ones that came out intact and didn't find anything. Anyway, the first anomaly triggered a new round of tests, and that included a new infrared search, and here we are. But you know all about this, don't you?"

He did. Even the drone tests, which he'd actually witnessed via videoconference one time.

"Yes, but I'm finding the longer you talk the easier it is to keep walking."

Another five paces, and Morris turned on the flashlight, and nothing happened.

"Oh, hang on."

He rummaged around in his jacket pocket and came out with two sets of plastic eyewear. They looked like the 3-D glasses handed out at movies.

They both put the glasses on. It made the sunlight look much more impressive, but only made the ship look blacker. It occurred to Ed for the first time that perhaps the hull of the vessel was more than *just* black. As if the light absorption rate was higher than it should be.

"If they can see us from those camper roofs right now . . ." Ed said.

"Ah, don't worry about them. Nobody puts much stock in what they have to say." He looked up and toward the road. "But I don't think they can. The angle's poor and we kept the trees near the road intact for a reason."

Morris waved the flashlight around. This time the termination point of the beam was visible. He directed it toward the ship, but the light became too diffuse too quickly to make a difference.

"Little closer," he said.

They went another five paces. The end of the beam began to co-alesce into a wide circle on the side of the ship.

Four more paces. The beam began to tighten and brighten, and then Morris began probing the surface looking for . . . something.

Ed realized he hadn't called his mother in nearly two months.

It wasn't really a big deal—they went much longer than that routinely, especially since the divorce. She'd been kind enough to wait until well after Ed had moved out and established a life of his own before telling both him and her husband—his father—how unhappy she was. A whirlwind divorce that devastated Ed's dad, and bewildered Ed, resulted in her relocating to Florida, opening up a yarn store, and cohabitating with "Aunt" Linda, a long-time friend of the family and (apparently) the lesbian lover of the former Mrs. Somerville. Then Dad died of congestive heart failure, because he never took care of himself, and that caused more than a little friction between Ed and his mom, but they patched that up a couple of years back and now he was used to hearing her voice semi-regularly.

She didn't even know he was in Sorrow Falls! Sure, it was supposed to be something like a secret, but not a *big* secret, not necessarily. Not the kind of thing a man should have to keep from his mother. It wasn't like he was going to tell her *why* he was there. He could say he was on vacation or something. But she'd get a kick out of it, knowing he was there, and he was standing right near the ship. Because in a way it was the ship that helped them reconnect. When it landed, and everyone thought the world was going to end, he picked up the phone and called her and ended up settling the mess that had gone on with Dad and the divorce and everything else. She should know where he was standing.

He stopped and turned around, pulling out his cell phone.

"Put that away," Morris said.

"I was just going to . . ."

"Yeah, I know. You suddenly realized there was something much more important you should be doing right now, way more important than looking at the side of a piece of extraterrestrial technology. And you have to do that thing this very second."

"I want to call my mother."

"And you should. A boy should always call his mother. But not right now. Congratulations, you had your first intrusive thought. Now look where the beam is."

"I . . ."

"Son, I've just become convinced I left the gun cabinet in my cabin in Nebraska unlocked. I'm about to drop everything to make some calls before someone gets hurt."

"Who?"

"Sheriff's a friend, he has keys and . . . dammit, look where the beam is."

Ed did.

"I don't see anything."

Morris waved the beam around. "Look at the difference," he said.

"Okay, there's a patch, kind of. It's a little brighter, I guess."

"That's right, and it's not true anywhere else."

It wasn't far up the side of the ship, not really. It was at about chest height for an adult male.

"Nobody noticed this before?"

"I think maybe someone did but thought like you did, that it wasn't anything, just a curiosity of shading or something. Or plant matter got on the ship."

"Something could have come down with the last snow."

"Maybe, but doubtful. Snow doesn't stack up."

One of the many minor curiosities of the ship was that snow melted off it. Yet the heat was almost undetectable. It wasn't so much that the ship generated warmth; it was that the snow failed to cool it.

"So there's a splotch on the side of the ship."

"Yeah."

"Did it turn up because of the first anomaly?"

"Unknown."

"I'm under-impressed."

Morris grabbed Ed's wrist and pulled him four paces closer.

"Look at it again," Morris said.

Ed realized he wanted to call his mother because she was dying. She hadn't said so, he had no evidence it was so, but it was as true as anything he'd ever felt. The damn ship wasn't going anywhere; he could look at it any time. But he had to call her.

He looked.

"Do you see now?" Morris asked.

"I have to make a call."

"So do I. Do you see?"

What Ed saw looked like a handprint. It contradicted everything they understood about the spaceship, and it was incredibly important, and in that moment he didn't care even a tiny bit.

"I see it. Now let go of me or my mother is going to die."

5

IN THE LIBRARY, WITH THE CANDLESTICK

*T*here was an enormous mural on the wall of the library. It greeted all persons upon entry, and was the subject of endless hours of scrutiny among the staff employees and volunteers, and many a patron. It was easily the most dramatic—and certainly largest—piece of art in town, if not the state.

The painting was called *Sorrow Fell*, and the most tragic thing about it—aside from what was depicted—was that nobody knew the name of the artist. The town commissioned the artwork to commemorate the foundation of the library, which was in itself odd, as there was nothing in the painting to imply that greater knowledge might be found through books. More curious, all of the historical records detailed the commissioning, installation, and aggrandizement of the mural's creator, but in every last document the name of said creator was either omitted or excised. He or she was only ever referred to as the Artist.

What the Artist painted was the tragic, mundane, and borderline comic founding of Sorrow Falls, which aside from a particularly unusual interpretation of the Bible was an extremely nonliterary event.

In the center of the piece was the heroic figure of Josiah Foster Sorrow, depicted not at all accurately. The Josiah of the painting was a strapping, powerful man with an open collar to reveal his impressive chest hair, traveling in a canoe in the most ridiculous way imaginable: standing, one knee up on the edge of the boat, hips squared, and pelvic region unquestionably augmented for artistic reasons. It looked vaguely like the pose one might expect of a man on the cover of a paperback romance novel.

The real Josiah Foster Sorrow was a cult leader of sorts. Over three hundred years earlier, Josiah fled what he considered religious intolerance in the colonies, taking along his family and many like-minded religious zealots. It was an inconvenient detail that the intolerance the Sorrowers fled was in regard to his peculiarly unpleasant set of beliefs. Such beliefs involved worshipping a God who told them to ignore property rights, marriage banns, and the social and legal standards surrounding the minimum age of sexual consent.

Like an earlier band of Massachusetts settlers, Josiah had been fleeing religious persecution for a little while, having first self-exiled from the Massachusetts colony for what would later be New Hampshire, then for what would later be Vermont, before heading down-river on the Connecticut, into Western Massachusetts and Native American tribal territory.

The Connecticut River was never one of those rivers that could be traversed at length via canoe. This was a detail lost on Josiah and his people, and made for slow going, as they frequently had to stop, beach themselves, carry their boats downstream, and get back in. It was frustrating, and Josiah's God was an impatient deity, so one night his God told Josiah to stop stalling and hurry on down to the Promised Land already.

According to at least half of the legends, what happened next was that Josiah and his Sorrowers came upon a large drop in the river, at dusk. When his followers began heading for the shore, as always, their leader excoriated them for their lack of faith and vowed the Lord would protect them from harm if they only stayed in their canoes.

There were doubts, as most of the Sorrowers—while being unswervingly dedicated to their leader—also had a passing familiarity with gravity and its consequences. So they recommended that Josiah go first.

He did, falling roughly twenty feet to his death upon a rock at the base of the falls—Sorrow's Stone, it was now called—and putting an end to the wanderings of the Sorrowers. For as soon as Josiah perished, the rest of them looked around and concluded that this must surely be the Promised Land they had been told to expect.

They named the place Sorrow Falls, not for the waterfall that claimed Josiah's life, but because this was the place where Sorrow fell.

That was not precisely what was depicted in the painting.

There was a second version of the story, one that saw Josiah not as a determined fanatic who thought he could defy the laws of physics at a very bad moment, but as a peerless leader who was unaccountably distracted at exactly the wrong time.

In the painting, the strong, square chin and determined blue eyes of Josiah Sorrow were pointed upward, at the sky rather than straight ahead. In his line of sight was a bright streak of light—a sign from the heavens.

Unfortunately, this sign's timing was poor. The river beneath Josiah's canoe was disappearing over the falls, but as he was looking up he didn't notice.

The depiction captured, almost comically, the moment just before his death: nearly half of the canoe was pointed over empty space, like something from a cartoon.

It was probably an apocryphal version of events, as the holders of the historical record—the founding Sorrowers—no doubt had cause to re-examine the suicidal last decision of Josiah Sorrow, and perhaps make it come off as less silly and more tragic. *No*, this version said, *there was no talk of God protecting Josiah, it was only that he was leading and became distracted by a light in the sky.*

The mural, then, paid respects to both versions. Yes, Josiah can be seen distracted by a light in the sky, but *look* at him. What an idiot. He doesn't even have his paddle in the water. Who would go canoeing like that?

Unsurprisingly, after the spaceship landed outside of town, the light in the sky responsible for Josiah Foster Sorrow's death became a lot more interesting to a lot more people, and the painting in particular ended up gracing the cover of enough magazines to convince the town council to put some money into getting it restored.

In a bit of irony, the restoration uncovered more of the fading tail of the meteor in the top left corner of the mural. The tail—surely nothing more than an accidental brush stroke by the Artist—had a thirty-degree angle in it.

The Artist, according to some, had predicted the future.

That was probably Annie's favorite part of the painting, or it was on that particular day. Other days she ended up transfixed by a background tree, or the symbolic renderings of wild men in the woods—horror-show versions of Native Americans with dull eyes, reaching out toward the water like the Karloff edition of Frankenstein's monster. Sometimes it was the chaos of the water, or the woman on a canoe way behind Josiah, barely given detail other than a bonnet and an open mouth, screaming to warn him.

Sometimes her favorite part was just that nobody knew who painted it or exactly how old it was.

"Stop staring at it."

Annie was at the library's front desk, directly beneath the enormous mural. When she sat on the middle stool her head was just below Josiah's impressively bulgy crotch. That was never one of her favorite parts of the painting.

She turned to discover a slightly paler version of herself.

"I can't help it," she said to Violet. "There's always something new to look at."

Annie and Violet were the same age, had the same basic physical shape and the same dark brown hair. Anyone filling out a document listing their attendant vital statistics would conclude that they were therefore very similar, and in those simple terms, they were. Annie even thought of Violet that way—as a lost twin sister or lab-created doppelganger, depending on her mood. At the same time, nobody who saw them together could ever mistake them for one another.

To the extent that anyone knew of Violet's existence, they would say she was a shy girl. Her body language said *stay away* under most circumstances, or perhaps *easily frightened*. She was reserved, did not express her opinions easily, assumed nobody was ever talking to her, and didn't like introducing herself to people. Violet was the sort of person that had to be dragged into a social setting and co-erced into interacting, but when she did so the people with whom she interacted usually wondered why the person who had coerced her to do so had bothered.

Vi was home-schooled. She moved into town six years ago, and as Annie liked to joke, if she hadn't discovered Violet, nobody would know she existed other than her parents. It probably wasn't true, but it wasn't that far off either. Vi didn't hang out with any kids her own age unless she was with Annie, and the only time she ever went into town was to hang out with Annie.

All of which made Annie feel as if she had a responsibility to get others to notice Violet. She appreciated that to a certain extent some people were just by nature unsociable and introverted, and as a highly sociable extrovert she would never entirely understand her friend's issues. Telling her to *just be friendly* and all that was probably not helping.

Annie still did it more often than she probably should. Violet was the smartest person she knew, and Annie knew a lot of smart people. (Annie was, by her own estimation, extremely smart. Violet was smarter.) If Violet were in the public school system a lot more people would know this about her, and then maybe Annie wouldn't have to spend as much time convincing other people how cool her friend was.

"It's kind of amateurish, really," Vi said. "The color composition is terrible, and the artistic style . . . I mean, what is he even doing with his . . ."

"The pelvic thrust for Jesus, right here?"

"Yes, the groin region. Someone rewrote a lot of history there."

"He did take several wives, maybe the man had the goods."

"I think it's more of a Methuselah touch."

"Explain."

"All the exceptionally wise men in the Old Testament ended up living extra-long lives. It was an artistic flourish to put a number behind exactly *how* wise they were."

"Methuselah didn't actually live nine hundred years?"

Annie began singing "It Ain't Necessarily So" in her head, which was a little curious only because while she knew the song was a show tune from *Porgy and Bess*, she didn't know how she knew that or when she ever heard the song.

Probably something we watched together, she decided.

She and her mother were always catching up on something older than Annie, and sometimes older than either of them.

"It was nine hundred and sixty-nine years. And no. If he was lucky, he lived to sixty-nine."

"I am shocked . . . *shocked* . . . that you would suggest a non-literal interpretation of the Bible. In front of Josiah, no less. And his enormous member."

"I'm pretty sure Josiah was sicklier than that too. He was seizure-prone and probably had syphilis."

"Source, please."

"Half of the Sorrowers were dead in a year from it and he had multiple wives. And it wasn't like they picked it up from the Indians."

"Native Americans, please."

"Noted."

"The court finds your argument in favor of Josiah Sorrow having syphilis unconvincing."

"On what grounds?"

"Speculation!"

She banged a hardbound copy of *Essentials of Gardening* on the counter to gavel home her judgment.

"If it pleases the court, what time is the judge getting the heck out of this place?"

"I can leave whenever. Nobody's here."

This was a common fact of the library, especially in the summer, when the high school that stood behind it and up the hill about a quarter of a mile wasn't in session. Annie went between deciding that was sad, and not worrying much about it. A lot of books could be found online nowadays, so what could have been interpreted as a lessening of interest in reading was maybe actually a change in the way information was obtained.

True, there were a lot of books that weren't available in any form other than print. The Sorrow Falls library had plenty of such books, and if it did — it was not in any real sense a large collection — there had to be a ton of such books out there. At the same time, a whole bunch of those books were perfectly dreadful. They were as relevant as historical artifacts, perhaps, like Methuselah's exaggerated age, but not as valuable resources in and of themselves. They had meta-historical value, at most.

"So what are my reasons for closing early?" Annie asked. "What do you have for me that could be better than this?"

She waved her hand at Josiah's package.

"I have the car, and cash, and the sun is still out."

"Oooh!"

"Does it please the court?"

"It pleases the court immensely."

⋮

Annie had a driver's license. She got it as soon as it was legally possible to do so, even though she had almost no use for one, because there was only one car in the family. Annie only drove it once, on the occasion in which she got her license. Since then, she'd driven Violet's family car twice and that was all. It was okay; she didn't enjoy the experience — it looked *much* easier when other people did it — but thought that this was perhaps because she wasn't a particularly good driver.

Violet, on the other hand, seemed to have access to the car whenever she wanted, and was clearly a better driver. Annie only sort-of knew Violet's parents and certainly not well enough to ask them what they did for a living or why that existence didn't require their use of the car, but that was clearly the case. Her mother—Susan—mostly stayed at home, and her father—Todd—seemed to have the kind of job that used a company car and had him leaving for extended periods, but beyond that it was an Adult Thing. Annie knew about plenty of Adult Things in the town, but this was one she never tried understanding.

Plus, the happy consequence was that Violet got the use of the car, which meant Annie got the use of the car. As long as that continued to be true, Annie wasn't going to ask any hard questions.

It took Annie about ten minutes to close down the library for the afternoon. The building was theoretically large enough for someone to hide inside of one of the stacks without being detected, but they would have to want to do it. Otherwise, it was impossible for this to happen by accident, because the library carried sound incredibly well. It was something only a few people realized, for the obvious reason that most people were trying to be quiet while inside. Once Annie walked from end to end loudly declaring her intention to bolt the door for the remainder of the day, only the deaf would have failed to hear her.

"Where to?" Annie asked, as she threw her bike into the back of Violet's incredibly unsexy hatchback.

"Your choice. Where do the youths gather?"

"The youths gather at the mall."

"Then we shall hie to the mall."

"Verily."

The engine kicked to life with tremendous reluctance, and they were off, pulling out of the library's modest parking area onto Main and then left, past the protesters, over the river, and out of town.

"Think something's up with Shippie," Annie said, as Vi took them toward the highway.

"Something's always up with Shippie."

Shippie was what the two of them called the spaceship, but only when they were alone. Annie tried using it on other people but nobody much cared for the nickname. The name was borrowed from

Nessie, because there seemed to be a certain kinship between Sorrow Falls's most famous visitor and Loch Ness's most famous lake inhabitant. The ship was very real, while Nessie probably was not, but that didn't seem like a huge distinction back when they were thirteen.

"Yeah, but this might be legit."

"This isn't from your friends on the roof, is it?"

"No. They had something too, but it wasn't really something."

"They're still seeing canals on Mars, those people."

Sometimes, Violet sounded uncomfortably like an adult, especially when she was judging the behavior of actual adults. In this case, she was referring to the erroneous sighting by various scientifically inclined persons in history of water-bearing canals on the surface of Mars. It was an optical illusion, which should have been obvious when the drawings of the canals were compared to one another.

Annie got the reference, because this was the sort of minutia one learned when hanging out with Violet, who was some kind of trivia savant.

"They're enthusiastic is all. It's good to be enthusiastic about something."

Violet smiled.

"I guess. So what's the thing?"

"I don't know yet. A guy turned up this morning asking for Joanne. I went and talked to him."

"You *talked* to him? Why'd you do that?"

"Dunno. He looked approachable. He didn't have the kind of skeeve a lot of those guys have. Clean-cut, laptop, young."

"Stop hitting on older men."

"Oh my God."

"I'm serious."

"I wasn't hitting on him, he's like thirty or something. He just didn't look skeevy is what I mean. He looked like a normalish guy with a normalish understanding of the modern world. He wasn't . . . what did you call them?"

"Ink-stained wretches."

"Yes, he wasn't like that. Except now I'm pretty sure he's not a reporter."

"All right, now you're confusing me."

"He never *said* he was a reporter. I talked to him about the story he was writing, and he talked back as if he was in fact writing a story, but he didn't say *reporter*. And when he gave me his name he didn't say anything about who he was writing for. I'm pretty sure I've never met a reporter who didn't give the name of his magazine or newspaper in the first thirty seconds. A lot of them say it before they even say their *own* names."

"Maybe it's a crummy paper and he's embarrassed."

"A writer for a crummy paper getting a tour of Shippie?"

"He's getting a tour? Like, they're letting him inside the fence?"

"That's what my sources say."

"Well, you're right, that would indicate some prestige, if not his, then the company he's attached to. He gave you his name?"

"Edgar Somerville. I looked him up, and either he gave me a fake name or the guy doesn't have a byline in any major publication."

Violet side-eyed her. "Uh-huh. What did you check?"

"The database in the library and the Internet."

"Did you check the scientific journals?"

"Of course I did."

"Government?"

"What, like position papers and bills?"

"Sure."

"Those don't really come with bylines."

"Hmm. I guess you'll have to go flirt with him some more."

"I wasn't flirting!"

Violet maneuvered the hatchback into highway traffic and stuck to the right-hand lane, both because the mall was only two exits down and because the car couldn't hold at sixty-five MPH without screaming and rattling, and every car on the road was going faster than that.

"So if he's not a reporter, what is he here for?" Vi asked.

"Not a clue, but like I said, he got to see the ship. Hardly anybody does that anymore. Dobbs and Mr. Shoeman will have to fill me in tomorrow about his visit. I'm assuming they recorded the whole thing."

"Yes or your army boyfriend."

"Sam? He won't tell me anything. No, I take that back. If something happened, he won't tell me anything. If nothing happened, he'll say so."

"How will you know the difference?"

"Oh, I'll know."

Vi laughed.

Off the highway exit, she followed the generously large signs to the parking lot of the Oakdale Mall, which was surprisingly congested for a weekday afternoon.

⋮

Sometime in the past ten years, some intrepid marketer got the idea that the word "mall" was a negative, so beginning with the shopping malls close to the downtown Boston area and radiating outward, the chain malls had been getting makeovers and new names.

In all fairness, the makeovers were sometimes quite impressive, in that they turned low-end strip malls into upscale centers with a higher quality of stores. The rebranding was a pretty effective way of signaling that change. Still, when it turned the Oakdale Mall into *the Oakdale Experience*, pretty much everyone laughed. Annie didn't know one person who called it that without irony. Even tourists weren't quite sure what to think.

Whoever was in charge of redesigning the mall did a fantastic job, though. What had been a large rectangular building surrounded by parking was turned into a rectangular parking area surrounded by shops, with a smaller rectangle of shops in the middle. From the air, it looked like an especially thick digital zero. This seemed like a catastrophic choice for a New England shopping center—who would shop at an outdoor plaza in the winter?—but it worked surprisingly well. The restaurants, movie theater, and bowling alley made it the kind of place people went to spend the day rather than visit in order to shop, and that turned out to be an important distinction.

Annie didn't have a lot of spending money at any given time, but she enjoyed going to the mall when circumstances conspired in her favor. A generation or two ago "the mall" might have been a place for someone of her age and/or economic level to go and "hang out," and perhaps use a skateboard and harass angry white adults like in the music videos from the '90s. (These videos looked as dated to her as the black-and-white films she watched with her mother. In fairness, everything pre-spaceship looked a *little* dated anyway, but these looked like especially quaint artifacts. Especially the clothing.) For her, hanging out at the mall, more often than not, meant figuring out who'd gotten a job where. It was basically the only place in the area that hired high-school-age kids on a consistent basis.

The Oakdale Mall (everyone still called it this) also benefited greatly from being the only shopping center of consequence within a twenty-mile radius of the spaceship. Sure, there were the authentic and semi-authentic shops on Main Street, but almost without exception those shops ended up being places to stop at briefly, and not to linger. Plus, one of the things that made Main so very authentic was a thorough lack of parking.

The typical activities arc of the Sorrow Falls tourist was, in order: see the spaceship; discover the ship was not all that interesting a thing to look at; visit Main; if lucky, find parking; shop for approximately forty minutes; hear something about "the Oakdale Experience" and conclude incorrectly that it was perhaps—with a name like that—an amusement park; head to the mall; spend remainder of vacation there.

One would think the town of Sorrow Falls would be interested in encouraging people to stay, perhaps by building a mall of their own, but after three years the town's attitude toward visitors was permanently affixed somewhere between blandly courteous and *get the hell off my lawn.* Just about any local, when asked, would tell a visitor, "You should really check out Oakdale!" and not think twice about it. They would even offer directions.

It was one of the only places Annie visited outside of Sorrow Falls on any kind of consistent basis. It was too far to bike, though, so she had to rely on people with cars. This was also one of the reasons she didn't have a job there, although not the only one. She also didn't want to be too far from the ship, for more or less the same reason Mr. Shoeman and the rest of the rooftop city people couldn't bring themselves to leave. She didn't want to be the one who gave up waiting on something to happen right before something happened.

She also didn't want to be too far from her mom for too long at a time.

⋮

Violet found a spot at the top corner of the plaza, right in front of a fiberglass model of the ship. It was an impressive replica, built to scale, with enough detail to pass as the real thing when one was squinting. It sat in the middle of an extra-large sidewalk in front of the movie theater, which was appropriate: it was one of the models used in the movie version of the Sorrow Falls story, donated to the town by the filmmakers as thanks for their hospitality. Naturally, the town thought the replica was tacky and immediately donated it to Oakdale.

The two things Annie thought particularly funny about the replica: first, everyone assumed it was not to scale because they thought the actual ship was much bigger; second, there was a glass case around the ship and a velvet rope around the case, to prevent anybody from touching it, meaning even when fake versions of the ship were put together, nobody could put a hand on it.

This was the most ostentatious of the dozen or so things in the mall that were meant to connect the Experience with the slow invasion happening up-road. That list didn't even include the gigantic souvenir shop.

"Hello, Shippie," Annie said to the model as they got out of the car.

"Don't talk to it, people will stare," Vi said.

"Ignore the olds, skatergirl, let's go smoke some cigs."

". . . what?"

"Never mind. C'mon, I think Rachel's working at VS now."

⋮

"Hey, did you hear?"

Sometimes Annie liked to pretend she was a sociologist, and her job was to evaluate her own life. It was a kind of meta-distancing trick she pulled under certain circumstances, in which she saw herself interacting directly with the world while at the same time standing back and taking notes.

In the ninety-odd minutes it took to nearly complete a full circuit of the outer ring of shops—with one brief stopover at the ice cream shop at the inner building—Annie encountered over a dozen people she might call friends. Sociologist Annie's notes listed them as *fellow tribal members*, with additional margin notes like *potential mate* and *competition*.

The standard greeting for this tribe would be *Hey, did you hear?* It was how they all said hello, and how they verified their tribal statuses. It was also the preamble to the transmission of vital social, political, and legal issues concerning members of said tribe, which were of critical import to the entire unit.

None of it mattered, while at the same time all of it was terribly important. This was what Violet—who was a much more authentic sociologist, really—never entirely understood. It was true that in the proverbial Grand Scheme of Things, it wasn't terribly important that Rachel broke up with Luke after hearing he made out with Lucy at Marko's party—which she wasn't even invited to!—and then got, like, *sick* drunk and passed out on the floor of Marko's pool house, especially since that wasn't half as earth-shattering as the news that Tina was *completely* gay for Nona, except Nona was only pretending to be a lesbian to piss off her parents while Tina was pretending to be straight so as not to piss off *her* parents, which was *amazing* news except for the much more amazing story about Dougie shaving his *entire* head for no reason at *all* except Dougie is a dork who thinks he's going to join the army, which is stupid because the army doesn't let in dorks, *besides which*, the army wasn't even all that cool, and oh, did you hear Rick thought he saw a vampire? *No joke!*

"I have an important question," Violet said, over two burgers and a shared milkshake. They were sitting in the dining area of the bowling alley, which was not at all like a typical New England bowling alley, for a number of reasons. First, the food was actually excellent. They had the best burger at the mall, only nobody knew it because when people wanted a burger they went to one of the two places that specialized in burgers. Second, it was 100 percent tenpin bowling. Most of New England bowled a version called candlepin, which used narrow pins and shotput-sized balls. It was about a thousand times more frustrating than tenpin, which meant it served an important regional purpose of teaching local children how to swear effectively.

"Hit me."

"Do you *like* any of those people?"

Annie laughed.

"How long have you wanted to ask me that?"

"About as long as I've known you. Or since you started trying to indoctrinate me."

"Ooh, indoctrination. That's definitely what I'm doing. No, come on, I'm just trying to, I don't know, insert you into the world a little."

"I'm perfectly happy with my degree of insertion."

In the ninety-odd minutes of their whirlwind shopping circuit (in which there was virtually no shopping) Violet had said approximately five words, and all five of them were *hi*. The people of Annie's tribe knew her exactly well enough to understand that Vi was meant to be ignored, and that she preferred it that way.

"I know you are, but it's not healthy!"

"I'm perfectly healthy as well."

"But I can't be your only lifeline to the world, what if something happens to me?"

"What's going to happen to you?"

"I don't know, but something could! And if it did and I wasn't around anymore, your meager social skills would just wither away. A decade from now you'll be like Nell, grunting in a cabin in the woods."

"I already live in a cabin in the woods."

"*That's my point.*"

Violet sighed grandly.

"All right, I will *try*. But seriously, the banality is difficult to stomach."

"You are so full of it."

"Me? How so?"

"Nobody is *actually* this pretentious. People have to work at it."

"I think I'm offended."

"See, that's what I mean, you can't actually even *be* offended, you have to announce that it's a possibility you may at some point develop a feeling, and that feeling if, when felt, might develop into a sensation akin to a quality reminiscent of offense."

"Well, I would never say that, but that was impressive. You should write it down."

Annie threw a balled-up straw wrapper at Vi, and then Rodney sat down.

"Hey, did you hear?" he said.

Rodney Delindo was either nineteen or twenty, which put him squarely outside of the tribal demographic of Annie's sociology study. He still had a spot inside her circle of friends, though, perhaps an even more important spot than most everyone aside from Vi. Rodney was, for a short while not too terribly long ago, quite possibly Annie's very best friend.

They hardly spoke anymore, because they both got older and things changed. Rodney's graduation from high school was one of those things. He was a manager at the bowling alley now, while he considered his higher-education options. This meant, in less polite terms, his grades were not fantastic and his ability to pay college tuition suspect. At the same time, the job still had to be considered temporary because nobody goes through life planning to be a shift manager at a bowling alley. Especially not one without a candle-pin lane.

He was Annie's first crush. She never said so, but he probably knew it.

When he sat down, he flipped the chair over so the back was facing the table, and then straddled it cowboy-style. It was a modestly stud-worthy maneuver.

"Hey, Rod. What were we supposed to have heard?"

"Yes, there's so much," Violet said. Annie shot her a look, and got back a *you wanted me to engage, so* . . . shrug.

Rodney more or less pretended Vi wasn't there. It wasn't even impolite; it was just what one did.

"About Rick."

"I heard he saw a vampire. But this is Rick we're talking about." Rodney laughed.

"No, no, it wasn't a vampire."

"Of course it wasn't. That's my point. Rick is Rick."

Rick Horton was a year above Annie, which made him seventeen and still four years away from the legal drinking age, when he could officially fulfill the role he'd been training for his entire life, that of the town drunk.

Wildly insensitive, Annie the sociologist wrote in her notebook.

Rick was the first local kid roughly Annie's age that had a self-evident drinking problem. It didn't seem possible for someone so young to exhibit alcoholic tendencies, but by most accounts, Rick had his first beer when he was twelve and hadn't stopped drinking since.

The last two or three times Annie spoke to Rick, it became clear he was also auditioning for town crackpot. He was working on a number of fascinatingly disturbing theories about the spaceship and the army that were a complicated synthesis of everything the trailer people had to say combined with the wild theories from the protesters. Just add alcohol and stir.

Literally anything could follow *did you hear about Rick?* She expected one day it would be *he died*, but not yet.

Vampires were right in his wheelhouse.

"No, I mean it wasn't a vampire, it was something else."

"Go on," Violet said. Rodney looked her way, confused momentarily, wearing an expression along the lines of *I did not know it spoke.*

"So you remember Mr. Granger?"

"From seventh grade? Sure."

"And do you know . . ." He looked a little uncomfortable, because the next part of the sentence was *that he died*, and it just occurred to him if she did *not* know this, the way he was breaking the news was probably a tiny bit insensitive.

"Yeah, so sad," Annie said. "He was young, too." To Violet, she said, "He taught English in middle school. He was really cool."

"He died?"

"Couple weeks ago. It was really sudden. Heart attack?"

"I think so," Rodney said.

"I think he was only maybe fifty. Used to jog, too."

"Yeah, we'd pass him in the morning, remember?"

"I do."

Rodney's family lived up the road from Annie. She used to hitch rides in the winter.

"So what about Mr. Granger?" Annie asked.

"Rick said he saw him."

Annie laughed.

"Was Mr. Granger the vampire?"

"Not a vampire. What Rick said was, he saw the undead. People filled that in."

"So, wait, okay, Mr. Granger is a zombie?"

"Where did he see him?" Violet asked.

"Uhm . . ." Rodney was still perplexed regarding the existence of Violet.

"He was drinking in the cemetery, wasn't he?" Annie asked. She thought this was hysterical, and couldn't really understand why nobody else did. "That's priceless."

"No, no it was . . . well, he didn't say exactly."

"You got this from him?"

"Yes, he told me himself. He was really spooked."

"So where?" Violet repeated.

"Okay, so the whole story, Rick said he was hanging with Ellard. You know Ellard?"

"I know him by sight. I don't think I've ever talked to him."

"He and Rick . . . they hang out."

"Ellard can buy alcohol."

Ellard Baron was twenty-two, and the kind of person young girls were told to steer clear of.

"Yeah, I'm sure that's a factor. So he and Ellard were going tipping . . ."

"Oh, good Lord."

"What's tipping?" Violet asked.

"Cow-tipping," Annie said. "Could they be more stereotypical? Did they also have moonshine in jugs? Jesus. I'm embarrassed on their behalf right now."

"So Rick and Ellard headed up Cedar in Ellard's pickup, looking for a cow. But you know how the farms are up there, not much to see from the road, especially at night. I guess they pulled off at some point and started wandering on foot."

Annie sighed. "I can see where this is going."

"I can't," Vi said.

"Once you leave Cedar, you're pretty much just hopping stone fences one after the other. It's really easy to get lost up there, isn't it, Rod?"

"It is. Story is, they settled down, edge of one pasture or another, and started drinking. Never found a cow. Then Ellard passed out. Sometime around who knows when, Rick heard somebody walking around in the trees. He was thinking farmer, shotgun, that sort of thing, so he ducked down behind the fence. That's when he swears Mr. Granger walked on past."

"In the dark, in the woods. Was there even a moon that night?"

"I don't know what night it happened. I guess I can catch up to him and check."

Violet had pulled out her phone and opened a maps application.

"Cedar Road. This here?"

She pointed to a small road surrounded on both sides by no

roads at all. Cedar was one of those poorly paved barely-two-lane roads that were commonplace in Sorrow Falls and large portions of the entire valley. It was the kind of tributary Spaceship Road used to be, before it was Spaceship Road.

"Yeah, that's it. By the way, I'm Rodney." He extended his hand. Conservatively, he had met Violet on six prior occasions.

"Violet," she said, shaking his hand. "How far up Cedar do you suppose they were?"

"Seriously, no idea."

She zoomed in on the map, pulled it left and right.

"Where was Mr. Granger buried?"

"Violet, seriously."

"I'm showing interest."

"You're creeping me out."

She turned to Rodney. "So you don't know."

"No, but I get what you're saying."

"What's she saying?" Annie asked.

"Peacock Cemetery's just over that hill."

"You are seriously both just messing with me on this, aren't you?"

"Yes," Violet said. "That's all." She swiped the maps image to one side and put it down in front of Annie without saying anything about it.

"I'm sure this Rick was just drunk," Vi said to Rodney.

Annie looked at where her friend stopped the map. Cedar Road ran more or less precisely between the cemetery and the field where Shippie rested.

This meant nothing, of course.

6

GUESS WHO'S COMING TO DINNER

*T*he conversation at the bowling alley soon devolved into an exchange of some of the gossip Annie picked up earlier that day, some of which Rodney even cared about. Then there was a pin jam on some far lane that needed immediate tending-to, and he was back to work.

They were on the road shortly after.

"Geez, Vi, I wanted you to engage in conversation, not act like a crazy person."

"Sorry. You know I'm not good at this. I just thought it was interesting."

"Yeah, well, now I'm freaking out over zombies, thanks. Vampires I can handle."

"Neither one is real."

"I appreciate that, but if I'm going to be afraid of something that isn't real I'd rather it be vampires. At least some of them are a sexy kind of not real. Zombies are just gross. Plus, what does the ship even have to do with any of this?"

"Nothing! I just thought . . . Never mind. I thought if this Rick fellow was going to make up something that happened in a certain place, he picked an interesting place."

"It's not *that* interesting. I can think of two other cemeteries and one pre-colonial burial ground around here, and I could pick almost any street and draw a straight line going from one of those sites, across the road I'd picked, ending at the ship. I mean I guess if I'm a zombie, and I really, really want to see the spaceship, I'd rather be buried in Peacock than Winterhill, so that's smart thinking by Mr. Granger."

"I doubt he had much say in it."

"I'm kidding."

"Oh."

Annie's phone vibrated. She pulled it out and discovered she'd been missing some texts.

where u?

u shd come home.

"Oops, Mom's looking."

"Is she all right?" Vi asked.

"Yeah, she just wants me home. No emergency."

With Vi. Heading home now. Driving.

It was ten minutes from the mall to the end of Main, and another twenty to the house. Violet went by way of Patience and Liberty instead of taking Spaceship Road, even though the route that took them past Shippie was largely clear of traffic by nightfall on most evenings. That may have been because it was harder to see the ship at night. The army had spotlights on it, but those didn't help as much as they should have. Plus, sightseeing in the dark just wasn't a thing.

It would have been faster, then, to take Spaceship Road, but Violet preferred the second route, or perhaps was just on automatic, since it also went past the road that led to her house. Vi's default excitement level in regard to the ship was also much lower than Annie's.

When they pulled up to the house, the spot behind the family Honda was taken by a black SUV.

"You sure no emergency?" Violet asked.

"We have a code worked out, you know that," Annie said. "And that doesn't look like an ambulance."

"No, that's a government vehicle. Look at the plate."

"Yeah," Annie agreed. "Army car. I don't really like this. Wanna come in?"

"No. Text me later."

"You're not curious?"

"I'm very curious. Text me later."

Annie jumped out of the car and waited for Violet to release the trunk so she could extract her bike. The driver of the SUV—military man in plain clothes, she didn't recognize him but he had the Look—was standing next to the car. He noticed her and pretended not to. She wondered if he called anyone indoors to notify them of her impending entrance.

She got the bike out after some work and wheeled it to the front porch, which was where it lived. The inner door was ajar, but this was hardly unusual. They lived far enough from proper civilization that they rarely locked up.

Annie's house was on a small street that got a decent amount of traffic only because it connected the northern side of a bowl valley to the southern side of the same valley. In the center of the bowl was farmland. The house was on the lip, so from her bedroom window on the second floor (above the front door) she could look down on the private farms of six families. It looked a whole lot prettier than it smelled, because someone was always spreading fertilizer down there, and the wind always seemed to blow it toward her room.

It wasn't the sort of place Annie would intentionally bring a guest. This was the first thing she thought of when finding Edgar Somerville in her living room. He and the army man who had picked him up that morning at the diner were both there, drinking coffee, and talking to her mother.

Annie didn't quite know what to make of this peculiar arrangement of humans, but she was pretty positive she wasn't okay with it.

"There you are, honey," her mother said. She got up and gave her daughter a hug, which got her close enough to whisper: *"What have you been up to?"*

Annie smiled and shook her head, to say *I have no idea.*

"Mom, you should sit down. Are you feeling okay?"

Her mother was the kind of thin that looked unhealthy, because it was. Carol Collins was not in any real sense a healthy woman, physically, and her mind was nearly as suspect at this stage. She was dressed in an assortment of scarves and a loose caftan and standing in a living room that smelled of pot smoke, which—if Annie's somewhat acclimated nose could smell it—meant she'd had a joint recently. It was not a good time for the military to drop in unannounced. Not that there was ever a good time for that sort of thing.

"Oh, I feel fine, Annie. Don't worry. She worries."

Edgar and Army Guy nodded politely. Annie could only imagine what they had been talking about before she got there.

The couch the guests were sitting on bore some similarities to the way Annie's mom was dressed, in that it was covered in blankets and sheets—plus a couple of towels—and was maybe even being held together by all of it. Most of the couch springs had surrendered all of their potential energy years ago and were just there to keep a little space between the top and the bottom of the seating area. Despite this, it remained superbly comfortable, although perhaps not the best thing to be sitting on should the need to rise quickly present itself. It was no coincidence, then, that a fire extinguisher was bolted to the wall next to it: if there was a fire it might take less time to put the fire out than to get off the couch.

The rest of the room was a collection of mismatched electronics verging on antique status, two floor lamps losing a battle with gravity, and an embarrassingly vast library of old movies on videotape. Every surface—the fireplace mantel, the end tables—was decorated with two or three porcelain tchotchkes, a drink coaster, a pen commemorating something, or an ashtray.

It wasn't the kind of place meant for guests, but when they had them it was the guests who tended to act embarrassed, because this was a room that suggested privacy and intimacy, and *not for public consumption.*

"These men were just here to, well, I guess to offer you a job of some kind, isn't that right?" her mother said with something close to a smile. It was impossible to tell if she was incredibly amused or if Annie was in a lot of trouble.

"It was her suggestion, actually," Ed said, somewhat louder than he meant to. "I just decided to take her up on it."

"I wonder, um . . ." Annie looked at Army Guy. "I'm sorry, we haven't met, have we? You are?"

He stood — this took some effort — and offered his hand. "Brigadier General Morris, Ms. Collins. A pleasure. Your reputation precedes you."

"My reputation? Okay. Okay, can I . . . ? General, I wonder if you could keep my mom company for a minute while I talk to . . . Mr. Somerville in private? Would that be all right?"

"Absolutely."

"Great. Ed, if you could just . . . no, not my room, let's go outside."

She led him out onto the front porch.

There were a great many reasons not to hold this conversation anywhere else in the house, because despite the inhospitable nature of the living room to all but close family and friends, the rest of the house was possibly even worse. About two years earlier they'd discovered dry rot in some of the floorboards on the first floor, and her father — who didn't live with them in any real sense — decided to tear out the floorboards to stop the rot from spreading. This was a good idea provided those floorboards eventually got replaced, and they hadn't been. He was due to return in October, at which time he would hopefully finish the job, but given that she and Carol had been saying that every six months for two years, there was a reason to think it wasn't going to be happening.

What it meant was that navigating the house to get to just about any other room aside from the kitchen (which had a direct exit from the living room) meant going down a corridor that opened directly to the root cellar in three different places.

Annie took Ed past her bike and down the creaky wooden porch stairs and around the side of the house. The entire time, he looked either confused or embarrassed, or something in the middle of both.

"*What are you doing here?*" she demanded.

"Calm down."

"Don't tell me to calm down, you showed up at my *house?*"

"I'm really sorry. I promise you, I didn't . . . look, I didn't know your mom was sick."

"Didn't know? It's none of your business. It's not *anyone's* business unless I . . ."

"I know, all right? I screwed up. Look, I mean . . . it's kind of your own fault, really."

"I didn't invite you here, how is this my fault?"

"You suggested it!"

"I suggested you hire me to show you around, I did *not* suggest a house call."

"Right, and I'm the idiot who's going to put a sixteen-year-old on the payroll without getting her parent's permission first. In this day and age."

"On the . . . wait a minute, you're going to pay me?"

"No, the army's going to pay you."

She shook her head and stepped back like he had just whipped open his pants. "Whaaaat is going on?"

"I can't really tell you."

"You gotta tell me *something*. Like why you're seriously about to turn me into a government agent."

"Don't get carried away, you'll just be drawing a stipend."

"I don't know what that means, does it mean I get paid money?"

"Yes, that's what it means."

"All right, so I'm in, but let's keep talking anyway and pretend you need to convince me, because I'm not necessarily going to be all that helpful if I don't like what I hear."

"All right."

"Why don't you tell me who you really are?"

"I gave you my real name."

"Super, but you're not a reporter."

"No, I'm not. That's my cover, though."

"A cover. You're a spy!"

"No, no, I'm not a spy. A spy would be better at this."
She laughed.

"I agree. You work for the army?"

"I work for the U.S. government. I'm an analyst. I do things called threat assessments and action plans."

"Sounds boring."

"It kind of is. But it means I'm sort of an expert on Sorrow Falls."

"That's an interesting distinction. Sorrow Falls, and not the spaceship."

"I'm sort of an expert on both, but yes, I made that distinction deliberately. I've spent about as much time studying the town in nearly every way I can as I have the ship itself."

"All right, all right."

Annie was pacing. This was partly because it helped her think, partly because she was in shorts and a T-shirt and the bugs were starting to discover her existence. Walking kept them guessing.

"So what I'm hearing is, something changed," she said.

"Yes. I can't tell you what."

"Right, but it was something. But why me? You aren't a reporter, and that was my whole pitch."

"Yes, but . . . look, Annie, I can't tell you exactly what's going on, but the reason I'm here instead of someone else is because I've been arguing for a while that there's something . . . different about Sorrow Falls. There are things here that don't fit together right. I can't pin it down, but it's something. And now . . . well. I need to talk to people, get my ear to the ground, that sort of thing. I have a good reason for doing it, and I can't tell you what that reason is. But based on everything I've heard about you in the past few hours, you're something like the local Tom Sawyer. I'm not sure why or how that's true, but it is."

"I'm not sure if I like the comparison, Tom Sawyer was only like twelve, and I'm—"

"Sixteen, I know. You have a tendency to mention it every few minutes. Why is that?"

She laughed.

"I've spent my life in this town, and I know a lot of people. All of them are friendly and most of them are much older than I am. Around when I started hitting puberty I noticed some of those people were looking at me a little differently, so I got in the habit of reminding them how old I was. It's nothing personal."

"I guess that makes sense. What will you do when you turn eighteen?"

"I'll start reminding them how old *they* are instead. So what are you looking to find out? In general."

"Anything unusual, basically."

"How unusual?"

"I don't know how to qualify that."

"All right, we'll work that out later. How long?"

"As long as it takes, I guess."

"School starts in a month, so I may need a note or something."

It was hard to tell, but he might have been blushing.

"You know, it actually didn't occur to me school would be an issue. I obviously can't get in the way of that."

"Sure you can. This sounds way more fun."

"I . . . okay, we'll figure that out if we need to. You'll, um . . . you'll also need to keep my cover, which will mean a little . . . lying. I already feel uncomfortable asking you to do that."

"Your cover as a reporter."

"Right."

"Let me explain something right off. Nobody's going to believe you, especially if you went and saw the ship today like you were supposed to. Not that it will make a huge difference."

"I don't understand."

"If you build up a good, solid lie, you'll be fine. They won't believe you, but they'll answer your questions anyway. You just can't half-ass the lie or they'll think you're insulting them. Who do you write for?"

"Well, I'm not really writing for anyone."

"You're never going to pull this off, Ed. Good God."

"Ahh, okay. *The New Yorker?*"

"Noo, no. Nobody's going to talk to someone from *The New Yorker* in Massachusetts. Follow baseball sometime. Try again."

"I, um . . ."

"Okay, here's what you say: you're writing a feature article on spec for the *Atlantic Monthly*. General Morris is your . . . let's go with uncle. He pulled some strings to get you onto the base and up close and personal with the ship."

"I've been meaning to ask, how did you know we were doing that?"

"Edgar, everyone knows everything in this town. So you're using your connections with Morris to get the kind of story nobody's written before, and that's why the *Atlantic* is interested in a spec piece from somebody who has no bylines in their own name. You're probably going to have to come up with a plausible backstory on how you're a thirty-year-old writer with no credits, too."

"You make it sound like I have to prep for a background check."

"That's exactly right. I checked up on you already. Took me about ten minutes to decide you weren't a reporter."

"You got my age wrong."

"That's because I'm guessing, because you have no public profile, and that's exactly my point. You can either build that profile tonight—it won't stand up—or come up with why you don't have one. Why, how old are you?"

"Thirty-four, but you had me looking younger, I'll take the compliment."

"Don't let it go to your head, I'm only sixteen."

"When do you turn seventeen, exactly? Just so I know when I can stop hearing you say that over and over."

"Not for another four months. Are you gay?"

"No."

"Then I'll probably keep saying it, sorry."

⋮

They went back inside to rescue General Morris from Annie's mother, or perhaps the other way around. Both appeared reasonably uncomfortable to have been left alone, especially when they probably could hear Ed and Annie arguing.

Morris had a number of documents for them to sign. According to the general, it was the same basic documentation the army used when putting translators on the payroll on foreign soil. This actually made Annie laugh out loud.

The whole thing took about an hour, which taxed her mom, a lot more than she let on. By this time she was usually lighting a joint and picking a movie to relax to, before either passing out in her recliner or staggering off to bed.

When it was all done, everyone shook everyone's hands, and Annie took over hosting duties for long enough to escort them out while her mother excused herself.

"Again, I'm really sorry," Ed said quietly as the general walked ahead to the car. "We didn't know. Is it cancer?"

"Yeah, it's . . . yeah. It's not going to get any better. The weed's for pain, and to help her whole 'power of positive thinking' thing. Look, I don't know if she even has a legal prescription for it. We grow it ourselves."

"Don't worry about any of that."

They shook hands again.

"I'll be by in the morning," he said.

"Yeah, hold up. Are you planning to go around in one of those?"

He looked at the car, then back.

"I was. Comes with its own driver, too. It's all right, right? That cover story of yours has me related to the general, so . . ."

"No, that's not going to work. Like I said, don't insult them. You parked a rental at Betty Lou's, you should take that."

Ed laughed. "You know where I'm staying and what I drove into town in. I'm starting to think none of this was actually my idea."

"Now you're learning. See you in the morning."

Inside, her mother had settled back into her chair and was searching her layers for a lighter.

"Well, he seems like a nice boy, dear," she said.

"Stop it. He's thirty-four."

"I can't wait to tell your father his little girl is working for the Man and being courted by a boy in his thirties. He'll be thrilled."

Annie held up a throw pillow as a threat. "You are not allowed to tease me about this."

"Oh, come on, this is the only fun I get."

"Did you eat today?"

"I did. Twice."

"Liar."

"All right, once, but it was a big meal."

Annie put down the pillow and threw herself on the couch.

"You have to *eat*, Mother."

"Yes, I know, I know."

"Oh, and don't worry, I made sure nobody's going to say anything about the . . . you know."

"The *dope?* Honestly, who *cares* anymore?"

"Some people do! The army does, I bet."

"I grow my own plants in my own yard for use in my own house. Let them come. I'll call the ACLU."

"Hippie."

"You are correct. I am too young to be one, but you are still correct. Now, I believe *North by Northwest* is already in the machine. Will you be joining your mother for a Hitchcock, or would you prefer hiding in your room and writing 'Eddie Loves Annie' on all your notebooks?"

"I swear to God, I will hit you with this pillow, lit joint or no."

"Ah, such violence. Find me the TV remote, would you?"

Annie started rummaging through the nearest collection of afghans, as this was the most obvious place to check. As she did, a thought occurred.

"Hey, Mom, silly question: did we ever watch *Porgy and Bess?*"

"That's Gershwin, right? I don't think so. If we did, it would have been a network airing. I'm sure we don't own that. Why, did you want to?"

"No. I was just curious."

7

THE MAN IN THE GRAY FLANNEL SUIT

*D*obbs hated using the bathroom in the camper.

It was a funny problem for a man who lived in a camper to have, but it was true. He'd been away from real plumbing for a long time and was growing to despise a lot of things about that fact, including the chem smell, the size of the john, and most especially the part where it had to be emptied regularly.

He had no decent solution to the problem aside from hoping the city would install public bathrooms in the field. (He had petitioned them to do exactly that, and received nothing for his efforts. Not even a port-a-john.) All he could control was the frequency in which the toilet needed emptying, and even then he had only so much say. He could make fewer contributions, certainly, which might cut down on the number of times Art asked him to change it, but it wouldn't eliminate the part where Dobbs did the changing.

Art asked him to do it *every* time. There were other things Dobbs had to do—or rather "had to" do, with air-quote scare quotes—presumably to offset the expense of giving him a place to stay while awaiting the inevitable, and he didn't much mind those other things. But the toilet?

That was why, whenever he could, Dobbs went for a walk instead.

Behind the campers was an open field, but at the far end of that field was a collection of freestanding trees, a forward-thrust first wave of vegetation with a larger column of forest bringing up the rear. A vanguard of nature's toilet, located only about a quarter of a mile away.

⋮

Learning how to dump in the woods—without either getting bitten by nature or coming into contact with something that caused a rash—was never on Dobbs's list of life goals.

He grew up in Minnesota. Not particularly athletic, he ended up in a common enough geeky-smart-socially-awkward niche that steered most young men in the direction of comic books and RPGs, but which took him on a side path to UFO fandom.

A child looking up at the night sky hoping to see strange lights will inevitably see strange lights, especially when one's definition of *unidentified* is fluid and poorly informed by astronomical and aeronautical minutiae. Most of his preteen years up until his extremely belated puberty was spent keeping a logbook of all the lights he saw, with important details like time of night, direction he was facing, and so forth. He wasn't technically proficient enough to measure the exact position of these objects, but that was okay because eventually he realized he was mostly recording one of the flight patterns out of MSP International.

The interest didn't wane as he grew up, though; it just became more focused. He became deeply involved in online groups, tracking sightings somewhat more genuine than the 9:42 p.m. to Chicago and, perhaps more important, developing real bonds with people as excited about UFO's as he was.

His favorite listserv quickly became the one run by UFOMAN, a legendary figure in the online version of the UFO-hunting community. It was through that board, and specifically from UFOMAN himself, that Dobbs first heard of the ship that landed in Sorrow Falls. This came out as an IMPORTANT bulletin direct from UFOMAN, citing TOP SECRET sources, CONFIRMING the existence of an alien presence in rural Massachusetts.

It was a big deal, being only the fifth time Dobbs had ever seen such an important announcement. (The other four, sadly, turned out to be hoaxes.) It was met with skepticism—some appropriate, some inappropriate and a little too personal, which was the nature of things on the Internet as regards nearly any subject. And since it came a full two weeks before the president informed the world, it was two weeks' worth of an unpleasant flame war. By the end of it, when UFOMAN—largely unflappable throughout—suggested "we all" get the nearest gas-powered vehicle at our disposal and head to northwestern Massachusetts, he was greeted largely with ridicule.

Dobbs believed him. He was also out of work, having just graduated with a degree in electrical engineering that wasn't getting him as far as it should have. So he was free. And it turned out UFOMAN lived in Minnesota as well. His real name was Art Shoeman, a widowed retiree who had just buried his life savings in a camper and was looking for another driver.

Art was also looking for someone to clean the toilet for him, but of course he didn't bring that up right away.

⋮

The walk from the campers to the tree line was considerable. There were closer trees across the street, but they went only a couple deep, there was a fence on the other side of them, and the soldiers didn't take kindly to people using that part of their perimeter for that sort of thing.

The walk across the field was over ground that was usually pretty dry, even after rains, which could explain why it hadn't been active farmland even before the invasion. But it had its share of snakes and rodents of unusual size, so it wasn't really a super-pleasant journey. Not that Dobbs would ever be mistaken for an outdoorsman who might otherwise appreciate a walk through nature. He had allergies, he didn't enjoy exercise in general, and he felt a lot more at home in front of a panel of electronics than just about anywhere else.

He did enjoy the stars, though. There was almost no atmospheric interference with the view of the sky in this part of the world, so it was a pretty great view. Some nights it made him want to be an astronomer. If he thought there was time, he'd teach himself how to become one.

That wasn't going to happen, though. People had learned to relax and stop worrying about the ship, but he knew better. Something was coming, it would be soon, and it would be bad. He couldn't prove it, though, and he'd been saying that almost constantly for long enough that he had lost a lot of friends who simply refused to listen. (Even the original listserv moved on, which was amazing. A UFO mailing list decided to stop paying attention to a verified alien ship. The world had gone mad.)

He didn't know yet what the end was going to look like. His current theory was that the ship was an unmanned probe that was reporting information on all of them via a means that science simply didn't understand and could not detect.

Or, they *could* detect it, and the government was keeping it to themselves. Dobbs went back and forth on this a lot. Art was inclined to believe in the super competence of governments when it came to conspiracies, so it was his opinion that they knew a lot more than they were letting on. He spent as much time watching the army as the ship, for exactly this reason. Dobbs often leaned in the other direction, toward a government that was so incompetent they didn't notice anything, but it was hard to tell if this was conviction or an instinct to present a contrary opinion for the sake of variety.

He made it to the trees. It was a cool night, but he was covered in sweat by the time he got there. *That's my workout for the day,* he thought. *A walk to the poop-trees.*

He had a pattern, a system that involved visiting the trees in a certain order. This was to allow his prior contributions to the environment to dry (he covered them, but that didn't always do much good) so he didn't inadvertently step in a fresh something of his own making. This night's visit was to tree number five, and he was on his way there when he thought he heard someone moving around in the woods.

"Hello?" he called.

It was unlikely anybody else from the trailers was out there; he'd have seen them walking.

"Someone there?"

He stood motionless and listened carefully, at first just to his heartbeat and to his breathing, but then to the woods around him.

There.

He heard it again, to his right. A rustling. Dead twigs, dried leaves . . . something with a little weight to it was moving around in the copse other than him.

It occurred to Dobbs for the first time that there might be wolves. He'd never heard of them out here, but that didn't mean they weren't there.

Wolves, or coyotes or bears. Or a giant deer.

But it wasn't a wolf, or anything else on four legs.

A man stepped from behind one of the trees, mostly hidden from the starlight by the shadows.

"Oh, hi," Dobbs greeted him. "Um, sorry, I'm just . . . these aren't your trees, are they?"

The man didn't move or speak. Or necessarily even breathe, as far as Dobbs could tell. It was a little unnerving.

"Of course they aren't your trees, the government owns . . . I'm Dobbs. I live in one of those trailers over there. I'm expected back soon."

Silence. In the trickle of moonlight and starlight and lights from the spaceship perimeter, Dobbs could see enough to tell the man had a suit on, which was just weird on top of weird. Who would go walking around in the woods at night in a suit?

"Aaand, you are?"

"Are . . . you?"

The man had a dry, deep voice. It sounded like speaking caused him pain. Dobbs jumped three feet when he spoke and nearly did the thing he was there to do, only in his pants.

"What?" Dobbs asked. "Am I what?"

"Are you?"

The creepy guy in the suit was either asking Dobbs if he was someone, or he was reciting the international country code for the Russian Federation. Dobbs was pretty sure it was the former, but the two words by themselves didn't make any sense.

"I don't know what you're asking."

"Not," the man said.

"I am . . . not?"

"Not."

"Okay. Okay, so . . . I'm going to go now?"

The man didn't move. Dobbs was covered head to toe in goose bumps and had dropped the roll of toilet paper somewhere it wasn't worth hunting down.

The man could have been one of the trees, or a cardboard cutout. He'd never seen a person so still before.

It was inexplicably terrifying.

"Nice meeting you, goodbye," Dobbs said.

It took five strides to get out of the trees and back into the open field. They were the most anxious five strides of Dobbs's life. And when he was back out into the starlight he more or less ran to the middle of the field before looking back over his shoulder.

The man in the suit wasn't following. Dobbs didn't know why he expected him to.

"All right," he said. "I'll clean the toilet from now on."

8
ORDINARY PEOPLE

*T*he vehicle Ed showed up in the following morning was a species of luxury town car Annie had never seen the inside of before. She passed them on her bike plenty of times around town, but had yet to come across one without tinted windows. She tended to spend a lot more time than was healthy speculating on the identity of the person inside.

"This is your rental?" she asked. Ed was standing at the passenger door, holding it open for her like a chauffeur who didn't know the guest was supposed to sit in back.

"Of course. Not like I had time to trade up."

She slid in. Plush seats, cushy. Computer in the dashboard. Localized air conditioning and heating for each seat. There was a butt-warming function. It had Wi-Fi.

Ed hopped in the driver's side.

"Better than getting driven around in an SUV?" he asked. Behind the wheel, he looked about 90 percent less geekish than he had at Joanne's. She began to wonder just how well it paid to be a secret government expert on things.

"I don't know what the interior of the SUV looked like," she said, "but I don't think I ever want to leave this car."

"It was nicer. Had a bar in it."

Ed started the car. She was so accustomed to the loud, complaining engine in Violet's car she at first didn't notice they were idling.

"I thought we'd start with the people in those campers," Ed said. "Is that okay?"

"If that's where you want to start, sure. I mean, what kind of weird are you looking for?"

"Two different kinds."

"Great."

He put the car in gear, and it felt more like gliding than driving. Ed saw her expression and laughed.

"It's just a car. Spaceships are cooler."

"Yeah, but I can't get inside of that, and anyway it never moves."

A right turn from the driveway took them to the junction with Spaceship Road, and all the traffic that came with that road. To the left was the ship. To the right was the army base. The road continued for several miles after that, out of town, until terminating at one of the Old Post Roads that striated the countryside.

Ed merged into the inbound traffic, and then it was stop-and-go for a while.

"When you said something's not right about Sorrow Falls, what did you mean?" she asked. "Or is that top secret too?"

"It's not. What I mean is, the town shouldn't still be here."

She laughed.

"Like, what, an impact crater?"

"No, I mean, have you ever asked yourself how you could be living within a mile of an alien ship?"

"Not really. I was here first."

"It's too dangerous, being this close. The correct reaction to this situation would have been to evacuate the area for as long as it took to ascertain the intentions of the craft."

"According to whom?"

"Me, mostly. But I wasn't the only one who said so. Every time someone with enough authority to act on that recommendation agreed with me, though, they were overridden."

"Because that's a crazy idea. The ship isn't doing anything to anybody."

"So far as we know it isn't. Except I think it is. I think the ship wants the town to stay put."

"That is one crazy theory, Ed. Do you get paid for that?"

"I get paid a lot for that. It's not that crazy. We already know the ship can implant ideas aggressively, in self-defense. I experienced that first-hand yesterday. I knew what I was thinking didn't really come from my own head, and yet I couldn't stop. It was jarring. What if the ship has a more passive version of that technology impacting the area at large? I mean, nothing in Sorrow Falls is really right for this circumstance. You all went about your lives, pretty much."

"I think you're underestimating the unflappable nature of the New England native mindset. Besides, the people you're talking about, the ones who would get to decide to evacuate the region, they don't live here. They're in Washington. Did the ship call them up or something?"

"Well, that's the thing. My first recommendation made it all the way to the desk of the president. He was ready to sign the order. He told me so."

He glanced over at Annie to see what kind of impact this had, thinking possibly that the idea he had the president's ear might be impressive. She knew about ten people who'd spoken to the president personally, and she once bussed his breakfast table, so she wasn't overly impressed, but thought she probably should have been. To the rest of the world, it was undoubtedly a big deal.

"What changed his mind?" Annie asked.

"Sorrow Falls did. He came here to visit before signing the order, because someone who'd already visited convinced him to do it."

"Maybe he decided against it after meeting all of us."

"Maybe. And maybe the ship decided it for him."

⋮

There was some confusion among the members of the rooftop camper city when Ed and Annie arrived.

Only one day earlier, a big black army SUV went through the

gate, and out popped an army general whose name nobody seemed to know—he was new, everyone agreed—and a skinny city guy in faux rugged clothing and glasses.

The second man inspired a daylong debate between the rooftops regarding his possible identity and purpose. The easy, obvious answer was that he was a reporter working on a new story who'd pulled strings to get a close-up. But insofar as this was easy, and obvious, it was rejected unilaterally.

Secret government operative worked for most of them as a convenient catchall. What kind of operative was not agreed upon, nor was the arm of the government he must have come from, nor even the government, but it fit most theories nicely anyway.

Brenda and Steve, for instance, had strong opinions regarding the United Nations, which was not in itself a government. But an operative working for the U.N. could be from any nation, nation-state, or territory. He could also be one of their nationless operatives, a super-secret police force whose members knew no allegiance to any one government. No such secret police force existed, and anyone who listened to Brenda or Steve for more than a few minutes realized they were really talking about the utterly mundane Interpol, if Interpol was bitten by an evil radioactive spider.

The trailer park collective had, conservatively, two hundred pictures of the operative, so a great deal of bandwidth was expended on facial recognition software. This same software gave them General Morris's name in about ten minutes, but didn't turn up any definite matches on the other man.

The matches rated the highest were: a background actor in the film *Every Which Way But Loose* (except he was too young); an ethicist from Manila (except he didn't look Filipino); a retired Olympic gymnast from Kazakhstan (except he didn't look like a gymnast). Winston had an interesting theory involving the grandson of one of the Joint Chiefs and some minor plastic surgery, but this didn't stick because nobody could quite justify using facial recognition software to identify someone as a person who didn't look like themselves anymore. It seemed like an explicit contravention of the logical basis of the program. Also, as more than one person pointed out, if he *was* the grandson of one of the Joint Chiefs, it made perfect sense that he would have access to the ship, perhaps even to write a story about it.

The matter remained unsettled for the entire day.

Equally unsettled was what the man and the general did while inside the ship compound.

There were one or two positions near the ship that were effectively invisible from the street. At night, it was usually possible to get an approximate idea, because people at night needed flashlights, and because the passive thermal imaging detection—two different campers had equipment that did this—could track their heat signature pretty well when the sun wasn't out.

The men used an infrared emitter. That was established right off, because as soon as they began using it a half-dozen alarms went off on a half-dozen roofs. But nobody knew why, or what it meant.

By the end of the day the only thing any of them could agree upon was that they couldn't agree on anything. This was more or less how they ended every day, though, so in that sense the strange man in the glasses and faux rugged clothing was just the latest in a series of debate topics.

But then came the next day, when the same man returned—new clothing, new car, same glasses—with Annie Collins in tow.

Nobody really knew what to do with that information.

⋮

"Can you hear the buzz?" Annie asked, as she joined Ed on the driver's side of the car. There was no parking on Spaceship Road, so he just pulled over in front of the gates. When the soldier—who looked at Annie, confused, for several seconds—asked what they were doing, Ed showed him an ID that said, basically, he could put the car anywhere he wanted in Sorrow Falls.

"Not sure what you mean," he said to Annie.

"Look at my people on the campers."

A cascade of heads popping up to look down at them, a murmur of conversation, camera flashes. Annie felt like she was in a *National*

Geographic special, except she was the animal being observed, and all the scientists were scrambling.

"I hear it now. This is going to be weird, isn't it?"

"You have no idea. Let's walk slowly, they're going to need time to delete all the pictures they took of you yesterday."

"You're joking."

"Not even a little bit. Welcome to Sorrow Falls."

"Morning, Annie!"

Art Shoeman popped up and waved them over.

"Morning, Mr. Shoeman. How's things? Anything exciting yesterday?"

"You should ask that fella next to you, he might give you a better answer."

"This is Edgar Somerville. He's a reporter. He had some questions for . . . well, everyone. Can we come up?"

"A reporter, is he?" Mr. Shoeman said. He gave Annie a wink he probably thought Ed didn't see. "Sure, sure, come on up. Do you need me to make introductions?"

⋮

"They're getting in through the water supply!"

It was four hours later. Ed and Annie were on the fifth trailer and eighth interview, and being shouted at by Earl Pleasant, a man whose surname was clearly ironic. Earl seemed both perpetually angry and permanently sunburned, giving his face a cartoonish shade that reflected his ardor.

"How do you mean?" Ed asked. Annie, who made this and every other introduction to this point, had perfected a kind of impassive expression, which projected some degree of belief and sincerity to these true believers. (This was a misleading phrase, as they all believed something different, but with great individual ferocity.) To Ed, her expression looked more like amusement.

"Through the water table. I have maps, I'll show you!" Earl disappeared into a back area, ostensibly the bedroom of the camper, behind a sliding door.

The inside of Earl's trailer smelled like laundered sweat and turned fruit. But it was cool and out of the sun, which was a welcome respite.

"You holding up okay?" Annie asked.

"I had no idea," he said. "I thought these guys were just waiting for something to happen."

"Well, they are, but they also want to be the first to know it's happening."

"It's like they're all making decisions based on some kind of dream logic."

"I'm not with you."

"They aren't getting any feedback from the ship, or the government, or anybody with the necessary scientific background, so their imaginations are just rolling along, ignorant of anything attached to reality."

"Yeah, don't let them hear you talk like that. And try to avoid the word 'ignorant.'"

"Here!"

Earl returned with a topographical map and slapped it down on the table in front of Ed. This was accomplished with an unsettling degree of violence.

"This is a USGS water table survey of the area. As you can see, the ship's location is just about the ideal spot for a well."

Without knowing a lot about the provenance of the map—it could have been a map of any part of the country, as there was no key or date stamp attached, only a Magic Marker dot marking the location of the ship—it still looked like there were a dozen excellent places in the area for a well.

"What would be the goal?" Ed asked.

"I told you, this is how they're getting in."

"Earl, I think what Mr. Somerville is asking, is what do they do once they've gotten into the water supply? What happens next?"

"Well, we don't know that. But that's why nothing's happened for so long, it takes a while to get down there, do what they gotta do. If you ask me, it's about turning us."

"Turning . . ."

"Species conversion! You might be part alien right now, if

you've drunk the water round here. I drink only rainwater, just to be sure. They'll probably get the livestock first. And the pets. But it'll move up the chain."

"Okay. Thanks, that's really good stuff." Ed stood and offered his hand, which Earl looked at but didn't take.

"Sorry, I don't touch people," he said. "It's not personal."

"I understand completely."

"This is for what magazine, again?"

"The *Atlantic*," Annie said. "It's big-deal story, Earl."

"Well that's good. People need to know."

"They'll know," she said.

She led Edgar out of the trailer by the elbow.

"You need a break?" she asked. "A cigarette or something?"

"Do you smoke?"

"No, but I think Mrs. Chen does, a few campers over. We could get you one."

"No, thanks, that's . . . an oddly specific offer."

"You look like a guy who needs a cigarette."

"I smoked in my twenties, but it's been five years."

"There, see? I have you pegged. C'mon, then. Laura and Oona are a trip, you have to meet them."

Laura Lane and Oona Kozlowsky, in the trailer next to Earl's, were indeed a "trip," as archaic as that description was. They were dressed in a peculiar kind of battle armor that looked like it was borrowed from the set of a *Mad Max* film. They appeared to be under the impression that the apocalypse had already transpired and they were the only ones who fully understood this.

That opinion was actually shared to a certain degree by everyone there. A kind of cognitive dissonance was taking place among these (as Annie called them) experiencers, whereby the spaceship actually had done a thing and they were already living in the aftermath of that thing. In that sense, they had a little more in common with Ed—who thought the ship actually was having an impact on the collective psyche of the town—than he was fully comfortable admitting to. But their version of "done something" and his varied drastically.

One particularly impressive iteration of this theme was espoused by a man named Gunter, who was convinced the world effectively ended when the ship landed and everyone was living in a kind of *Matrix*-like artificial reality. His proof was that he could find no proof, which proved the program was so seamless it could only be designed by a superior alien intellect.

Laura and Oona were a little less dramatic, but only a little. Their camper, normal-looking on the outside, was a reinforced tank on the inside, with a bomb-shelter store of canned goods and at least ten guns. Ed didn't know much about guns but was pretty sure two or three of the ones they had weren't legal for private ownership.

Annie made the introductions, and then went into the preamble.

"Mr. Somerville is doing a story on the ship, but what he's really looking for is the whole picture. Everything, just from your perspectives. Like, when you got here, what you're here for, what you've seen, what you think. All that stuff."

"Sounds like a goof hunt," Oona said.

Oona described herself as "the big butch dyke of Sorrow Falls," which appeared to be a deliberate attempt to embrace what might be said about her behind her back. She was a heavyset woman with a buzz cut, wearing an appreciable quantity of studded brown leather.

"It's not a goof hunt," Annie said. "He's talking to everyone in town, I just brought him here first."

"What's your part in this, sweetie?" Laura asked. Laura introduced herself as a "lipstick lesbian," but was only stereotypically effeminate in contrast to Oona. She was more petite, certainly, and kept her hair longer. The hair even had a barrette with a plastic flower. But she favored the same leather clothing; she just wore it a little better.

"Tour guide. Mr. Somerville's interested in the people nobody's talked to before, and not the ones *everybody's* talked to. I know everyone, so . . ."

Laura laughed. "You sure do."

"Still sounds like a goof hunt," Oona said.

"I'm sorry," Ed said. "What is a goof hunt?"

"It's when a reporter shows up and promises a fair perspective, then goes on back to New York or wherever they're from and writes up a goof piece. *Look at what these dummies believe.* That's a goof hunt."

"Oh. No, this won't be anything like that. Promise."

"Well, I don't trust you, mister." Oona turned to Annie. "This is on you, girlie."

"You won't see any goof stories coming from Ed," Annie said. "I promise."

"All right. So what do you want to know?"

"Hey, we should tell him about the thing," Laura said.

Oona glared at Laura. Laura was either oblivious or deliberately ignoring her partner.

"Something cool started happening about six weeks ago," she said to Annie and Ed.

Annie said, "We can just start at the beginning and—"

"Actually, let's start there," Ed interrupted. "What happened six weeks ago?"

Annie shot Ed a look, and all of a sudden there were three conversations going on at once in the trailer, and only one of them was a verbal conversation.

"Nothing," Oona said, her eyebrows screaming at Laura.

"Oh, for goodness' sake, if we keep secrets we're just as bad as *they* are." The "they" was conveyed as meaning the government but, tellingly, she pointed at Ed when she said it. "Come on, you guys, let's go to the roof, I'll show you."

⋮

The only way to the roof was up an internal ladder, which distinguished Oona and Laura's trailer from all the others Annie was familiar with.

It was easy to understand why the women preferred this design:

their roof was a gun tower. A three-foot wall augmented the edge, making it possible to crouch down and—assuming the wall could stop bullets—hide from an attack on the ground, and there were four rifles mounted on hooks at strategic points. A Gatling gun would not have been entirely out of place.

Annie had never been to their roof before, and only really seen it from a distance, from Gunter's roof two spots over. (Gunter was nuts, but he was also really nice.) It drove home the paranoia she'd seen in small doses before from the women.

"It's over here," Laura said, attracting the attention of a suddenly eager Edgar Somerville. This was an enormous annoyance to Annie, although she couldn't say why. She already knew he wasn't telling her things, because he told her specifically he couldn't, so there were no surprises here. Still, this was the first time he'd responded this way. Dobbs thought the ship moved two inches a few days ago, Johnny Nguyen insisted he saw the ship alter the migratory patterns of geese ten days ago, and Mika and Morrie said the ship's aura turned "more purplish" fifteen days back. Ed didn't even raise an eyebrow then.

What happened six weeks ago, Edgar? she thought.

"What's all this do?" Ed asked Laura, referring to a large bank of equipment. Already, they had seen multiple arrangements of electronic toys. Ed asked the same question each time, and the answer was almost always disappointing. Either what the equipment did wasn't all that interesting, or it would have been interesting if it did what the owner thought it did.

Behind them, Oona lumbered up the ladder. She fit through the opening only barely. It was close enough for Annie to wonder if they had plans on either widening the hole or reducing the size of the owner anytime soon.

"Well, it's pretty basic. I know we've got, what, a hundred gadgets pointed at that thing, right? All together?" She looked to Annie for affirmation. She was still ignoring Oona, who was actively glowering in a way that would have made angry Earl proud.

"At least a hundred," Annie agreed. "Plus the ones on the other side of the fence."

"Right, the government sensors. That's some state-of-the-art stuff, isn't it, Mr. Somerville?"

"I wouldn't know."

"You should know if you're going to write about it. You didn't ask General Morris when you were over there yesterday?"

Ed blushed. Annie nearly laughed out loud. She warned him.

"No, it's . . . it's all classified."

"Everyone loves that word," Laura said. "*Classified.* Anyway, we're all playing the same game of 'let's see what the invaders are going to do,' like it's going to make a difference."

"It isn't going to make a difference?" Ed asked.

"Maybe I'm being naïve or . . . help me out."

"Fatalistic," Oona said. She was settling into a beach chair near one of the rifles. "That's what dear old Daddy called us."

"My daddy, not hers," Laura whispered.

"Go on, give up the whole story. I'll just be over here cleaning the guns."

Ed had the good sense to look alarmed.

"Don't worry about her," Laura said. "She's a big teddy bear."

Oona giggled.

"Where was I?"

"You were being naïve," Ed said.

"Yes, so everyone's hung up on what they're going to do, and from where I'm sitting, well, whoever the invaders are, they did something we may never know how to do. Interstellar travel, right? Who does that? Not us."

"It doesn't matter if we know what they're going to do," Annie said.

"*Right,* honey. Who are we to stop them? The ant doesn't stop the boot, the ant gets out of the way of the boot."

"You're pretty close to the boot," Ed said.

"Right, but we still want to know when it's going to move."

"Let's dispense with the boot analogy," Oona said.

"What we decided was that maybe we don't care as much *what* the ship is here to do so long as we have a good idea *when* it's going to do that."

"That's what this equipment can tell you?"

"It tells me about sound."

Ed looked visibly disappointed. "Oh. You mean like what Art Shoeman's doing?"

Oona laughed. She had a laugh designed specifically for maximum derision. "UFOMAN doesn't know what he's doing. Neither does that kid of his, Dobble."

"Dobbs," Annie corrected.

"Whatever. Every time a truck climbs the hill they're running for the bunker. Metaphorically."

"We don't have a bunker," Laura said to Ed. "Don't write that we have a bunker."

Annie was suddenly convinced they had a bunker.

"So let me show you," Laura said, turning on a monitor. The markings of a three-by-three grid appeared on the screen. Laura pointed above her head.

"We have an array at the top of this pole. Right now it's pointed across the street."

The array she spoke of was nine parabolic microphones in a configuration that matched the screen grid.

"It's not focused. This is . . . it's like a wide-angle shot if it were a video. You get it?"

"Sure," Ed said.

"Now, we figure, everything makes noise, right? This is how we'll know if the ship is about to do something. It'll make a noise. Art's thinking the same way, but he's lousy at it. I'm gonna turn on the array."

She flipped a switch. Nothing changed, aside from a light on the underside that turned red. The screen came to life, though.

"Each square in the grid is a different quadrant. You can see the sound waves."

It looked like a black pond with green ripples from invisible stones.

"How sensitive is this?" Ed asked.

"It's on a starter setting, so not very. The ship is the middle grid, though. Do you see it?"

The middle grid had little wave splashes at the corners, but nothing in the middle.

"It's not making any noise," Ed offered.

"It's not that simple," Oona said. "This is how we were goofed. Some ass from the *Times* wrote about how we flipped because the ship wasn't making a sound, but that isn't the point."

"Even at this setting, everything makes noise," Laura said. "Look top left. You know what that's picking up? The wind through the leaves, or a bird, or cricket a thousand feet off. *Everything makes noise.* Except the ship. The ship is a hole in the sonic signature of this field."

"Why is that?"

"It's sucking up the sound," Oona said. "Always has done. That's why it pisses me off when people talk about how it's not doing anything. The hell it isn't. Something in there is absorbing sound waves."

"It's always done this?" Ed asked.

"Up until six weeks ago," Laura said.

She punched a command into the system. The sound array expanded, the parabolic microphones spreading away from one another and refocusing on a single point.

"When we target just the ship the whole system goes silent," she said.

The screen reflected the point, showing no ripples.

"Now let's turn up the sensitivity."

The screen remained uncluttered, until . . .

"Whoa, what was that?" Ed asked. A tiny ripple appeared on the top center grid. It dissipated quickly, and then recurred.

"It's on a five-second pattern. Silent for three, audible for two, and so on. Started six weeks back, like I said."

Annie crowded in to get a better look, but there wasn't much else to see.

"Never did that before?" she asked.

"We do a narrow scope check once a day and the first time we picked it up was last month. I can't speak for what may have gone unnoticed before we got here."

"What does it sound like?" Ed asked.

"Hold on," Oona said. "How about a little quid pro quo?"

Ed looked at Annie, confused. She had nothing for him.

"What do you mean?" he asked.

"How about if you tell us what you were doing with that infrared scanner yesterday?"

Hello, Annie thought. Ed looked surprised. He was a terrible poker player.

"I don't know what you mean," he said.

"Nope, sorry, we're done here. Annie, he seems like a nice man, but don't you trust him."

"Hold on," she said. "Ed, why don't you just tell them?"

"I can't, it's . . ."

"He's embarrassed," Annie said. "Ed had this stupid idea that the ship was . . . what did you call it? Glowing, but only outside of the visual range. And I was like, c'mon, I'm sure someone thought of that already, but he insisted nobody had. So then he goes out with the general yesterday and he was like, let me tell you what *I* think, and then he whips out these lights and . . ."

"And glasses," Ed said. "Special glasses."

"Right! And Morris was like, okay, whatever, let's get this over with. Funniest thing. I guess they were making fun of him all night. But, you know, everyone has their pet theory, right?"

"Well, that's stupid," Oona said.

"That's, like, the first thing anybody checked," Laura said. "Who was it?"

"Larry was doing spectroscopic testing first, before, well, you know. Have you met Loony Larry yet?"

"Not yet."

"He doesn't do it anymore, but trust me, someone else is. Laura and I don't even bother, we'll hear about it. Don't remember who told us about your little infrared test. Did you find anything?"

"No," Ed said.

He was lying. Annie could tell. She was a little surprised nobody else could.

"Like I said. It's been done." Oona bobbed her head at Laura. "Go ahead, play the audio. This'll blow their minds."

Laura typed in a couple of commands, and the audio kicked into life.

Ed leaned forward, squinting, perplexed, not quite sure of what he was hearing. Annie felt about the same.

"I'm sorry," he said. "Is that . . . breathing?"

"That's what it sounds like, yes."

"You're telling me the ship is breathing?"

"No, I'm telling you the first time sound has ever come *out* of the auditory black hole that is the ship, it resembled the sound of a person breathing. But the significance of this . . ."

"It's a signal," Oona said. "We don't know what it means."

"Maybe it means the ship has grown a pair of lungs," Ed said.

"It's not *actual* breathing, you dummy. It's the *sound* of breathing."

"Fine, it's a signal. Who's it for?"

"Well, we don't know that either, do we?"

⋮

"What was that?" Annie asked afterwards.

Ed was supposed to have a number of interview-like questions for Oona and Laura, to at least preserve the idea that he was doing a piece of journalism and not looking for a surreptitious way to question an entire town. Annie was becoming less comfortable with not being told things.

"I don't know what you mean."

"So many things. You didn't tell me about the infrared, you didn't tell me you were looking for something that happened six weeks ago, and those two no longer think you're writing anything as far as I can tell."

"I'm sorry, I went a little off script. But you said nobody was going to believe me anyway."

"Right, but I have to pretend I do, and not look like a moron at the same time."

"We don't have a lot of time."

"What's *that* supposed to mean?"

"It means I'm on deadline, that's all it means."

"That's not what it sounded like."

"Look, I don't know what to think. Either their sound equipment works correctly and the ship is now *breathing*, or it's *not* working and they're delusional. Or, they spoofed all of that."

"They didn't spoof any of it."

"Then they know damn well I'm not a journalist, and a whole lot more."

"Why do you say that?"

"They just showed us. If everyone was as curious about me as you said, well, they could have eavesdropped on my entire conversation."

Annie thought about this.

"You talk about super-top-secret stuff in the field?"

"Not really, no. Except for . . . mostly no."

"All right, where were you standing when you *were* talking about super top-secret stuff?"

Ed looked across the road at the ship, same as it ever was.

"Behind it. We were behind it."

"Then you're fine. Like Laura said, that thing is sucking up all the sound."

"Right. If their equipment does what they say, they didn't hear me and the spaceship is breathing. Or, they might have heard me and the thing isn't breathing. I don't like either of those choices."

9
PLEASE STATE YOUR EMERGENCY

*T*wo weeks passed, during which the most exciting thing to happen was that Annie got her first paycheck. It was a decent enough sum to leave her wondering how long she could prolong things. To that end, she did not have a willing partner in Edgar Somerville.

It was hard to tell sometimes if they were even on the same side. She spent most of her days facilitating his introduction to various individuals, and then listening for clues as to what he was really after. So far, he hadn't given her enough to assemble anything like a complete picture. She had tantalizing bits, but that was all. It gave each day a modestly adversarial angle, like they were playing a bad game of chess with one another.

In a lot of ways, she was learning more as a consequence of whom he was asking to speak with than she was by what he was saying to the people she lined up. They spent the first week at the campers, but the second week was with a subset of the Sorrow Falls population that consisted of all persons who lived in the town when the ship landed and hadn't left it since.

The questions he had for the trailer park collective centered mostly on *tell me your crazy and how you arrived at it,* but the stuff he had for the other group suggested he was after a completely different thing. For the camper denizens it was all about what happened in the past six weeks. For everyone else—tacitly *not* the people in the campers, who arrived well after the ship landed—it was questions about what had changed in the town, overall, in three years.

Annie knew he had his theory that the ship was manipulating people at a distance, but these weren't just those kinds of questions. He was after something specific.

It would have been nice if he could just tell her everything, and it was obvious it bothered him that he couldn't. But apparently granting top-secret clearance to a sixteen-year-old was a hassle.

The second-most-exciting thing to happen in the two weeks was that Annie got a chance on more than one occasion to hang out at the military base.

⋮

The base was established in a field originally owned by the Tarver family. Annie knew a couple of the Tarvers back before they sold the field and moved away. All she remembered about them was that they weren't all that good at farming—they'd been at it for five generations by then—and didn't much enjoy it. The spaceship was basically the best thing that could have happened for them. Last she heard they'd opened a string of boutique coffee shops in San Diego.

The Tarvers were pretty lucky, not only for owning land the government wanted, but for being happy to sell it. More than a couple of Sorrow Falls families were considerably less fortunate. Ed's theory that the town was entirely too idyllic under the circumstances ignored the many times locals were briefed on eminent domain laws and the terms of the martial law agreement between the state and federal governments. Admittedly, it would have looked a whole lot worse if they'd actually evacuated the area like Edgar wanted to, but that didn't mean everything in town was puppies and rainbows from day one.

Unlike where the ship came down—on hard, rocky ground that wasn't being used for anything—the base was built on top of fallow farmland. The ground took in moisture well, grew things (weeds) with great aplomb, and didn't offer the sort of bedrock support needed for large, temporary buildings on wheels. Those were the only kinds of structures at the base for the first year, lasting until someone decided everybody could exhale and expect the ship to spend a while not doing anything. Then they started putting up permanent buildings, with solid foundations. They also put up a taller and more imposing perimeter fence, and paved their auto yard. Most important, as far as Annie was concerned, they built a basketball court.

Annie was not, under all but a few circumstances, particularly girlish. This sort of hinged on her personal definition of the word, which relied heavily on how Beth behaved whenever someone attractive and theoretically age-appropriate was in the diner. It was only theoretically because Beth was both playing in a higher age bracket than Annie and because Beth liked men in a higher age bracket than she herself was. It was also higher than Annie was comfortable with. Beth would probably think Ed was too young for her.

Beth's girlishness consisted of swooning, flirting, blushing, and gasping, and being just in general very Marilyn Monroe about everything. Annie wasn't like that. She tended to adopt a sort of Katharine Hepburn–ishness on a day-to-day basis, and was straight up Rosalind Russell when flirting, which was almost never.

(Beth wouldn't have understood any of these references, except possibly the Marilyn one, which she probably would have liked. Annie didn't have any friends who would have gotten them, actually, aside from Violet. Interestingly, Annie never watched movies with Violet aside from Vi's favorite film, *The Wizard of Oz*, which they watched at least once a month together. Violet never explained why she found the movie so appealing, but since Annie never seemed to get bored of watching it with her, maybe there was no reason to explain.)

Annie made one exception to the girlishness rule, and that was the army compound's basketball court in the summertime.

The court wasn't exactly a secret, but it was right in the middle of the compound, which made it hard to see. What was known about it was that on certain days, men from the base would play basketball on the court, wearing camo pants and combat boots and hardly anything else. (Unstated and unknown was whether any of the women on the base partook as well. This may have been because there were hardly any women on the base, period. Annie wasn't sure why this was so, but it was clearly so.)

For the population of teenage girls in Sorrow Falls—already surrounded by attractive, polite young men in uniform—the basketball court had obtained a kind of mythic status. And as Annie sat at a courtside bleacher in the late-August sun watching those polite young men lumber around under the hoop, she had to say that the mythos was entirely earned.

"So that's all you've been doing?" Sam asked. He was sitting next to her, an appropriately chaste distance apart, while the game was going on. Like half the court, he wasn't wearing a shirt, and seemed to think this wasn't mind-numbingly distracting.

"Pretty much, yeah. Just going around town and asking the same questions to different people. What are they saying about him around here?"

"Ah, we don't trade in rumors so much on the base."

Annie laughed. "No, seriously."

"Nobody knows who he really works for, but his credentials . . . Someone said his credentials give him the authority to do some things to the general that would be illegal in most states, let's just say. I'm cleaning that up for you."

"I appreciate that. He told me he writes classified reports."

"Yeah, and he probably does. Wonder what he's going to write about us?"

"I don't know."

What she did know was Ed had a propensity for saying ominous things about *running out of time*, then refusing to say what would happen when they *ran* out of time. She didn't share this with Sam because she didn't want to talk about it. Hopefully, Ed was just worried about the start of the school year, because if he were counting down to the evacuation of Sorrow Falls, she'd rather not know it.

Plus, there was a basketball game to watch.

There was no apparent score-keeping going on. The game was three-on-three and it was only half-court, and nobody was trying all too hard, but that didn't make it any less compelling.

"Why do they keep yelling *pickles?*" Annie asked. She'd heard it four times now, and kept trying to tie the word to a particular play being run or something, but it didn't appear related to one.

"That's his name," Sam said.

"Someone out there is named Pickles?"

"Nickname. Hey, Pickles, come here and introduce yourself."

The shortest guy on the court stepped away from the game and came over. He was replaced immediately by another soldier, just so the rest of them could keep playing.

"What're you talkin' about me for? Is it because I'm so pretty?"

"You know it is, Soldier," Sam said. "Corporal Dill Louboutin, this is Annie Collins."

Louboutin gasped and clutched his heart.

"Not *the* Annie Collins! Why, I do believe I have been instructed not to converse with you, young lady."

Dill Louboutin had a drawl that reminded her of the villain from a half-dozen B-films in her mother's collection. Oddly, this made the soldier before her seem a little more charming.

"Have you really?"

"Yes ma'am, we were notified that on occasion, you might find yourself among our company, and that we are to compost . . . did he say compost?"

"Comport," Sam said. "Compost is something else."

"That we are to comport ourselves as gentlemen at all times on account of your delicate age and temperament."

Annie raised an eyebrow at Sam.

"He's making this up," she said. "Right?"

"Tell her the rest," Sam said.

"Oh yes, and also to not engage you in conversation."

"And why is that?"

"Something about devil or seductress or . . . you know, along those general lines."

"Because you know things and you find things out," Sam said. "They don't want anyone telling you something they shouldn't."

"You mean, like you do?"

"I'm hurt. That hurts me."

"I'm guessing they don't have a problem with all the dirt I get out of you. Or maybe you just don't know any of the good stuff, like Pickles here does."

"Please don't call me that," Dill said.

"You're digging around the wrong shrub, he knows even less than I do," Sam said.

"That is true, young lady. I in fact know just about nothing. Why *are* you here, anyway? See, I don't even know that."

"Ed's in his top-secret batcave. He'd rather I hung out here because I guess he's just bathing in confidential files or something."

Ed's batcave was actually one of the few remaining temporary structures from the initial move-in. It was a steel-paneled eyesore that was towed in on a flatbed, now sinking slowly into the mud. The window faced the court, possibly so he could keep an eye on her while working with his decoder ring and invisible ink.

"Yes, but why you, exactly?"

"My girlish good looks, Corporal. Of course. Also, because I know everyone and everything in town. I thought you'd been briefed already."

"All right, I feel a test is in order."

"Dill . . ." Sam said.

"No, go ahead, this should be fun," Annie said. "Give me your best, Pickles."

Dill looked over her shoulder.

"Right now I am looking past the fence at some little twerp who stands on his porch every damn day watching us. What's his name?"

She laughed. "I don't even need to turn around. That's Dougie. I've known him most of my life. You guys must be bored if you care that much about him, he just wants to grow up and join the army like any redblooded American boy."

"Aww, come on, I don't even have a way to check if you're right."

"Should have thought of that sooner," Annie said.

Her cell phone vibrated with a new message. She snuck a peek at it.

"Hey, guys, I gotta go."

⋮

Ed spent a lot of time on a lot of army bases, and for some reason had it in his head that the Sorrow Falls base would be different in some way from the others. That it felt exactly the same despite a fundamentally different mandate just made his head hurt.

The army didn't know exactly what to do with the soldiers. They had daily drills, and an obstacle course, and important duties both public and private. (Publicly, for instance, they guarded the ship and manned the checkpoints on the roads. Privately, they had ten lightly manned outposts ringing the town, which hardly anyone knew about.) What they didn't have—or know how to provide—was training for the thing that brought them there.

It was true nobody had any idea what to expect on the day the spaceship finally executed whatever directive it was there to complete, so having drills along the lines of "how to reload a laser gun" or "what to do if there's an alien attached to your face" didn't make a lot of sense. At the same time, Ed could think of no better example of the axiom "generals are always fighting the last war."

One of the things Ed hoped to accomplish in his visit was to give everyone an idea of what to expect, and then maybe the base outside his window would be full of people knowing what to do with their time aside from pickup games of basketball.

He turned back to the desk, which was large—thankfully—and overfull of documentation. Between the two weeks of notes from the interviews, the documents provided when he arrived, and everything he brought with him, there was a decent amount of material. Granted, if he wished he could stack all of it together and form only a very small pile, but that was somewhat contrary to his method.

The material was arranged in something approximating a collage. It was the only effective method he'd ever found when collecting disparate bits of information that had to be arranged in a comprehensive whole.

It was failing to arrange, however.

Nothing connected. He had the event of eight weeks past sitting next to the notes from the interview with Laura and Oona, even though Ed put almost no weight on the latter and a great deal on the former. Everything else sat in an unassociated pile, an archipelago of independent territories associated only by virtue of existing on the same desktop. There was the folder holding photographs of the handprint on the outside of the ship, alone on the corner of the desk. It should have been associated in some way with at least one of the resident interviews he'd conducted, but it wasn't.

There were all the rooftop trailer people, but none of their theories crossed, or went anywhere near anything else. They also contradicted one another and sometimes contradicted themselves. He had little Post-it notes attached to each file, summarizing the contents: zombie, hybridization, Matrix, David Bowie, and so on. In cases where there was no theory, he wrote the specialty of the interviewee. When that didn't work, he just wrote their first name and "???" and left it at that.

He picked up the folder marked "zombie." This was the interview with the man everyone called Loony Larry. Larry wasn't even his name—he was born Vincent Allen—but everyone called him Larry, and that was how he introduced himself. He didn't mind being called Loony, either. He seemed to think it was a compliment.

Larry had a theory that incorporated a flute, the migratory pattern of monarch butterflies, and something about Sauron from *The Lord of the Rings*. There was no sense to be made of any of it—even after Larry showed them the flute, as if that would help—but the conclusion was an actual zombie apocalypse.

When Ed asked him when this was going to be happening, in his considered opinion, Larry said, "Soon," and then strongly indicated that it might already be happening.

Larry was actually the most cogent of the crazies in the crowd. A woman named Margo theorized that the reason nobody could touch the ship was that it wasn't there at all. It was actually a piece of negative space in the shape of a ship, and to get too close was to fall through to another universe, "like into a cup of coffee," she explained not-at-all-helpfully. A man named Zeno spoke for an hour about spiders and never explained how they had anything to do with the spaceship. He didn't seem to know why he was there.

Ed came into this worried that one of them had managed to detect the same thing the scientists had. Two weeks later he would have been overjoyed to hear just one mention of Cherenkov radiation. It would have been bad news, but it also would have meant at least one of those people had found something real.

He glanced back out the window to see how the basketball game was going.

Annie was enthusiastic about coming back to the base and letting him hide with his documents while she visited with the soldiers. He was probably doing something wrong by leaving her unsupervised. That was provided the definition of *unsupervised* included leaving her in the charge of a corporal named Corning, who was currently at the basketball court shirtless. Ed wasn't the best reader of people in the world, but he understood just fine that Annie wanted Ed gone once she saw Sam Corning without his shirt.

It was just as well. Better she see Corporal Corning without his shirt than any of the confidential stuff on his desk. Annoyingly, he had a feeling if she *could* see it, she'd have an insight or two that would be helpful. She had a talent for that.

And, she was gone. He was looking at the soldiers playing their game and not at the bleachers. She wasn't there.

He jumped to his feet and ran to the door, jerked it open, and nearly ran her over.

She stumbled into the room.

"Jesus, Ed, where are you going?"

"To look for you."

"I'm right here."

"I see that now. I'm—"

"Forget it. We have to go." She was holding her cell phone in her hand. She looked terrified, and—for perhaps the first time since they met—like a young girl.

"Is something wrong?"

"My mom. Please."

⋮

The closest thing to a hospital in Sorrow Falls was a walk-in clinic on Main. The clinic didn't have overnight services, or anything like an ambulance bay, and was really established primarily to deal with accidents happening to or caused by tourists.

When someone needed a real hospital, they ended up at one of two such facilities, both located within thirty miles. Which one a person ended up at depended upon where they were picked up by the ambulance, based on an invisible demarcation line running through the middle of the town, southwest to northeast. People who found themselves in unexpected emergencies while in the southeast half of the town usually ended up at Saint Mary's in Carrel, which was two towns over. The northwest half—which had the army base, an alien spaceship, Annie's house, and a lot of farms—was supported by Harbridge Memorial, which was one or two wrong turns away from the Vermont border.

Ambulance services were more diverse, and closer, but not in all cases 100 percent devoted to emergency support. Annie knew this, but Ed was a little alarmed to find a hearse in front of the house when they got there.

They were already inside, and the door was open. Annie jumped out of the car before Ed even parked it, and ran up the steps.

"Oh hello, dear!" her mother said as soon as Annie breached the living room.

She was in her chair with an oxygen tube in her nose. A paramedic—his name was Lee, Annie knew his younger sister Zoe from school—was checking her blood pressure. His partner, a woman Annie didn't know, was sorting through her mother's pharmacopoeia with a blue-gloved hand.

"What happened?" Annie asked. It wasn't addressed to anyone in particular, just whoever felt like they could provide the best answer.

"It's nothing!" her mother said.

"It wasn't nothing, Carol, you sent a 9-1-1."

Getting the full attention of Mrs. Carol Collins was often a challenge, whether one was a paramedic trying to assess her stability or her daughter trying to get a straight answer. Her daughter had one trick that almost always worked, and that was calling her by her first name.

"All right, I had a thing, but I'm okay now."

"What sort of thing?"

"Nothing, I panicked is all. I'm actually fine. I'm sorry I worried you."

Annie turned to the female paramedic.

"What kind of thing?"

"Difficulty breathing was the call," the paramedic said.

"Is she out of danger?" Annie asked.

"Oh, I'm fine now."

Annie ignored her mother, the woman paramedic silently deferred to Lee, and nobody said anything else for a few seconds because he had a stethoscope plugged into his ears and was busy jotting down notes.

"Not sure," he said, on realizing he was expected to answer. "But we're going to need to bring her in. You know how this goes."

Annie did. So did her mother.

"It's nothing!" she said.

"Shut up, Carol, they're taking you to Harbridge and you're going to be nice about it," Annie said.

"But—"

"Be nice!"

"Fine."

Carol threw her hands in the air in mock surrender.

Ed was standing at the door, looking unsure about whether he should even be in the room for this.

"Hey, I could use a lift to the hospital, if you're not doing anything," Annie said. "I hate to ask, but I have a thing about riding in ambulances and—"

"Of course."

⋮

"Does this happen a lot?" Ed asked, en route. The flashers from the ambulance lit up the evening, which reminded Annie a little bit of the spaceship, even though the ship glowed white on entry, while the dome lights were red.

"No," Annie said. "Well, once or twice. Maybe four times. Not a lot. Last time was in winter. That sucked. Took the ambulance forever to get to us, even. I was home for that one."

"But she was okay?"

"On top of everything else she has going on, she's prone to panic attacks. I guess that's what they are. Not like she doesn't have a *reason* to panic. I think the weed's in part to keep her from freaking out. She says it's for pain, and that's true, but it keeps her moods stable too. So, but last time, they sent her home with the number for a psychiatrist she never called, and she didn't tell *me* what the diagnosis was, but I'm guessing it was something more in her head than her body."

"Well, that's good. Not *good*. You know what I mean."

"Yeah. They'll take her in and make sure someone with malpractice insurance looks at her before deciding it was nothing. The paramedics sure aren't going to make that call. But they know. Look, they aren't even speeding."

Annie remembered when old Rooney Kazmarek passed. He had an apartment above Kazmarek Hardware, right up Main from the diner. She saw them loading him in the back, then heading down the road. They drove slowly then, too, but that was because Rooney was already dead of a heart attack. There wasn't any rush.

Annie shivered, and shook the memory free. Her mother was fine. They were driving the speed limit because Carol was in the back telling them to.

"Is there . . . anyone else you need to call?" Ed asked. He was asking a different question.

"I'll call Dad if I have to. You know, if it's anything. It's *not*. Same thing happened last time; she just freaked out and couldn't breathe. It was scary."

"Your father lives around here?"

Annie laughed.

"Sure, when he's in town. That's just not all that often. It's his job. He works for Hollis."

"The paper mill?"

"Yes, that Hollis. They used to use trees from New Hampshire and Maine to make the paper. Someone up there would cut down the trees and then roll them into the river and float them down. On this end there'd be guys whose whole day was spent on the riverbanks, catching logs before they hit the falls. Cool job."

"Sounds dangerous."

"Oh, wildly dangerous. They have these giant hooks on the wall down at the mill. I'll show them to you, you'll want to talk to the people there anyway, right?"

"I've been trying to get a meeting with Desmond Hollis since I got into town, actually."

"Seriously? You should have asked, I can get you in."

Ed laughed.

"Right, I should have figured you'd have a way into a room with the richest man in town."

"I think he's actually third-richest now, but yeah, I can get you in with Desmond. What was I talking about?"

"The hooks on the wall."

"Right. They're mounted right above one of those 'It's been X days since the last accident' safety signs, because someone down there has a sense of humor. Anyway, my dad's the one fetching the logs now, but not from the river. The lumber comes in from Canada, and on trucks. Safer, not as good for the environment, probably."

"So he drives a rig."

"Kind of. He supervises the driving of rigs. Trucks come through all the time, but he's not behind the wheel more than once every six months or so. He'll come down for vacations and whatnot . . . anyway. He's around, just not *very* around."

Annie didn't feel a need for further clarification. It should have been obvious that her parents were separated. Dad effectively lived in Canada. He kept an apartment there, and the last she heard he had a girlfriend staying with him in that apartment. He and Carol weren't divorced in part to keep her on his health insurance, a decision reached shortly after her cancer diagnosis and about six months before they formalized their separation by notifying their only child.

He still kept a room in their house, and stayed in that room when he was in town, but that was about all.

Ed seemed to get all this without it being explained, and he looked like he wanted to share a story about his life or something, which is what adults did when they talked to kids about serious things. She'd been getting a range of *things will get better* life lessons stories from adults since Carol was diagnosed, and Annie hated every one of them because they always ended up being a lot more self-serving than helpful. Yes, she knew things would get better, and yes, she was coping. She coped by keeping incredibly busy, and being positive, and getting so involved in the town the military warned its soldiers about her. She didn't need to know someone else's tragic backstory to figure out how to do that.

Annie was glad, then, that Ed opted not to go that route. Perhaps it was the confused not-divorced status of her family. Or maybe he just realized that drawing a comparison to his upbringing in Whatever-Land U.S.A. wasn't going to match up well with the girl who was raising herself with a UFO for a neighbor.

"Hey, thanks for doing this," Annie said. "I could have followed in the family car, probably, but I haven't had a lot of practice and this didn't seem like the best time to work on it."

"No, I imagine it isn't. Don't worry about it."

The ambulance eventually pulled up to a dock at a building that looked only nominally hospital-like. Annie was mostly used to it, but the first time she'd been to Harbridge Memorial she asked the paramedic (she'd ridden in the ambulance that time) why they were stopping at a warehouse.

"Looks like we're here," Ed said. He rolled the car past the dock and into one of the "Emergency Room Only" spots. "I can stick around, if you need me to."

Annie hadn't thought past getting to the hospital, but now that she had and he was asking, she realized she should have given the family car a more thorough consideration.

"It may be a couple of hours."

"That's okay. Do they have coffee in there?"

"It's something that looks like coffee. I can't attest to the taste."

They were taking her mother out of the back of the ambulance/hearse. Carol was sitting up and her mouth was going, so she was probably complaining about having to leave home. That was a good sign, Annie decided. The day Carol stopped fighting was going to be a rough day for everyone.

"I'm sure it'll be fine," Ed said. Probably referring to the coffee and not Carol, though both worked. "Doesn't seem right to leave."

⋮

The emergency room of Harbridge Memorial was unreasonably small for a hospital servicing such a large geographic area. There were only about fifteen temporary beds, separated by curtains on rollers attached to the drop ceiling. It wasn't a great place to spend a lot of time when one was healthy, and especially not when one was a healthy sixteen years. Consequently, while waiting for the barrage of preliminary tests to begin producing results, Annie did a lot of walking around, drifting between the beds and the waiting area where Ed was taste-testing the coffee and reading magazines about the latest Christmas movies from last season.

Carol mostly slept, which was another good sign. When she was really worried about something, she didn't sleep; she talked, and when she didn't talk she watched old movies.

"Do you have a girlfriend?" Annie asked Ed. They were alone in the waiting room, it was approaching midnight, and there wasn't anyone else there. Annie had counted all the ceiling tiles, twice, and discovered every pattern irregularity in the tile floor. There was nothing left to do but sleep, and she didn't want to do that.

"Right now? No." He closed the magazine he was pretending to read.

"Of course right now. I'm assuming you've had one or two in your life."

"Yes, that too. But not at the moment."

"Why not?"

"I don't know. I guess I haven't been looking all that hard. Not since the ship landed. Nothing serious. How about you?"

"Oh, I have prospects. Looking for a guy who can keep up with me. Haven't found him yet, but the list of suitors is long, let me tell you."

"I bet it is."

⋮

The doctor finally returned, after another hour of waiting. Annie was pretty annoyed by then, because this was going to end up being the same news as always: nothing appeared to be newly wrong with her mother, they see no reason for her not to be released, call if something changes in the next twenty-four hours, and so on. Keeping her waiting for three-plus hours to hear that was just silly.

The doctor was working from a different script, though, which ended up explaining the delay.

"I'd like to admit her overnight," the doctor said. This was outside the curtained area where Carol was sleeping.

The doctor's name was Chao, and she had such a pleasant way of saying not-pleasant things that it took Annie a second or two to absorb the information, then another second or two for her to deal with the lump that fell out of the back of her throat and into her stomach.

"I'm . . . sorry, what?"

"Oh, it's just a precaution." She was holding a thin folder that had, at minimum, the outcome of a blood test. "Her white blood cell count is elevated, and I'd like to hold her over until at least to-morrow, and get her going on an antibiotic."

"So it's just an infection."

"It may be, certainly. I'd like oncology to have a look. To rule out some things. Do you have a guardian?"

"A guardian?" She was picturing a guy in armor, following her around. That would be sort of cool.

"Is someone waiting for you? You have a place to go?"

"Oh, yes. Yes, I have a friend . . . my boss is here. He'll take me home."

"All right, good. Let's go have a conversation with your mother."

10
CHOKING HAZARD

*orporal Sam Corning checked into the barracks at twenty-two hundred hours, after a briefing on the latest info regarding the ship. Said briefing lasted a solid hour, and at the end of it he felt no more enlightened than he was before it started. He did walk out a little more worried—in a non-specific sort of way—than when he walked in, and that was certainly a change.

Part of the issue was just that he had no classification level to speak of, so any information being delivered to him had all the interesting stuff removed ahead of time. Most briefings it was seamless, but there were days when very specific information suddenly became very general information, and any efforts to get greater detail were met with the classic *need-to-know* line.

All of which was pretty amazing, since the way Sam saw it, if that thing jumped up and started mowing people down with a ray gun, he would be one of the first to go. That was something he thought he probably needed to know.

There were other times in briefings when it became abundantly clear the real information had been removed and replaced with fake information. Sam and the other men of his squad called these tofu briefings, where the meat was substituted with something that only looked like meat. The briefing in which they were informed of the impending arrival of Edgar Somerville was a tofu briefing, because nobody really believed he was a journalist doing a story. Even Sergeant Phineas rolled his eyes when he read it.

That particular tofu briefing was especially annoying, because inside of a week Annie Collins had more accurate intel than Sam did, which was just insulting.

The briefing that ended at twenty-one-forty-five was not a tofu briefing. It wasn't really even a briefing, since no new information was imparted. It was a lecture on the importance of drilling, maintaining order, holding position, keeping equipment at the ready, and staying "awake and focused." It followed a terse reminder that Sorrow Falls was a de facto war zone and they had to remember that, even if the war was not apparent and the enemy unresponsive.

It was a little terrifying.

By twenty-two-fifteen, Sam and the others had talked it over and, after a few valid points on the subject of getting a little lazy about perimeters, focused on two or three details from the meeting that could be made fun of safely. For instance, Phineas was unreasonably fond of the word *perambulate* and used it—incorrectly, they were sure—so often it became their own little drinking game. (Not that they drank on the base during a briefing in front of a superior. They mimed each drink when the occasion arose.) So they went through every instance of the word, and that seemed to calm everyone down. Then it was time to bed down, as some of them—although not Sam—had sentry duty down the hill at oh-six-hundred.

For a couple of soldiers, that only meant talking in whispers, rather than sleeping.

"What do you think, Sammie?" asked Dill Louboutin in that bayou drawl of his. Dill was two years younger and five inches shorter than Sam, and seemed to think those two years and five inches made Sam someone to look up to, metaphorically. Dill was new to the base and to anywhere this far north. His first three weeks were spent talking almost non-stop about the hilly terrain.

Sam didn't appreciate just how flat Louisiana and Texas were—he was a West Virginia boy, and knew from hills—until Dill came along to explain it to him.

Dill had a lot of theories about the ship. Probably everyone did, but Dill had a mouth that kept going when his brain had long stopped, so he extemporized on the subject at length. And since he was newer to the base than Sam was, every time there was a briefing, Dill wanted to know if it was unusual.

This was the first time the brief actually was unusual.

"What do I think about what?" Sam asked.

Dill was on the top bunk, looking down. He could rain words on Sam for hours, and had.

"You know what."

"I think we've gotten sloppy of late is all. Hard to stay focused when nothing's happening. Sarge isn't wrong, there are soldiers on war games more alert than we are."

"Yeah, but what did it *mean*."

"It didn't mean anything, Dill."

"I think it means something's coming."

"Like what? Aliens? We already have that."

Dill shook his head, which shook the whole bunk.

"I'm telling you. Something's in the air. I can smell it, like ozone."

"Ozone? You don't even know what that is. Go to sleep, Pickles."

Dill didn't like the nickname, which was a little strange because his full first name was Dillard. He could have gone by that instead and skipped the obvious *pickle* reference.

"Ahhh," he grumbled, and disappeared over his bunk.

There was quiet for about two minutes, but then he was back again.

"Hey!"

"Dill, I swear to God . . ."

"No, look! Who is that?"

Sam rolled up onto an elbow and looked along the row of bunks. Someone was walking down the row, which was not in itself unusual. The latrine was at the other end of the tent. He was only in his boxers, and that was a little odd, but just a little. It was a warm night.

"Think that's Vogel. What of it? Man's gotta go, man's gotta go."

"Don't think that's where he's going. Watch what he's doing, brother."

There *was* something distinctively odd about Vogel's movements. His gestures were halting. Jerky, almost. Somewhere between Frankenstein's monster and a marionette.

Hank Vogel had a few years on Sam. He was a stocky kind of big, not super bright, but friendly enough. Sam would never say Hank was graceful, but he wasn't usually as stiff as this, either.

He was stopping every few feet along the central corridor, standing at the end of each cot and looking at the occupants. The stare lasted eight or ten seconds, it seemed.

"Holy crap, I bet he's sleepwalking," Dill said.

"Could be."

Hank's eyes were definitely open. It was hard to tell if he was awake behind them.

"What should we do?"

"Maybe leave him be, I'm sure he'll go back to bed soon enough."

"*Hank!*" Dill whispered.

"C'mon, leave him alone."

"No, this is too good. *Hank!*"

Vogel turned at the sound and sleep-wandered his way to the base of the bed.

"How you doin', Hank?" Dill asked, waving his hand in front of Vogel's face.

Hank didn't respond. It was just about the creepiest non-response ever. Sam was beginning to dislike this. Dill felt no similar qualms.

"You in there, Corporal Vogel?"

Hank opened his mouth.

"Dill . . ." Sam said.

"Shh. What is it, Hank?"

"Are . . . you . . . ?"

Hank spoke like he had a mouthful of food and didn't know where his tongue was supposed to be.

"What's that?" Dill asked. He hopped off the bunk. Hank—who was taller than both of them—towered above.

"Are you," Hank repeated.

"Sam, should we wake him?"

Sam remembered being told to never awaken a sleepwalker. He thought it was probably just one of those things people said that weren't actually true, but Hank wasn't hurting anybody, so why risk it?

"No, leave him be."

"Are you," Hank said again.

"Am I? No. I don't think I am."

"Dill . . ."

"Well, I don't know how else to answer."

Hank lowered his gaze from Dill and turned to head down the aisle, and then Dill did something dumb. It was, in all fairness, something that only came off as really stupid in hindsight, but still.

When Vogel turned, Dill put his hand on the sleeping man's shoulder.

"Hold on, Hank, let's talk this . . ."

Corporal Vogel's reaction was sudden and alarming. His left hand lashed out and clamped around Dill's throat.

Dill emitted a gurgling shout, with both his hands around the larger man's arm.

"Choking . . ." he cried. "Choking me . . ."

"Hank!" Sam exclaimed.

He was up in a second, his arm around Vogel's, trying to peel the fingers loose. Dill was beet-red already. Vogel was going to kill him.

"HELP!" Sam shouted. "HELP US!"

Four men from neighboring bunks stirred, realized what was wrong, and jumped in, but Vogel's grip was like iron, and efforts to tackle him were proving strangely impossible.

"Wake up, Hank!" Sam said. "Come on, you're killing him!"

Arms and legs and bodies were pulling and shouting, but Vogel was like a rock. A rock that wanted to crush Dill Louboutin's windpipe.

Finally, someone had the idea to slap Hank Vogel across the face.

He trembled, his eyes blinked, and he released Dill, who fell gasping to the floor.

It was said later that in this moment, it looked as if Corporal Vogel became aware of himself and his surroundings. Like he'd been away for a while and just returned to discover himself in entirely the wrong place. Then the moment passed, and Hank started to convulse.

"Hold him, hold him," Sam said. Vogel was falling backwards, arms flailing madly. His eyes, still open, had rolled back in his skull and there was foam coming out of his mouth.

They got him to the floor, where he continued to seize.

"Get him something to bite down on!" somebody shouted. Sam was on top of the larger man, trying to hold his body still before he broke himself or something else.

"Like what?" someone else said. Half the barracks were awake now.

"I don't know!"

Sam said, "Get the medics in here, for Chrissake!"

Then, quite dramatically, Hank Vogel seized up, held his entire body stiff in a huge inhale, and then stopped and collapsed. His arms and legs fell limp and his eyelids fell shut.

Sam put his finger on Vogel's neck and listened to his lungs.

What the hell just happened?

"I don't think he's breathing!" Sam said. "Where's the medic?"

*T*he phone call that was supposed to come from the hospital the next morning—the one notifying Annie that her mother was being released momentarily—didn't come. Not that there was no phone call, only that the one she received involved a very different conversation.

Annie didn't realize exactly how much she failed to pay attention to the information being recited over the phone until it came time to repeat it to others. Ed, and later Violet, and after that her father, all received partial bits of things that didn't entirely add up to a comprehensive whole. It didn't fit into her head that way either, so that was only fair.

The short version was that Carol wasn't coming home and she wasn't staying at Harbridge. She was being transported to Boston, where a medical facility with first-class oncology support was located. There, she would be tested and an approach would be devised, and the question of chemo came up, and phrases like *as comfortable as possible* and *managing the condition* were bandied about, and just about all of it made Annie's eyes burn.

As she explained to the doctor—his name was either "Doctor Benson" or "Doctor Ben Song," she couldn't tell—Carol did a round of chemo before, when she was first diagnosed, and it nearly killed her. It was Annie's understanding that there would be no more chemotherapy. Her mother would rather die on her own terms than live on theirs, and that was that. She asked the doctor if Carol repeated this declaration.

She had, but Doctor Bensomething had a lot to say on that point, along the lines of therapeutic changes and options and the importance of thorough diagnoses, and Annie gave up trying to figure out how it all ended up playing out because at the end of the call her mother was still heading off to the city, whether she wanted to or not.

Annie was tacitly *not* going to Boston.

She could have. Even though she was only sixteen and had neither the money nor the wherewithal to get a hotel room, and even though she had no relatives in the Boston area, there were options. She'd done this before, the last time Carol ended up in the city for a chemo session. The hospital had a program in place that could put her up short-term in something like a halfway house that was a cross section of people going through outpatient cancer screenings and their family members. When she did it, a guardian was appointed to keep an eye on her, and she hated every second of the experience.

It was terrible to admit, but when her mother exited chemo and swore she would never go back, Annie was glad to hear it. Carol was essentially saying she'd rather die at home sooner than in a hospital later, but all Annie could think was that she'd never have to go back to that halfway house again.

She was being incredibly selfish, and she knew it. If she had a therapist, that therapist would undoubtedly be all over her. Nonetheless, the reality was unchanged: Annie had no intention of going to Boston. In the event she *had* to get to the city—for instance, if Carol took a "turn for the worst" (this was her least-favorite euphemism for dying)—Annie could always reach out to Desmond Hollis, who would probably send her into town by helicopter if he had to.

Annie deciding to stay in Sorrow Falls created a new set of problems, though.

In hindsight, the whole issue could be placed at the feet of Carol

Collins, because sometime after the last chemo session and the current emergency, Carol decided to eradicate all negative thoughts from her life. In a very basic way, this made sense, because there was some evidence to suggest cancer patients with positive outlooks tended to do better. The idea of being healthy could impact the health, essentially.

But there was a difference between trying to be positive and refusing to anticipate a circumstance in which that positivity would be inadequate. Specifically, Carol made no concrete plans for her daughter in the event she wasn't there to perform her duties as the Adult.

Anyone who met the two of them in the past two years would have drawn the entirely appropriate conclusion that Annie was playing the role of the Adult, but the problem was that this wasn't in any real way a legal designation. If her mother was unavailable to perform her duties as guardian, the task fell to her father, but when she spoke to him about Carol's condition he made it clear he would be unable to return to Sorrow Falls in anything like a reasonable period of time. (He said he was in Manitoba, which wasn't just north of them but considerably west. Annie wouldn't have time to appreciate this until later, but clearly Hollis's paper trees made quite a circuitous route to the mill.)

All of this meant she had no available adult to pretend to tell her what to do and make sure she didn't set herself on fire or subsist on chocolate bars and vodka, or wander into traffic, or whatever it was she was supposed to end up doing if unsupervised. It was completely crazy, because anyone who knew her at all knew she could take care of herself perfectly fine.

Her initial efforts, then, were to deflect the concern of the people holding themselves responsible for her.

At first, the hospital was pretty easy to fool. Doctor Ben asked if there was an adult guardian, and Annie said yes of course, her father lived with them, and this was technically not a lie because he had a room there. Carol backed her up, too.

Someone blabbed. Annie thought it was probably Lee, the paramedic, although just about anybody from Sorrow Falls could have been the source, as it wasn't exactly a secret. So then they told her she had to have an adult in the house when the ambulance people came by with Carol, to verify that a legal adult was there, even if that adult wasn't her father.

The adult ended up being Ed, which turned the day into possibly the most awkward thing in the history of awkward things. Because when Annie asked Ed to come into the house she didn't tell him he was donating his services as guardian, right up until someone handed him a document to sign.

He *did* sign, which was great, because that meant one set of adults was going to leave her alone. But as with many of the things that made sense in her head, this did not solve Annie's problem.

⋮

"I'm sorry, did I just adopt you?"

"Don't be so dramatic. Of course not. I just needed to get rid of those guys. You can take off now, I think they have a big enough head start."

"No, I can't."

It was Saturday, and they had no plans to continue the interviews again until Tuesday, at which time they would be visiting city hall, talking to some of the long-term resident/owners of the area businesses and, at the end of the day, Desmond Hollis. Annie was expecting it to be far less interesting than, for example, talking to the picketers at the end of Main might be, because *those* guys were entertaining as hell. Although Desmond was always worth the time.

Anyway, they had no place to go for the weekend, so he had no reason to stick around.

"I have plenty of food and everything, if that's what you're worried about," she said. "We keep a well-stocked freezer. We pack for long winters around here."

"I'm worried that I just agreed to make sure a minor is being taken care of. If something happens to you, I'm in a ton of trouble."

"Okay. A little self-centered, but okay."

"In addition to it being bad that something happened to you.

Annie, you just maneuvered me into being your legal guardian until one of your parents gets back, did you even read what they made me sign?"

"Well, yeah, but, I mean, c'mon, do you know how long I've been taking care of myself? Ask anyone."

"Your degree of self-governance was something arranged by your mother, and I guess your father, if he's . . . wherever he is. Now I'm the one who gets to make sure you don't die in a fire or fall through a hole in the floor. And no, you cannot stay on the base, and you definitely can't stay in the B&B with me."

He had clearly visited the part of the house where there were holes in the floor.

"I wasn't going to ask to. I'm fine."

"You can't stay here, Annie."

"You can't make me leave."

"Actually, I just signed some documents that say I can do exactly that."

Annie sighed. "Well, that's not gonna work. Do you want to stay here? I'll show you where all the holes in the floor are."

"That's not going to work either. You keep telling me everyone in town knows you, and so far that's ended up being true. There *must* be someone you can stay with."

And that was how she ended up at Violet's house.

⋮

The handoff was a lot stranger than it should have been, mainly because, somehow, Annie had never spent the night at Violet's house before. Vi spent many a night at Annie's, hanging out with her and Carol and watching movies, and doing things girls did, like talking about quantum theory and orbital mechanics.

And boys, sometimes. Especially before the ship landed, when there wasn't much else going on in Sorrow Falls aside from the Coming Puberty.

This was not to say Violet had anything particularly compelling to offer when engaged in a discussion of boys and girls and how they might interact socially, sexually or academically. It was perfectly understandable for someone home-schooled to have effectively no opinion on boys she'd never met, met only once, or only seen from a distance. At the same time, her lack of interest in developing a more robust understanding of the available local options seemed to go beyond her innate social awkwardness. At times, in other words, Annie wondered if her friend might be gay.

As explanations went, it was a pretty good one. She'd never asked, in part because she wasn't sure if Violet even knew yet. It also seemed sort of rude. It was one of those things you waited for the other person to bring up.

The ship was sort of a welcome icebreaker, in that sense. Once it landed she and Violet had a ream of other things to discuss. It was an almost bottomless pool of things, actually, because Vi was some sort of genius. This was another thing Annie didn't really come out and just ask, but unlike the gay thing, the genius aspect of her friend was more or less assumed.

In home-schooling their daughter, Violet's parents decided early on to concentrate on science and math to the virtual exclusion of all other disciplines. How they got away with this, Annie didn't know — she was pretty sure the state required some sort of testing for the home-schooled, and could only assume Vi tested out okay since she'd not heard otherwise. Anyway, it didn't seem as if Violet had any issues with reading and writing, and if her grasp of history was a little general (aside from movies) it was still good enough to convince whoever regulated these things to let her slide.

Her understanding of science — physics more so than biology — was, in Annie's opinion, the coolest thing about her friend. It was also incredibly helpful; Annie learned way more from Vi than from school or from her friends at the campers. It was Violet's information that helped Annie sort out the good theories from the bad.

While it was true their conversations about applied and theoretical science were frequent, they didn't generally take place in Violet's home, a place Annie had only been inside of a few times. She'd seen the kitchen, the living room, and Vi's bedroom, but only in passing.

Carol probably should have made arrangements for Annie for this kind of thing. Carol met Vi's mom—Annie always called her Susan, as this was one of those households which eschewed titles like "Mr." and "Mrs."—two or three times and had nice things to say about her and all, but at no point did anyone discuss an emergency plan. This was (again) pretty much Carol's fault, as her *think positive!* attitude sometimes precluded a *but plan for the worst!* corollary, but Mrs. Susan Jones could have also stepped up and volunteered.

This was what Annie was thinking as the parties Edgar/Annie and Violet/Susan met in Vi's kitchen to work out the care and feeding of Annie Collins, Defenseless Child.

"You want her to stay?" Susan asked. She was literally repeating what Ed just asked, right after the two of them went through the hospitalization of Carol and Ed's accidental guardianship. Susan came off as dully shocked at his temerity, which was a little odd given that anyone could have figured out why they were there before they even made it to the kitchen table.

"Yes, you see . . . if that's all right . . ." Ed stumbled.

"Of course she can stay," Violet said.

"Yes, of course," Susan said. She smiled.

Then nobody talked for a few seconds. It was incredibly awkward.

Annie had little direct experience with Susan. She was a thin woman with—according to her daughter—an enthusiasm for macrobiotics coupled with vitamin supplements that pushed her body somewhere past healthy and into so-healthy-she-might-be-unwell territory. There were moments, in speaking with her, in which she sometimes seemed to check out a little, as if her mind were on something more important. This happened at the oddest of times, such as this particular one.

"I'll go get the room ready," Violet said.

"I'll help," Annie said, very much ready to get out of the room.

"No, you stay. I'm sure you have to work out everything with . . . Edgar, isn't it? It's nice to meet you."

"And you," Ed said. "I've heard a lot."

This was just him attempting to be polite, as he'd heard almost nothing. He was only slightly less socially awkward than Violet's family.

Annie tried to shoot Vi a *please don't leave me here alone* look, but Violet was already gone.

Ed was gamely trying to keep the conversation at the table going as he pulled the documents from his jacket pocket. "I understand Annie and your daughter have known one another for a long time, and..."

"Yes, yes, sorry," Susan said. "I'm so sorry, Mr. Somerville, I was thinking about poor Carol." To Annie, she said, "Are you all right, dear?"

She'd never called Annie *dear* before, or anything even distantly maternal. It was jarring.

"I'm okay, thank you."

"Well, of course, you can stay as long as you need. Violet will set you up in the guest room."

"That would be great."

"Good," Ed said. He was visibly relieved.

"Do I need to sign something?" Susan asked.

"Yes, actually, I have a form here. I'm still her guardian and all, but... let me just add a little legalese at the bottom here. If you could sign it, that would be great."

"Absolutely."

Ed jotted a few words under his own signature, probably along the lines of, *if something happens to me, check with these people for Annie.* Then he drew a line on the bottom and handed it over.

Susan skimmed what he'd written, signed it, and handed it back.

"Great, thank you so much, Mrs... Jones?" He was reading her signature.

"Susan, please. We don't concern ourselves with formal titles around here."

"Susan, then. And you can call me Ed." He slipped the paperwork back into his pocket and stood. "Annie, are you okay with all this?"

"Sure, Ed, I'll be fine."

"Great. I'll be back Tuesday, usual time, but call me if anything . . . you know, with your mom. Or anything at all."

"You'll be by to pick her up?" Susan asked.

"Yes, on Tuesday. We have a busy day ahead."

Already, Annie was thinking of ways she could continue to live at her house but get picked up at Violet's when Ed needed her, but she couldn't come up with an uncomplicated way for that to work. At minimum, she would need Susan to be complicit, which was a pretty big ask.

Ed stepped around the table to say goodbye to Annie, which was another species of awkward because he wasn't sure what halfway between a handshake and a hug was supposed to look like, so it managed to be a little of both. Then he saw himself out.

"Thanks for this, Susan, I appreciate it," Annie said.

"Don't worry yourself. I just hope everything will be okay with Carol."

"I'm sure it will. I . . . I'll need to go home and pick up some things, though. All my clothes and stuff are there. And my bike."

"Of course," Susan said. "Violet can take you. She needs to run to the store today as it is."

⋮

"I'm sorry," Annie said, as soon as she and Violet were alone. They were in the car and on the way to the grocery store, as it turned out one of the things Vi's family didn't have enough of was food. Guest bedroom, yes. Food for guest, not so much.

"It's fine."

"I didn't know where else to go."

"It's okay, I understand. A call ahead would have maybe been cool. A text, even."

"It happened fast. I didn't know what else to do. One minute I was like, looks like I'm dipping into the frozen pizza stash for the next few weeks, the next minute Ed was looking to make me a ward of the state or something."

"He's just looking out for you. He seems like a good guy."

"You talked to him for all of ten seconds."

"Are you saying he is not a good guy?"

"No, no, just you didn't have a lot of time."

"I'm a quick judge. Mom seemed okay with him."

Annie didn't want to point out that Violet's mother was perhaps the most inscrutable person she'd met in her life, as that seemed rude. But it was impossible to tell, without employing precise scientific equipment, what reaction Susan had to Ed, good or bad. Perhaps her dad was the expressive one in the family.

"Well, I don't want to disrupt anybody or be a burden or whatever. I'll stay out of everyone's way, so you guys can do . . . you know, whatever."

Violet laughed.

"Yes, the goat sacrifice at midnight is really a family thing."

"I mean . . . I don't know. Whatever home-schooling you've got going on."

"It's summer."

"I know, but still."

"Is this your way of saying you think my family is a little weird?"

"No, no. Not a *little*."

"I'm scandalized! I've a mind to just bring you right back home for that."

"And that's where I wanted to be in the first place."

"Okay, forget that, Brer Rabbit. No guest bedroom now. You can sleep under the stairs."

"All right, I take it back. Your family isn't weird."

⋮

Vi lived in an actual cabin in the woods. To get to her place one had to head down Liberty Way to a left turn at an unmarked, well-hidden dirt road, right to the point where you reach the conclusion that you've made a navigational error and decide it's time to turn around. Her place was another two hundred yards past that.

The road extended beyond their house, up into the hills. Annie didn't know where it ended: possibly Narnia. She never tried finding out.

To get to the grocery store meant going back down the dirt

road to a left on Liberty, then a trip through farmland—staying north of the traffic on Patience and Spaceship Road—until reaching Durgin Ave. Durgin went east-west across the northern part of Sorrow Falls, hooking up (indirectly) with the north end of Main. It would have been a viable route for Annie to take on her bike if she wanted to avoid the mess caused by Shippie, but Durgin was a narrow, shoulderless road people treated like a highway. Legally, she could have biked on it. Intellectually, it seemed a foolish idea.

At the western edge of Sorrow Falls, right off of Durgin, was a shopping plaza that had a Super Shopper; a chain pizza place everyone despised and still ate at; a home goods store; and an empty storefront that used to have a steak house, and still had a lot of the signage up for it.

The plaza was kind of typical for the region, which is to say it was a pavement-heavy consumer oasis that made everyone a little sad about capitalism. The Super Shopper was the largest grocer in the area, though, and while the locals had a lot of good things to say about farm stand produce—of which there was a lot—most of them got the bulk of their goods (food and otherwise) at the Super.

Annie knew it well. Carol hadn't been strong enough to make a proper meal more than a couple of times a week for a year or two, but she *was* strong enough to shop at least one Saturday a month, so on that Saturday she and Annie stocked up on frozen food, canned food, food that came in kits requiring only water and perhaps the addition of ground beef, and so on. It was all processed foods all the time: the anti-macrobiotic diet.

Violet and Annie ended up filling a shopping cart with the kind of goods that only made sense for a frat house freezer, and then Violet paid for all of it, which was incredibly embarrassing. There was cash sitting in a box in Carol's bedroom, and that money was for exactly this situation, but Annie forgot all about getting it before leaving. She still couldn't believe she wasn't going to be spending the night in her own bed, which may have been part of the problem.

Annie didn't recognize Dougie at all until he said hello while bagging their one-week supply of tater tots.

"How's it going?" he said, with that half-nod guys their age thought was cool and affecting. It was almost a shrug, almost a nod, almost nothing at all, as if to say *I do not wish to expend the effort to fully acknowledge you but I can do* this.

"Oh, hey!" Annie said. "I didn't recognize you, sorry!"

He smiled and rubbed his hand over his head. It was not, as claimed by the gossipers of the Oakdale Experience, a completely shaven head. He had stubble up there. It was an army-standard crew cut, more or less. Still, it was a very different look.

Doug Kozinsky — Dougie — was the same age as Annie, and in a lot of ways was a kindred spirit, in that he was a town kid of limited means, eclectic tastes, and above-average intellect. But where Annie could merge with just about any clique, Dougie could barely handle eye contact. She knew him pretty well because his dad was a long-haul trucker for Hollis, and worked either with or under Annie's father. Growing up, when her dad and Carol and Annie did things together like going to family barbecues and whatnot, they usually ended up with Dougie's family. That made them bona fide "childhood friends."

They no longer hung out, which was more of a reflection of the change in Annie's family dynamic than in anything Dougie did or didn't do. She was pretty sure he saw it differently, but there was little she could do about that. She always said hi, and took the time to chat with him when he was around, and that was a lot more than most.

"What do you think?" he asked, regarding the haircut.

She thought he was spending too much time idolizing the local army men.

Rude, she wrote in her imaginary sociology field notes.

"Looks good!"

"Thanks."

He blushed. Dougie was an extremely white young man, and with his light brown hair no longer fully disguising his scalp it was possible to answer the question: does blushing happen over the whole head or just the face? (The answer: yes, the whole head can blush.)

Violet finished paying, and Dougie finished bagging and placing the bags in the cart. Annie was struggling with the question as to whether or not she should introduce him to Vi, when he grabbed Annie's elbow.

"Hey, you have a second?" he asked.

"Sure, what's up?" Annie's eyes darted to the register and then along the bank of registers; communicating the obvious *don't you have work?*

"I'm on break in a minute, meet me out front?"

She looked at Vi, who shrugged.

"Sure thing, Doug."

They loaded the food in the trunk of the car and reconnoitered at the entrance. A few seconds later, Dougie appeared and quick-walked them around the corner, as he pulled out a cigarette.

"You *smoke?*" Annie asked.

"Yeah, you want one?" He extended the pack. Annie shook him off. He offered one to Violet, who also declined.

"So I, uh, I don't know how up to date you are on things, but something's *definitely* up with the base," he said.

Annie considered herself remarkably up to date in that regard, but didn't share.

"Yeah, how so?"

"Well, here's what I heard. I guess there was an attack last night."

"An . . . attack? What, did the Russians arrive?"

"No, no, no. On the base. Some grunt went nuts, and now he's dead, and I think they're covering it up."

"How do you know this?" Violet asked.

"I know," he said. He addressed Violet as if she had been a part of the conversation from the outset. "She knows how."

"Doug's house is near the base," Annie said.

This wasn't a fully adequate explanation, but it was okay for the moment. A more complete version of the story would be to say that

Dougie's back yard terminated at the army base fence on one side and at the fence to the Winterhill graveyard on the other side. According to some of the more reputable gossip, Dougie also spent an unreasonable amount of time hijacking army radio frequencies and taking notes about what he heard. A couple of years ago he got in a little trouble for marching along the perimeter of the base and pretending he was a soldier too. It would have been cute if he was still eight — they'd both played "army" when they were eight, coincidentally in the same field that now housed the base — but he was doing this at fourteen.

"So what do you think's going on?" Annie asked. She did not, truly, think anything was, but he did, and that was what counted for the moment.

"Space flu," he said.

"I'm sorry, space . . . flu?" Vi asked.

"It's what they call it when . . . never mind, I'll explain later," Annie said.

"Yeah, I think it's starting to affect them, like, badly. What I hear, this guy went nutso in the barracks, and they ended up choking him or something. He was trying to kill people with his bare hands."

"So we should be thankful the space flu hasn't inspired anybody to use their service revolver, you're thinking."

"I'm dead serious, Annie, you should be careful. They're already talking about a change in their training protocols. They're also tightening things. Altering shifts and stuff. This morning they were running drills on the base I haven't seen them run since the base went up. The bad kind of drills, like, suppression fire, crowd control, those sorts of things. I think things've been changing for a while only we didn't really notice. Do you know Tina?"

"Sure." Tina Henneker was a classmate who'd been driving since March and was unofficially voted by the class as Most Likely To Lose Her Life Texting While Driving. It was unlikely she said anything to Dougie Kozinsky directly, but news traveled a lot of different ways.

"She got stopped at a checkpoint, a couple of days ago."

Annie laughed. "C'mon, Doug, nobody gets *stopped* at those. I don't think the arms on the gates even come down."

"I'm serious. Ask her yourself. They're getting ready to close off the town, I'm telling you."

"I'll keep my ear to the ground, dude."

"Look, I . . ." He looked around in case one of the pigeons or trashcan rodents in the nearby Dumpster was feeling curious, then leaned forward and took his voice down to a whisper. "I know you were there. On the base. I saw you."

"Oh, that, I was just—"

"I don't wanna know. I'm sure you had reasons. I just want to warn you, you know. Be careful. Whatever you've got going on in there . . . I think they're hiding a real problem. And I don't want anything happening to you."

"Aw, thanks, Doug. That's sweet. Thanks. Don't worry, I'll stay aware. And hey, let me know if you hear anything else."

⋮

Dinner was chicken nuggets and fries, two popular frozen delicacies in the Collins household, rendered slightly less edible in Violet's home by the absence of ketchup or any other species of condiment. It was something they hadn't considered needing when at the Super, because as far as Annie was concerned every house had ketchup or at least a jar of prepared barbecue sauce or vinegar, or *something* that would pair effectively with fried things, while Violet didn't usually eat like this at home and so hadn't considered it.

Susan didn't join them. Annie assumed she'd eaten already or had plans to eat later, and until then elected to remain in the house's study, reading a book by lamplight.

The study was the most impressive part of the house, and Annie resolved to spend more time in it. If her own living room was an unconscious homage to old Hollywood, Violet's study was a paean to unusual books. Annie spent a lot of time around books as a library volunteer, but Susan and Todd's collection (Todd was Violet's nearly-always-absent dad) had stuff she never heard of before. It was like an alternative history *Twilight Zone* library, covering a lot

of less-than-respectable subjects, like cryptozoology and nutso as-
sassination theories. There were also books on since-debunked scientific ideas and books on subjects that would never make it into
the public library, like eugenics. It was, in short, a vast collection of
wrong things. Annie couldn't wait to jump in.

After they ate and cleaned up—dishes were done by hand in Annie's household, so when it turned out that was the standard in Vi's
house as well she was already prepared—they retired to the guest
bedroom, where Annie tried to get used to the idea that she was going to be spending the evening there.

The room was small, but clean. It smelled like an alien room,
though, and the sounds were all different, the air blew wrong, and
basically this whole thing sucked.

Violet seemed attuned to her friend's discomfort.

"Maybe we can work something out," she said. Violet was sitting
at the foot of the bed across from Annie at the head. It was a queen-
sized mattress, bigger than the twin in Annie's own room. If this
were a hotel and she were there under different circumstances,
she'd be pretty happy with the larger bed. "You can sleep over there
on weekends or something. I'll stay over too."

"You're the same age as me."

"Sure. But we've been there alone before."

"Look, I'm probably gonna be pissed at Ed about this for a while,
but that doesn't mean I want him to get in any trouble, either. If he
says I need to stay here with you and Susan, I probably have to."

"Yes, I guess you're right."

⋮

Annie couldn't fall asleep, which was more or less as expected. After Violet left, she talked to Carol on the phone for a half an hour
or so. This was a challenge, because only one part of the bedroom
got any cell phone reception, and it was a part with no place to sit.
It was good to hear her voice, though. Annie imagined her mother
was at home and Annie was the one on the trip, and that idea made
it easier for some reason.

Carol found a channel running *Bringing Up Baby* and the two of them spent a good amount of time quoting lines to each other. But then her mother had to get some rest, and Annie was left alone in the big strange bed with the wrong noises and smells and breeze.

Sometime around midnight she decided to stop staring at the ceiling and tried staring out the window instead. The window was on one side of the bed, so it was possible to look through it while still retaining the comfort of being in bed, which was nice.

The isolation of the cabin was jarring. Her own bedroom window faced the street, and while their street was essentially empty—she looked out on farmland on the other side, with the nearest neighbors to the left and right on the same side of the road—there was still a paved road there with a line down the middle and an expectation of periodic traffic.

Violet's place was completely secluded, and until midnight, looking out into the dark woods and listening to alarmingly loud insect and animal sounds, Annie didn't entirely appreciate what true seclusion really was. This was Stephen King–level isolation. Cujo was surely about to emerge from the brush.

No sooner did she have that very thought than something large moved in the trees on the other side of the clearing in front of the porch. In a mild panic—mild because she was pretty safe where she was—she ran through all the obvious options from wolf to deer, then drifted to less obvious ones, like bear, moose, and (on loan from one of the cryptozoology books in the study) Bigfoot.

Then a man emerged from the trees, and Annie's heart stopped for a solid five seconds. He stood at the edge of the clearing, this man: motionless, like statue-motionless, like she couldn't even see him breathing.

The terrifying possibilities regarding who he was and what he was doing there were only beginning to churn through her already-over-imaginative brain when he moved again, two steps, enough for his face to be seen in the moonlight.

It was Todd, Violet's dad.

Why he was wandering around in the woods at midnight was only one of a hundred questions. Another was, what was he even doing in Sorrow Falls, when as far as Annie knew he traveled for his job? And where was his car?

She turned away from the window and went back to staring at the ceiling again.

"I take it back again, Violet. Your family is really weird," she said.

*I*t happened like we told you," the corporal said, with a trace of irritation. This wasn't the best attitude to have when being questioned by a general, but he looked like he wasn't working on a lot of sleep. General Morris didn't seem too put off by it.

"We have your statement," Morris said. "And you're not in any kind of trouble here, son. Mr. Somerville just wants to go over it. Nobody's accusing anybody of anything."

"Begging your pardon, sir, but that's just what people say before they start accusing people of things."

Ed stifled a laugh. He decided he liked Sam Corning, and could understand why Annie spoke well of him.

Sam turned to Ed, but spoke to the general.

"Has Mr. Somerville read our reports, sir?"

They were sitting in Morris's office, which had a surprisingly understated and temporary feel to it. The table in the center of the room and all the chairs were of the collapsible variety, and the room itself was the interior of one of the temporary-to-permanent trailers the base had. He wasn't sure if this meant Morris thought this was only a brief assignment for him, or if he just didn't have any things.

They had already questioned the other men who were a part of the incident, most recently Corporal Louboutin. Dillard Louboutin stood at attention the entire time and refused to comment on any element of his original statement other than to affirm the words contained within it. If it hadn't been obvious from the behavior of the other four men they'd already spoken to, Dill's attitude drove home the point: they all thought the army was looking for someone to blame for Hank Vogel's death, and Ed was the man with the power to make that accusation.

The men were closing rank and backing each other up. Usually, with something like this, at least one person would start in with dark hints that maybe someone did something they weren't supposed to, but that hadn't happened. It spoke to the six men having a strong leader at their center. Ed was pretty sure he was looking at that leader.

"I've read the reports, yes," Ed said. "Can I walk through your statement with you?"

"You can do whatever you want to, sir."

"You don't have to call me sir, I'm not an officer. I'm not even army."

"My mother raised me to be polite to my elders regardless, sir."

Ed caught Morris stifling a laugh of his own.

"Son, you can relax," the general said.

"Yes sir, thank you, sir," Corning said, visibly not relaxing.

Ed sighed.

"According to . . . well, everyone, Corporal Vogel was sleepwalking," Ed said. "Had he ever done that before?"

"Not that I'm aware of, sir."

"You knew Vogel for some time, didn't you?"

"Knew of him, sir. We were neither friends nor foes. It's a large base. I knew him by sight."

"Did he know Louboutin?"

"You'll have to ask him that."

"We did that, yes. As I'm sure you know."

"Not sure what you mean by that, sir."

"I only mean Dill Louboutin thinks highly of you and would confide if given the opportunity. So Vogel was sleepwalking, and nobody remembers him ever doing that before. Does anybody else have that problem?"

Corning hesitated. It wasn't a question he'd been expecting. "In the world, sir?"

"On the base. In the barracks. Has anyone ever sleepwalked before?"

"I'm sure I don't know, sir. That might be a question best asked of the doctor."

"You're right, it is. I'll take it up with her. What I'm getting at, Corporal, is that I'd like to know just how unusual it was, seeing Vogel walk around like that."

"Not sure what you mean, sir. People get up and down all through the night. We roll three eight-hour shifts, people are always about. I'm sure I wouldn't be able to tell if one of them was sleepwalking or running to the toilet or heading off to guard duty. I was trying to get some sleep myself."

"Yet there was something different about Vogel that night."

The corporal looked as if he were about to deny this, then thought better of it. His testimony and Louboutin's were united on this point: Dill Louboutin thought something was wrong with Hank Vogel and attempted to engage Vogel because of it. Sam Corning couldn't very well turn around and claim otherwise.

This was the line of questioning that had been missing from the original testimonies.

The statements from the six men were pretty straightforward. Four only reported on what happened *after* Vogel began choking Louboutin, because before then those soldiers were uninvolved. The two other statements—from Sam and Dill—were so nearly identical they sounded like they'd been memorized ahead of time . . . which was probably exactly what happened.

"Not sure how to answer that, sir," Sam admitted.

"According to both of you, Corporal Louboutin tried to get Corporal Vogel's attention by touching Vogel on the shoulder. Vogel responded by attempting to murder Louboutin. What I'd like to know is *why* Dill wanted to get Vogel's attention in the first place. As you said, people were up and down all the time, and you wouldn't necessarily know if one of them was sleepwalking or running to the bathroom or going out to howl at the moon. But Pickles knew something was up with Hank Vogel."

Corning blinked at Ed's use of Louboutin's nickname. It implied a level of familiarity with the soldiers Sam was perhaps not expecting.

"You'd have to ask him," Corning said.

Ed met Sam's gaze and considered the best way to proceed.

"General," Ed said, "this is a little unorthodox, but I wonder if I can speak to Sam alone for a few minutes? I know it's *your* office, but—"

"Not at all." Morris stood, which made Sam stand. "Remain at ease, Corporal."

"Sir."

"I mean sit down."

Sam sat.

"Answer the man's questions," Morris said.

"Yes sir."

The general left, and an uncomfortable silence took his place.

"Just you and me, Sam," Ed said. "There aren't any listening devices in here, you're not on camera, and my word holds no particular weight with the brass."

"Yes sir. But if I can ask . . . all that being true, what are you doing here? Seems to me you just ordered a general to vacate his own office."

Ed laughed. "I guess I did, at that. Annie can pick 'em, can't she?"

He looked confused, which was perhaps the first non-soldierly, human emotion Ed had seen him register. "How do you mean, sir?"

"I mean, she speaks well of you, and she has high standards."

"Well, I appreciate that, sir."

"Look, I just want to know what Dill noticed about Vogel. I'm asking you, because I think you noticed too, and because Annie told me I could trust you."

Annie told him no such thing, but he had a feeling if he asked, she would. He also wished she were there with him, but bringing her to a military interrogation—for, as informal as this was, it was still an interrogation—would have been impossible. Plus, she had enough to deal with.

She'd have gotten an answer by now, though.

"Why are you here, Mr. Somerville?" Sam asked.

"Well, some of that's confidential."

"Which part isn't?"

Ed smiled. "The part that really needs to know what happened to Hank Vogel isn't. At least, not yet. Look: I think something's going on in Sorrow Falls. Or maybe not some *thing*, so much as a lot of little sort-of somethings that add up to one big something, only we don't know what things to add together yet. I've got a lot of pieces that don't make sense yet, and this is one of them. Nobody here did anything wrong. Hank Vogel died of a brain aneurysm, and medically speaking everything that happened in his skull that night would have happened if he'd remained in his bunk. But he didn't remain in his bunk, and I'd like to know why, and what his last few minutes of life on earth looked like to someone who was there. Can you help me with that?"

Sam didn't answer for long enough that Ed was ready to give up.

"He looked empty, sir," Sam said. His eyes, which had been directed either straight ahead or locked with Ed's, had fallen to the floor.

"Call me Ed, please. What do you mean, *empty?*"

"Empty like he wasn't in there." His eyes drifted back up. "Nobody home. I've been thinking about this a lot, sir."

"Ed."

"Ed. I've been thinking about this a lot, because I . . . I can't stop seeing his face sometimes. It wasn't that he was sleepwalking. He was moving wrong. That's what Pickles saw. Up close you could see . . ."

He trailed off.

"Sam, trust me when I tell you, there isn't anything you could say here that I haven't already heard. I've been speaking to a lot of people around town and I've heard a lot of pretty out-there things. At this point I'm willing to take all of it at face value. What could you see?"

Sam fidgeted uncomfortably in the folding chair.

"It's hard to be honest about something like this. Not sure now if what I think I saw is something I'm just remembering wrong. But thinking about it now, it was like . . . like he was already dead. Like he wasn't in there anymore, and someone else was driving."

"A zombie."

"I didn't say that."

"No, you didn't."

"He didn't want brains, either. I mean, if we're going with zombie."

"How do you . . . did he speak?"

". . . Yes. We didn't want to tell anyone, it was too weird."

"What did he say?"

"He said 'Are you.'"

"The letters? R and U?"

"No, like it was part of a question but he couldn't say the rest of it. I mean, it was flat. He said it flat, but he was asking, I think. It was almost as if he couldn't figure out how to make more words than that."

"I wonder what he was trying to say?"

"I don't know. But I think he was looking for somebody."

"Why do you say that?"

"It was what Dill noticed. Hank kept going bunk-to-bunk and staring at people. That's what was happening before Dill called him over."

"Some*body* and not some*thing*?"

"That was my take. I don't think it was Dill he was looking for, though."

"And he responded to his name? When Louboutin called him?"

"He responded to someone looking at him and making a sound. Everyone else was asleep or trying to be, pretty much. Could've been like with a bull. Wave a red blanket in front of him, and it's not that he's reacting to the color red, he's reacting to the movement. Can I ask you something?"

"Sure."

"A lot of the guys are thinking what happened to Hank is . . . you heard of the space flu, right?"

"You want to know if I think the space flu was what killed Corporal Vogel? Sam, I don't think the space flu is real. The effect the ship has on people when they get close to it is real enough, but I don't believe that has a long-term impact, and I don't believe it harms at a distance. What's happening now is the same thing that can happen in any situation like this. For every malady or accident, someone's going to wonder if the big unexplained phenomenon at the bottom of the hill is the culprit. But at the same time, I'm here to piece together that phenomenon, because at the end of the day there actually *is* a spaceship down there, and we still really don't know what to expect from it."

"So maybe."

"Maybe."

"Which means what happened to him could happen to us."

"I didn't say that. Vogel died of an aneurysm. Those are pretty rare in healthy adults under forty."

"Sure, and that's the problem, isn't it? Someone dies of something they shouldn't have . . . that's what gets people worried."

"Are you worried, Sam?"

"Of course I am. But if you want to know what's keeping me up nights, other than the memory of Hank's face, it's that I don't know when the aneurysm killed him. Either it was before he got out of bed or after we tried to wake him up, and to be honest, I'm not sure I like either answer."

⋮

Having involved himself in the army's investigation of Vogel's death, Ed ended up pulled into a series of meetings with higher-ups that lasted the entire day. He had no say in what was to become of the six men, or what the report Morris was supposed to file on the incident would look like. He had *thoughts*, though, and if there were people in uniform who wanted to hear them, he was there.

Those thoughts were disjointed, and hardly involved Sam and Dill and the other four. Ed was starting to put pieces together, and now he had a word to use when talking to people. It was a preposterous word, but that was exactly what gave it value.

It wasn't until Monday that he had a chance to employ it. That was in the Sorrow Falls sheriff's department.

One of Ed's first top-secret papers on Sorrow Falls leaned heavily on data from the sheriff. Even then, he was trying to prove something was amiss with the town by pointing out what was *missing*, and in this case what was missing was criminal behavior.

Crime statistics before the ship landed and after the ship landed remained essentially the same in Sorrow Falls, which was just not possible. For one thing, the number of people inside the town line doubled. A concomitant doubling of criminal acts would have been too much to expect, but an *increase* was appropriate, and it hadn't happened. For another thing, reported criminal acts in every town outside Sorrow Falls *had* gone up, and not just in Massachusetts. It was a nationwide phenomenon.

Those numbers alone were enough to convince Ed something subtle was happening in the town, but they didn't convince anyone else. *The army's presence is discouraging criminal behavior,* he was told. When he pointed out that even when he added the reports of local peacekeeping actions to the sheriff's statistics, the totals were still too low, he was told that the existence of a military force was a natural deterrent.

Ed had mountains of evidence from every police action and war zone in history that said this wasn't the way the world worked, but nobody would believe him.

All that research meant he was very familiar with the sheriff's department, even if they didn't know him at all. He knew they remained in the same spot as always, just a half block from city hall on the northern end of Main, in a small set of offices with a parking lot roughly the same size as the building beside it. They had only two cells, ten desks, and two offices. The total number of deputies was the same. They worked in rotating day/night twelve-hour shifts, and for the most part they handled minor area complaints like vandalism and domestic disputes. A tremendous amount of scholarly legal work had been performed by a number of very smart people to settle the question of who might investigate a murder in Sorrow Falls, but none of that work had been applied because in the three years since the local suspension of Posse Comitatus there hadn't been a murder in the town.

Yet somehow, Ed was the only one who thought this was weird.

The sheriff's name was Pete, which was short for Patricia Gallardo. Nobody called her Sheriff Gallardo or even Sheriff Patricia. She was Sheriff Pete.

This began as a joke. Whether it was because the sheriff when the ship landed was a male (he retired only six months later, wealthy from a succession of speaking engagements, a book advance, and a movie deal) or due to some innate sexism which interpreted the title "sheriff" as belonging to the male gender, everyone assumed the sheriff was a man. People coming into town—journalists, typically—kept asking to speak to "him," so the deputies started calling her Pete and telling whoever was asking that "Pete will be right with you," specifically so they could appreciate the look on their faces when they met her.

Unlike the discovery that there was no Joanne behind Joanne's Diner, Ed was aware that Pete was a woman. This was undoubtedly one of the reasons he didn't get the runaround when showing up at the office Monday morning asking for her.

"Mr. Somerville, is it?" She met him at the small waiting area, having only arrived a few minutes earlier with a large coffee from the doughnut shop up the street. "Come on in."

Her office was one of the two the building had, the other being for interrogations and private waiting and whatever else they could think to use it for. His research led him to the conclusion that it was barely used for much at all. On this morning it held two boxes of doughnuts.

He sat down and closed the door, which got a raised eyebrow from Sheriff Pete.

"You're the journo interviewing folks around town, am I right? Everything okay?"

"Yes, sorry, I just wanted to talk in private. I'm sorry, I should have asked about the door."

"No, it's fine, I close it half the day. It's just a little early. I'm not ready for real problems for another couple of hours."

"I should have scheduled an afternoon meeting, then."

She laughed a deep laugh that didn't sound fully genuine.

Patricia Gallardo was a lot more petite than the person she replaced, and that was mostly a good thing. The old sheriff was a large guy in most every direction. Pete was in excellent shape, and someone Ed would call pretty if he didn't think it might get him shot. She gave off that kind of vibe.

"But yes, that's me," Ed said. "I've been in town a couple of weeks now."

"Annie Collins is working with you, I know. Heard about her mom. Is she doing okay?"

"Yes, she's fine. She's staying with friends for now. Do you know Violet Jones? Susan and Todd are her parents."

"I can't say I do. But when you see Annie tell her Chuck and I are praying for Carol."

"I'll do that."

"So you aren't here to ask if I know the Joneses."

"No, I'm not. I want to say a word, and I'd like to know what you think of that word."

Her brow wrinkled.

"Sure, try me."

"Zombie."

Pete didn't blink.

"Go on," she said.

"That's the kind of word that makes people laugh and look confused to be hearing it in a real-world setting."

"Maybe I've been hearing it a lot in a real-world setting. Are you actually a journalist, Mr. Somerville?"

"Let's say I'm not."

"All right, let's say that."

She opened a desk drawer and pulled out a small stack of folders inside a larger folder.

"Maybe you know this, but local property issues tend to get reported to this office instead of the one you spend so much time at up the hill. Did you know there are four cemeteries in Sorrow Falls?"

"I did know that, actually."

"Good for you. People have been living here since Oliver Hollis struck that deal with the five tribes, and they've been dying here that long too. There's a lot of property out there devoted to burying our dead."

She singled out one set of folders.

"These are reports of gravesite vandalism. Six different graves at three of the cemeteries. If you're not a journalist, maybe you're someone who can help me figure out what this is about."

Ed took the files from her and started flipping through.

"Nothing at the fourth cemetery?" he asked.

"Nope. Fourth one's an old burial ground. Flip through those folders, you can probably figure out why we haven't had an incident there."

"Hm. This isn't really desecration or vandalism," he said, halfway through the cases. "It's theft."

"The bodies are all missing, that's true."

"Oh, I see it." He closed the folders and handed them back. "Nobody's been dead for longer than a year."

"Ten months. Whereas Holly Hill Burial Ground last hosted a funeral eighty-two years ago. As you can imagine, the logical approach to this—assuming these six are related, which we are assuming—was to find out who the six deceased men and women had in common. Who, and not what, because that who was probably the sick bastard digging these people up, punching through their coffins, and taking their bodies somewhere. And after a little analysis, we added *making it look like the dead climbed out on their own* to the list of sick things this hypothetical who did. But we never found that person."

She slid the second set of folders along the desk.

"These are nine different reports filed with my office of people seeing the dead walk in Sorrow Falls. Four are assault cases."

"What kind of assault?"

"Bruising, scratching. Nobody trying to eat brains, if that's what you're looking for."

"Did they say anything? The . . . the undead. Did they speak?"

"All four of the attack victims said it seemed like the, um, zombie attacking them wanted something but they didn't say exactly what. One young woman insisted the man who assaulted her asked if she was a whore. But supposedly the one asking used to be one of her teachers, so I took that with some salt."

Ed flipped through until he found that report. *Are you a whore?* was the question. He wondered if that was the rest of the sentence Hank Vogel was trying to get out, and if so what sense that made in the context in which he was asking.

"So now, Mr. Somerville, I appear to be the second sheriff in this town to have to deal with something no other sheriff in any other town has had to deal with. Either someone has concocted an extremely impressive hoax, or we're looking at a zombie problem. To be honest, I'm considering all possible explanations, so if you've got one I would love to hear it."

"Not yet," he admitted. "But I know two things. One, the ship is probably causing this, although I don't know why or how yet. Two, we have to hope this is confined to the dead."

"Why wouldn't it be? Being zombies and all."

"Let me share what I can. It begins with a soldier named Hank Vogel."

13
MEET THE JONESES

*E*verything slowed down for Annie.

Even in her own house, she was unaccustomed to sitting still and staying put for even a day. Sure, she spent most of her evenings in the living room, rewatching one of the films her mother clung to (somewhat inexplicably, as the movies were not from *her* childhood at all) until bedtime. But her days were usually new adventures with each sunrise.

Or so she liked to tell herself. The truth was, in the summer she migrated between the same three or four places, and in the other nine months most of her day was spent at school. Still, that was high excitement compared to anything happening in Violet's day-to-day.

First, there was the Sunday morning awkwardness.

Annie waited until she was reasonably certain her friend was awake before knocking on Vi's bedroom door to ask about Todd.

"Oh, no, he's not . . . he's on vacation," Violet said, rubbing sleep from her eyes. "I'm sorry, it didn't even occur to me to . . . I mean, you're used to not having your dad around, so you probably assumed Todd wasn't."

I assumed he wasn't because he never has been before, Annie thought. This was maybe the second or third time she'd seen him, in six years.

"Maybe, yeah. I don't mean to pry, Violet, I really don't, but what was he doing wandering around in the woods at midnight?"

Violet adopted an expression familiar to anyone who'd been embarrassed by their parents at one time or another.

"Oh, that. He does that, I don't even understand. He has this whole 'back to nature' thing he does when he's on break. He says it's to compensate for being behind a desk all day. I should have warned you but I don't even think about it anymore. Not that I imagined you being up so late. Didn't you sleep?"

"A little, yeah. I'm a mess, Vi, don't mind me."

"Don't worry about it." Violet gave her a quick hug. "Now let's go get some food."

"Okay. But you'd tell me if your dad was a werewolf, right?"

"No, probably not. It's not a full moon, though, so I think we're okay."

⋮

Breakfast was just the two of them. Annie wasn't sure what part of the house Susan and Todd slept in—there were only a couple of options, really—but wherever it was, they hadn't emerged yet. That was provided Todd wasn't out wandering somewhere.

Annie wasn't sure Susan's diet even involved food. It certainly didn't involve condiments.

After breakfast, they returned to the Super to pick up more things, and then back to the house. It was late afternoon, when Violet asked Annie if she wanted to help in the garden, that Annie realized her best friend in the world was impossibly boring in her natural habitat.

"Sure, I'd love to garden," Annie lied.

She did a lot of the gardening at her own house because her mother wasn't strong enough to do everything, but they only grew one crop. She was admittedly curious about what a garden that grew something *other* than marijuana might look like, but not curious enough to get her hands dirty.

Nonetheless, that was what she ended up doing. It was that or try to find a book to read in the library, but that would have meant getting past Susan, who'd taken the time while they were out shopping to decamp in there once more.

First, Annie tried getting on the Internet. She brought a laptop from home, and knew Violet had one as well, yet when Annie tried connecting to the Wi-Fi, the computer kept failing. So did her phone. Yet with the same password, Vi's worked fine.

When she asked Violet to help her figure out what was wrong, she said she'd talk to Todd the next time she saw him. When Annie followed that up by asking if she could use Vi's computer instead, she said, "I'd rather you didn't," without elaboration.

Annie wasn't sure what the big deal was.

Like most Sorrow Falls kids, Annie had only a limited social media presence as herself. (Many of them, she was sure, had pseudonymous identities, although she didn't.) From the day the ship landed onward, pretty much anyone online who could be identified as a denizen of space invasion ground zero was a target.

Annie kept her public profile low and her interactions few, and gossiped face-to-face instead. But that didn't mean the Internet wasn't an excellent way to keep track of the rest of the world, especially from her tiny corner of it. She knew Violet treated the Internet much the same way, albeit with an even lower profile. She couldn't imagine doing anything on her friend's computer that Violet would disapprove of.

By late Sunday, then, Annie had literally nothing better to do than work in the garden.

Violet's garden was a lot larger. It took up enough of the plot in the back of the house to nearly qualify as a proper farm, Annie decided. It was a gross exaggeration, but she was sticking with it, especially after an hour into the weeding. She and Vi did this mostly in silence, broken by periodic "Is this a weed or are you growing this intentionally?" conversations brought about by Annie's general unfamiliarity with vegetable plants.

Todd walked by about eighty minutes in. He came from the woods and headed right through the center of the garden, not apparently noticing either of them.

"Hi, Todd," Violet said.

"Hello," he answered, without turning. He went inside.

Annie decided yes, he was exactly as creepy-weird as he seemed the night before.

"Hey, do you remember a lot about your birth dad?" Annie asked.

Vi seemed taken aback by the question. Maybe it was the timing of it — Todd having just walked past — or that it hadn't been a subject of discussion for a long time. Mostly, Annie was just looking for something to talk about.

She and Vi had been friends for six years. They were perhaps two years into that friendship when Annie became aware of something that would have been obvious sooner to someone with an adult-level grasp of genetics: Violet didn't look anything like Susan or Todd. It was another two months before she brought it up.

The short version of the explanation was that Violet was adopted. The longer version was that her birth father was a scary man. It wasn't something twelve-year-old Annie ever thought to ask, but there were times when she wondered if the Joneses weren't living in isolation entirely by choice.

"Objection," Violet said.

"Grounds?"

"Irrelevance."

"The court recognizes your objection but asks that the witness respond to the line of inquiry."

"Annie, you can't be the attorney and the judge at the same time."

"Overruled."

Violet sighed, but was unwilling to face a contempt-of-court charge.

"I remember a lot about him. Why do you ask?"

"I dunno. Part of me always imagined you were secretly in witness protection up here. And your dad was some mobster and you testified against him."

"That's a good story."

"Thanks, I've been working on it for a while."

"It's not true, but it's still a good story."

Annie threw a chunk of dirt at Vi.

"C'mon, it makes so much sense!"

"You think that's the answer to why we live up here? The home-schooling, the macro diets, all that?"

"Yes!"

"Sorry. Todd and Susan wanted a certain kind of life and built that life, and I happened to agree with their choices. I like it out here."

"All right, fine, if he's not in the mafia, what's his deal? Is he the president? Is your dad the president?"

"Like Grover Cleveland's love child? Yes, that's exactly it."

"I'm gonna throw more dirt."

"You make everything so complicated. He isn't anybody. He just wanted me to have a different kind of life than this. That's all."

"And you aren't hiding from him."

"I'm not hiding from him. That doesn't mean I ever want to see him again, either. He had a temper . . . Annie, I really don't want to talk about him. Is that okay?"

"Yeah, I'm sorry. I was just looking for something more interesting than gardening to talk about."

"There is nothing more interesting than gardening."

"I object."

"Overruled."

⋮

Sunday night was spent somewhat normally, in terms of their friendship: movie night, featuring *The Wizard of Oz*. There were a hundred-plus films from which to choose sitting in Annie's living room at home, but they all required a VCR, which Violet didn't have. They agreed that going over to Annie's to watch something else would end up with them being tempted to just stay overnight there and return in the morning.

Perhaps Ed's somewhat paranoid concern was rubbing off on Annie, but she decided even if Susan gave them a pass it still wasn't okay. *In case something happened.* Nothing was going to happen, but once it was in her head she couldn't get rid of the idea.

Violet had a copy of her favorite film in a format even older than VCR: she had an honest-to-God 8mm movie theater copy of it, and a movie projector to watch it on. It meant projecting it on the wall of Vi's bedroom, and changing the reel halfway through, and dealing with the crappy speakers on the projector—so actually, every aspect of the experience was inferior to every other way they'd watched it—but it was fun. It was a new experience, and even though she'd seen the movie a hundred times by now, the technology gave her a chance to pretend it was a new adventure.

Monday was the worst day. There was no more shopping to do, and no more gardening to get done, and Violet couldn't get the Wi-Fi to let Annie's devices in. After two hour-long conversations with Carol, Annie gave up and wandered into the library—ignoring Susan—for long enough to grab whatever book she thought might be worth an hour or two of her time. It ended up being a collection of Lovecraft stories.

She knew four or five profoundly nerdy kids who spoke of Lovecraft with the quiet reverence less nerdy kids reserved for Kurt Cobain, *The Catcher in the Rye*, or the Bible. (Depending on the kid, obviously.) Annie knew exactly nothing of Lovecraft, but his was the only name she recognized on any of the books in the library, so she grabbed it, and spent the afternoon trying to figure out what the big deal was.

She came out of the book a few hours later with a greater appreciation for Poe and a diminished opinion of her nerdy friends. Then she called Carol one more time, went to bed early, and had at least one nightmare involving ancient gods with unpronounceable names.

When she got downstairs the next morning Ed was already there, in the kitchen, chatting with Susan.

She could have kissed him.

"Morning, Annie, how are you?" he greeted her.

"Great! Let's go!"

"I was just . . . okay," he said, as she was already past him by then and on the porch. She sat in the passenger's seat of the car—she was possibly even happier to see the car again—while he finished up having whatever boring conversation he was having in the boring house with boring Susan.

"Everything okay?" he asked, starting the car.

"Super. I'm losing my mind here; let's go do exciting things. Did you have a fun few days? Tell me every last detail."

"Um, okay. I saw your library yesterday."

"Did you? Did you see the mural? What did you think?"

"I've seen it before, in pictures, but —"

"Actually, forget that. What happened at the army base? I've heard stories."

⋮

"So zombies, that's what you're telling me."

"I'm telling you what the information we've been collecting has led me to think," Ed said. "I appreciate how crazy it is."

"No kidding."

"But you live in a town with an interstellar vehicle parked in it. Why not zombies too?"

"Sure. And I mean, I've been hearing the same stuff, but not from anyone I took seriously."

Annie told him about Rick Horton and his late-night undead encounter in a cow pasture. Meanwhile, on the other side of the diner, Beth kept shooting glances her way.

They were in a booth in the back of Joanne's. It was the same one Ed had sat in the first time they met. They drove to the diner directly from Violet's, after Ed figured out Annie hadn't eaten yet (all Vi knew how to do in the kitchen was burn bacon) and before they realized they didn't have as busy a day as anticipated. The meeting they were supposed to have with Desmond Hollis was pushed to the end of the day, and the plan to head to city hall to speak to a couple of councilmen got blown up when the council canceled the day's session. No official reason was given for this, and if there was an unofficial reason, Annie had been away from town for too long to hear what it was.

Beth, hopefully, had something on it.

"How long ago was that?" Ed asked.

"I heard the story the day you and I met."

"I mean, when did your friend see this?"

"Not sure. And he isn't my friend. I could ask him if I run into him, or we can call Rodney and see if he knows. Might come off as kind of weird, though, dialing him up to ask that."

"You can't look up Rick?"

"Like I said, he isn't my friend. And he's not easy to track down."

Ed smiled. "Annie Collins, I thought you were friends with everyone in this town."

"I said I *know* everyone in this town. I don't happen to like all of them. He is one such person. But, I can find him if you really want to talk."

"It's okay. Probably not important enough to go through the trouble. It's only that he might have the earliest reported sighting. I thought we might want to establish a timeline."

"Yeah, well I'm about 50 percent not sold on the zombie theory right now. And I'm not even supposed to be the adult in this partnership. I'm gonna go say hey to Beth. Maybe come up with a vampire angle instead, while I'm gone."

"I'll see what I can do."

Beth stepped around the counter when she approached, put down a coffee urn, and gave Annie a big hug.

"You snuck in here without even a hello first!" Beth said, releasing Annie only to smack her on the arm. "I was so worried! When I heard about Carol . . ."

"She's fine. She'll *be* fine, I mean. I talked to her three times yesterday; she's in good spirits. Everything positive all the time, you know how she is."

"Where are you staying? Not home alone, right? I know it's not with your reporter friend, I would have *heard* about that."

"Stop it."

"Look, any time you want to stay with us, I mean, you know my parents already want to adopt you . . . I mean . . ."

Beth blushed furiously.

"Not that you need adopting," Beth said quickly. "I mean Carol . . . !"

"It's fine, oh my God, calm down. I'm staying with Violet, but I'll let you know if I need any help, don't worry."

"Oh, okay. Have I met Violet?"

"I think probably. She's a neighbor. Hey, so we were supposed to talk to a few folks down at city hall this morning, but it sounds like they're closed. Is something up?"

"I don't think so, I think people are just sick."

"Like, collectively?"

"No, but there's something going around. It's not like they have a lot of hugely important votes going on anyway."

This was true. Local government's central function was to make sure the trash was collected and the streets were plowed in the winter. Aside from that, they planned the occasional festival and put up commemorative plaques. The first year after the ship landed, the council was extremely important and extremely busy, because every day there were five new businesses looking for real estate, and there were liquor licenses and building permits needed everywhere. Not a lot had changed since that year, though.

"Okay, thanks. Hey, we have some folks to talk up down at the mill, can we leave the car around back?"

"Sure, nobody'll care."

"No towing today?"

"No need, it's Tuesday. Nobody's around."

"Thank you, girl. We'll talk later."

Annie returned to the table.

"I guess city hall called in sick today," she said.

"What, all of them?"

Annie shrugged. "It's a part-time job, they probably didn't have anything cool to vote on, and Beth said there's something going around."

"What kind of something?"

"I dunno. Want me to ask? Maybe it's a zombie plague."

"You're not going to drop that anytime soon, are you?"

"Looks like no."

14
BANG THE DRUM SLOWLY

𝒜 drum sat in the corner of Desmond Hollis's office, on a small stage, in a glass case. The drum was — depending on who was asked — either a smaller replica of the original, or the original itself, miraculously preserved for over three hundred years.

The latter claim was within the realm of the possible, only because the Hollis family could trace its bloodline back to the original Sorrowers, which was a statement pretty much nobody else in town could make. It gave the claim some legitimacy.

However, much like the spaceship up the road, most people thought the drum would be bigger.

The story was, when Josiah Sorrow's followers picked this spot in which to settle (or Josiah did, when he decided to die nearby) they inadvertently wandered onto ground that was considered either sacred or cursed by five different regional Native American tribes.

There were enough competing historical claims on this particular detail that it was effectively impossible to tease out the real story. In some accounts, it was the site of a great war between the tribes and was subsequently considered haunted by the natives. In another, there was no war, but the crops always failed, so it was cursed. A third had the tribes keeping away because of the wrath of an angry local god, although the expression of this wrath was unspecified. The most benign version held that the weather in this part of the valley was simply too harsh for people who lived lives which didn't include modern winter gear. This one had merit for being the least condescending toward the belief systems of the regional Native Americans—who were, in most respects, quite practical—if it did somewhat discount the ingenuity of a people who lived year-round in New England.

What all iterations of the story did have was the drum.

The drum used to rest on a tree stump in the middle of a field a short walk from the shore of the river. That field was now a parking lot and the stump was long gone, but a plaque was erected—by the same committee that funded Josiah's mural—and that plaque was still standing at the edge of Main in front of the parking lot.

As it went (in most of the stories) when there was an intertribal dispute, any one of the elders from any of the tribes could travel to the stump and bang on the drum, which would signal all of the tribes that a meeting was required. The other elders would show up shortly after, and the matter would be resolved peacefully, with no bloodshed, due to the sacred/cursed nature of the land on which the drum sat. It sounded like a great way to avoid a war in an era before telephones and treaty organizations.

Given this description it was reasonable to assume the drum was larger than the one in Desmond's office, because the real thing had to be something big enough to be heard throughout the valley. This was a very modern idea, though, because in truth, Main Street ran through a midpoint in a natural concavity. If one took away all of the buildings and the cars somehow, added some more trees, and got rid of the parking lot, it was possible that the sound of a drum could carry pretty far if one faced in the correct direction. Even a small one.

In the early going, it was to the Sorrowers' benefit that the locals—who surely would have otherwise slain them for their encroachment—were afraid to shed blood on the ground they'd elected to call home. Sorrowers were also considered cursed peo-

THE SPACESHIP NEXT DOOR · 163

ple by a couple of the tribes, not specifically because of where they were living but because when they arrived the first thing they did was shed blood (Josiah's) in a place where that was taboo.

The tribes mostly left them alone, then, and figured it was okay so long as none of the Sorrowers did something stupid, like touch the drum.

Then came winter.

Josiah's cult had some experience with winter, certainly. All of them were born and raised in the Americas, and they'd toughed out two prior winters isolated from the larger settler populations to the southeast. But half their summer was spent in canoes, which left almost no time for preparing the sorts of things a community needed to survive a winter in this climate: shelter, adequate provisions, and so on. They also had no horses and hardly any weapons, and half of them were dying from what turned out to be syphilis. (The Sorrowers called the disease the God's Wrath Plague, and in this instance that was probably accurate.)

One evening in the first winter, with a quarter of their number already dead, a young man decided, on his own, to trudge through a foot of newly fallen snow to the drum, which he banged furiously for an hour. His name was Oliver Tempest Hollis.

Young Hollis likely had no idea what the drum was for and just wanted something to hit, although later it would be said this was a divinely directed action, and who was to say?

Assuming his goal was to alert the neighbors that the tribe of white men residing on cursed soil was about to perish, he succeeded. Within two days multiple representatives of each of the five tribes arrived at the stump.

Pretty much nothing was known about what happened in the conversation that followed, between the elders and their clansmen and Oliver Tempest Hollis. As the banger of the drum, Oliver was presumed by the natives to be the man who spoke for all of the Sorrowers, and so he did. He had no authority to do so, but the deal he struck ended up being one that saved the lives of everyone else living in Sorrow Falls, so the others had little choice but to roll with it.

One thing that came out of the talk was that young Hollis was promised to an age-appropriate woman from one of the tribes. This was in exchange for food, clothing, and shelter, and a long-term co-existence between the Sorrowers and the natives, so the implication was that Oliver Tempest Hollis was one hell of a catch.

This also may have been true, in that the elders appeared to have considered him a great man to survive on cursed land and to bang the drum without being struck dead by their gods for this impertinence.

There was an accompanying Disney version of this tale that held that the woman Oliver wed—her name was Aquena in most of the texts, and the daughter of one of the elders—was there the day they found him at the drum, and they fell in love on sight.

This was probably not true. But it was a neat idea, and neat ideas almost always made for better stories.

⋮

Hollis's office took up a third of the top floor of the mill, which made it about level with Main Street out of one window. Another window presented a terrific view of the Connecticut River, and the sudden disappearance of said river over Sorrow Falls.

Annie had been in the office a half-dozen times, and liked to imagine the view from there wasn't all that dissimilar to the last one Josiah had.

"I'm glad we finally had a chance to talk," Desmond was saying to Ed as everyone took their seats.

Desmond Hollis was the youngest of the three brothers. Desmond, Richard, and Louis, and their sister, Katherine, were the children of Allan Hollis and his wife, June. Allan was, in turn, the only living son of Calvin Hollis, the founder of Hollis Paper Goods. Calvin's great-great-great-grandfather was Oliver Tempest Hollis, meaning the Hollises were one of the oldest families in America, and certainly the oldest that virtually nobody knew a thing about.

They seemed to like it that way.

"Well, I don't know what you heard," Ed said. "It's not a big deal, really."

"Nonsense, a reporter in town to write a big story on our special visitor? I wouldn't turn you away. We want everyone in Sorrow Falls to feel welcome, isn't that so, Annie?"

"It certainly is."

"How's your mother, hon? You know if you need *anything* at all . . ."

"I know, Desmond. Thank you. I'll tell Mom you said hey."

"You better."

Desmond was approaching sixty and had plans to hand over the business to whichever son he felt would do right by the town. That was how he ended up running the mill over his elder brothers, although word was they showed little interest one way or the other.

There were a lot of bad stories about industry in New England, but the Hollis paper mill was one of the few consistently good stories. It remained a family-owned company with its own way of doing things. Sometimes that way of doing things was contrary to what was most profitable, which was why choosing the right successor was so important, to Allan Hollis before and to Desmond now.

Ten years ago there was a fire, which gutted a large part of the factory beneath them. Desmond could have been made whole for the loss by insurance and kept the mill closed indefinitely at no additional cost. It was the profitable thing to do. Instead, he nearly bankrupted his entire family by using most of the insurance to rebuild and compensate all of the employees while rebuilding. Anything other than that would have ruined most of the town, and he knew it.

Annie was pretty sure he was paying for the care her mother was receiving in Boston, too. Their health insurance was good, but it wasn't *that* good.

"So what is it I can do for you, Mr. Somerville?"

"Well, Mr. Hollis, I'm talking to as many people as I can around town who were here back when the ship came down."

"Yes, so you told Missie. I'm happy to talk about that, but you know, I've told these stories a hundred times. If you've done your homework, you already know I didn't see it happen. Wish I had! I'm a restless sleeper."

"He's trying a new angle," Annie said.

"Oh, is that so? Well, good, I'm tired of my own stories."

"The people who've been around as long as we have . . ." Annie caught herself, because she realized she was about to compare life stories with a man who had almost fifty years on her. "I mean, those of us here since the ship landed, how we never left . . . The idea is, maybe we have a better perspective on . . ."

"On anything new," Ed said, finishing the thought. "Anything you may have noticed that's different. Ear-to-the-ground stuff. Annie says you like to keep well connected."

"Anything at *all*? That's a pretty broad question, Mr. Somerville. Annie, is this a fishing expedition?"

"Kind of. But this time's different."

More than one reporter had blown through town looking for a tiny thing to exaggerate into a huge story that ended up not being true. This was how it was reported, a year earlier, that birth rates had fallen in town because the ship was making everyone sterile. Another time, no lesser entity than the *New York Times* claimed the residents didn't celebrate Halloween, and the cars in Sorrow Falls no longer required gas.

"How's it different?"

"Because something's actually happening this time, Desmond."

Ed shot her a panicked look, which she ignored.

"Well, all right, that's new," Desmond said. "What is it that's happening?"

"Why don't you tell us first, and Ed here will tell you what he can."

"I actually can't . . ."

"Just what you can, Ed, don't have an attack."

Desmond fixed her with a long stare. "Don't be mad at her, Mr. Somerville, she's more shrewd than all of us combined. She knows I knew you weren't a reporter before you even walked in. Now she's playing my curiosity against me."

"That's why I'm here," she said. "So have you noticed anything, Desmond?"

"Broad question, young lady, as I said."

"But you have."

He shrugged.

"Maybe. Productivity's been down a lot lately."

"That's a cyclical thing, isn't it?" Ed asked.

"It can be. Middle of summer, people are on vacation in their heads already, sure. We still use a punch clock around here, did you know that? It's computerized, but it's still a punch clock. People come to work, punch in to record their arrival time, then hit the floor and get to work, or hit the break room and start their coffee. We're not real strict about most details because by now, people know how to do their jobs and we expect them to answer to themselves about it. Just the same, I know what time every one of my mill employees checks in, and I know when each of them is *supposed* to check in. What I'm seeing is, in the past six weeks, people are punching in late by an average of six minutes."

"That's unusual?"

"Compared to any other time of year, it is. Average is two minutes *early* except during winter storms. They're coming in late, they're not sleeping well, and they're groggy half the day. If it was one or two folks, I'd maybe sit them down, ask if everything was okay at home. But it's everyone. We're also seeing a lot of people down with the late-season cold everyone seems to catch toward the end of summer, but that's an annual thing. You probably want real numbers."

"I . . . sure, whatever you think you can share."

Desmond awakened his desktop computer with a wiggle of the mouse and began tapping away at it. "I can give you numbers, I just need to strip the employee information off the sheets. Probably all of this is confidential, but what the hell, I own the place."

"That's great."

"It'll give you an idea of what we're looking at over here. It's not much but it's something. Reminds me of farm animals before storms, to be honest. Those of us around long enough to be attuned to the changes in the atmosphere know something's coming."

"I think you're probably right," Ed said. "But what's coming?"

"Unless I miss my guess, that's what you're here to answer, Mr. Somerville. Now, give me a few minutes and I'll run this to Missie's printer. Annie, has the man seen the drum? Show the man the drum."

Desmond's gaze, and all his attention, went to the computer screen. He was two-finger typing, so this was likely going to take a few minutes.

Annie walked Ed over to the display with the drum.

A plaque was on the podium, describing it as *the actual drum of the five tribes.* So far as the Hollis clan was concerned, there was no dispute regarding whether this was the real thing or a replica.

"He's being awfully helpful," Ed whispered.

"Of course he is. He's as curious as anyone. I bet he's been wondering about those numbers for days."

The window behind the drum faced the river, which was a view a lot more interesting, to Annie, than the one in the display case. The sky had clouded up over the course of the afternoon, and now they were looking at what could be a rain shower rolling in from the east. Sunset wasn't for another two hours, but it already looked dark out.

"This isn't the real thing, is it?"

"What?" She got lost in the weather for a second. "The drum?"

"Yes, the drum. It's much too small."

"Could be."

She could see it, not resting in a case but in a recess in the stump.

When people talked about the stump what they thought of was the kind of dead tree stump of the current times, a flattened base making a tiny stage just above the earth, but the real thing was wide and as tall as a man. The tree, when it existed, was enormous and ancient, maybe the oldest thing in the valley before it fell. The drum fit in a knot that was eye-level.

The snow was deep that day, when the tribes rode to the stump. The wind blew hard over the river, the clouds were thundering, and the piles of white held everything down, including sound and warmth. It was unwise to go anywhere as long as the gods were raging like this, but still they went, because the drum called them, and they had to answer it.

The little pale man curled up in the stump with the drum was not what anyone expected. One of them mistook him for a tree god and nearly bolted in fear. When the little man spoke he used words none of them knew.

But then a little girl stepped forward.

"Annie."

Annie shook her head, and the room spun a tiny bit more than it was supposed to. Ed had her by the shoulder.

"Hey," he said. "You okay? Where'd you go?"

"What?"

"I was talking to you and you just sort of checked out, are you all right?"

"Yeah. Yeah, I'm fine, sorry. What were you saying?"

"It doesn't matter. You're probably tired; it's been a long day. I should get you back."

"No, I'm okay."

It had actually been a very long and largely fruitless day. With only the Desmond interview officially on a calendar that was supposed to be much more full, she and Ed ended up walking the length of Main, popping into stores along the way both to speak with long-time residents so Ed could ask his usual reporter-ish questions (a new one was whether anyone had been sick recently, since he seemed to think this was relevant) and to get out of the heat and into some air conditioning.

When she was at Violet's house, she imagined herself to be missing all sorts of amazingly important stuff. So far, all she'd gotten out of the day, though, was a few interesting chats with people who all wanted her to know they were praying for Carol, one very entertaining conversation with Pammy, the racist hairdresser who wanted Ed to know that reggae music was an alien invasion, and—apparently—an extended hallucination from Desmond's drum.

Desmond wasn't at the desk anymore and the door to the office was open.

How long has he been missing?

Ed saw her confusion.

"He said he had to fetch it from the printer. You didn't hear that either, huh? Maybe paper mill employees aren't the only ones losing sleep around here."

"I said I'm fine."

Desmond walked back in the room with a manila folder. "Here we are," he said, handing it over. "If you know how to read a spreadsheet, it should be pretty obvious what this is saying. I put my business card in there too if you have any questions. Private line, skips right past Missie. You call me any time."

"Well, thank you, Mr. Hollis, that's incredibly helpful."

"I have selfish motivations. I want to know what's going on, and I'd rather I heard about it beforehand instead of during. Hard to game-plan in the middle of it all."

"You make it sound like something big's about to take place," Ed said.

"Isn't it? Sure feels that way to me. But maybe you know more than I do."

Ed looked distinctly uncomfortable.

"We don't know a lot more than this, Desmond," Annie said. "Just rumors right now. But you knew that too, didn't you?"

"Seemed like a good bet. You know my number too, Annie. If the apocalypse arrives and I haven't received a call, I'm going to be very disappointed in both of you."

⋮

With the car still parked behind the diner, Annie and Ed had a hike ahead of them, because everything from the mill to Main was uphill. The best way to approach it was to reach the approximate same altitude as the parking lot and then take the nearest side street running parallel to Main. It was far less scenic, but a good deal more efficient, and the humidity was just not getting any better. The weather had reached that point where everyone caught outside was hoping it would just rain and get it over with.

The clouds indicated it was about to do just that.

The streets between the river's edge and Main were almost entirely residential or contained a building belonging to Hollis. There wasn't much else. The residences were row houses—tall, three-family buildings with a small footprint and almost no yard—that from Hollis's window looked like a series of stairs for a giant. On the street level, the buildings blocked out the sun and made the roads seem narrower.

Annie's preference was to drive through this area if possible. She hardly ever walked it. She did bike it a couple of times, but the climb back was brutal enough to discourage her from making it a habit.

They mostly climbed in silence. Ed was preoccupied with whatever he had going on in his head, stuff he annoyingly hadn't bothered to share with her yet. She was still trying to break down whatever it was that happened when she was looking at the drum.

Overactive imagination, she thought. That was what the teachers used to accuse her of, as if a vivid imagination were a bad thing. She would have been okay with the idea that that was all it was, but it *felt* different.

It felt like a memory. The problem was, it wasn't her memory.

Who else is in my head?

In any other town, the idea that something appeared in her mind that didn't also begin there would have been entirely nonliteral, but Sorrow Falls had an alien ship that put terrible thoughts in the heads of anyone who came too close to it. Also, if Ed was in any way correct, the entire town was behaving civilly to a statistically impossible degree. If the ship could reach out and make people unusually law-abiding, it could reach Annie's head and put someone else's memory in it. That wouldn't necessarily even make the list of top-five screwed-up things going on.

Ed stopped.

"Did you hear that?" he asked.

"Hear what?"

"I thought I heard a scream."

"Maybe one of your zombies . . ." She stopped talking, because then she heard it too.

It was a woman's scream, it came from directly ahead of them, and Annie thought she recognized the voice.

"That's from the lot behind the diner," she said. "And it sounds like Beth."

They were already running by the time they heard a third scream—the quite clear "HELP ME!" in a voice that was unquestionably Beth's.

The street they were running down took them to the lower back side of the lot, which was blocked off by a chain link fence that was too tall to get over.

Beth drove a Jeep with gold trim—Annie used to joke that Beth should paint it in pink so it would look just like the one in the Barbie playhouse set. It was memorable enough to identify quickly.

Through the fence, they could see Beth lying on her side next to the Jeep. She wasn't moving.

A man was briskly walking away from Beth. Annie could only see his back, but he looked familiar.

"Hey, HEY! You leave her alone!" Annie yelled. He was, to that point, already doing so.

"How do we get in?" Ed asked.

Annie grabbed him by the elbow and pulled them back the way they'd come, up a side street, to a spot where there was no fence in their way.

Just then, the skies opened up.

It was not the polite kind of storm, which started with a light drizzle and worked its way up to something serious before pulling back and settling in on a decent rain-to-not-rain ratio. It was the angry kind: dumping all the water it had as fast as it could as if the clouds had someplace to be.

It completely destroyed their visibility. The fleeing man, the Jeep, Beth and all but the nearest parked cars vanished in the downpour.

The Jeep was at the far end of the lot, a courtesy parking job so the customers had the spots closest to the restaurant. Annie raced straight to it, her biggest fear, strangely, being that her friend was about to drown in the middle of the lot. She lost track of Ed.

"Beth, Beth! Hey!" Annie knelt down and lifted Beth from the pavement. She was breathing, and once Annie pulled her off the ground, her eyes fluttered and opened.

"Annie, run! We have to . . ." Then she started crying. "Oh, it's awful, it's so awful."

"What is it? What happened to you?"

There was blood on the pavement. Beth had an open wound on her head, but most of the blood was coming from the keys in her hands.

"It's his blood," Beth said. "I stabbed him. Maced him too, but he . . . Annie, I sprayed mace right in the eyes and he didn't care."

"Who was it?"

Ed ran up.

"I can't find him. I can't see anything out here. I called Pete, she's on her way."

"She needs an ambulance," Annie said.

"They're on their way too. Did she say who it was?"

"No, but . . ."

Beth squeezed Annie's arm tightly.

"It was Mr. Blake, Annie," she said. "I think he wanted to kill me."

"Blake? Okay, I'll tell Pete," Ed said.

"Put away the phone," Annie said.

"But Pete can send someone to pick this guy up."

"Ed, he lives in Peacock Cemetery. George Blake has been dead for five months."

Ed stared at Annie for a five count. Then he put the phone away.

15
THE CONVERSATION

The deluge stopped by the time Sheriff Pete and two of her deputies arrived at the scene, which is to say that the rain didn't last long at all given the station was only a few blocks away. It actually took them longer than Annie would have guessed, only because it never seemed like there was an actual emergency in this town so they had nowhere else to be.

The ambulance came a minute later, and then Annie was in the back of the ambulance with Beth while Ed tried to explain what they knew to Pete, and Pete's men began to scour the area for a man who had been blinded by pepper spray and stabbed in the thigh by a pair of keys, and who might also have been a zombie.

"I had the late shift today, you saw," Beth said. She was lying on a gurney while a paramedic Annie didn't recognize wound a bandage around her head.

"I did. Last one out?"

"Last one out, check the lights and lock the doors, that's the drill."

"I know it."

"I got out here, and it was about to rain so I was hurrying, and then this . . . guy comes up like from out of nowhere. He was, I think he was behind my car, like, waiting for me maybe."

"He jumped you?"

"Not really. Not at first. He just like, stood there, and looked at me, and it was sort of murky out, right, so I couldn't see his face, I was just like, 'Can I help you?' And he took a step forward and said . . . what did he say? He asked me a question. I can't remember what. By then I had my mace in my hand, and I didn't know really what to do because he was between me and the car, but I was like, I don't know what you want but . . . oh, I remember! 'Are you?' That was his question."

"'Are you?' That doesn't make sense."

"Right? But I was like, I do not know what you're talking about, but back off. That was when he grabbed my wrist."

Beth looked up and away from Annie, because she was welling up. Her shoulder was already in a temporary sling, and as soon as her head was taken care of and she was strapped in, they'd be moving her to the clinic up the street to see if she needed to continue on to one of the hospitals for an overnight. Annie was about to perform the unenviable task of calling Beth's parents to let them know where to find their daughter.

"He grabbed your wrist, and then what?" Annie asked.

"He asked me the same question, only, I don't know, more aggressively. Then I sprayed him with the mace and it didn't *do* anything. He just, like, blinked, and tilted his head like, like a curious bird, you know? It was . . . anyway, that was when I recognized him."

"Beth."

"I know what you're thinking. It was dark, the rain was about to start, I was scared, but I waited on Mr. Blake for four years. Over easy, crispy bacon, side of hash, wheat toast, strawberry jam. I know my regulars."

"But . . ." Annie shot a glance at the paramedic. She was clearly listening, even if she was pretending not to. Annie leaned forward and whispered. "But he's dead."

"I don't care. That's who it was."

The paramedic coughed. It wasn't a real cough; it was one of those *I am interrupting politely* coughs.

"I'm sorry," she said. The woman was in her forties, and if Annie didn't know her that likely meant she was a stringer with the ambulance company and from one of the nearby towns. "I'm just about done here, but . . . I wanted to say, regarding what you two are discussing? It would not be the first story I've heard like this, not lately."

"Mr. Blake attacking other people?" Beth asked.

"No, honey. People being attacked by people who aren't exactly people anymore."

Oh, I do not have time for zombies in my life right now, Annie thought.

"All right, so maybe we have a zombie George Blake running around. He grabs you, barks an incomplete sentence, and then what?"

"I screamed a lot. You probably heard me."

"Yeah, that's what got us running. Then what?"

"I balled up the keys in my fist, remember how they taught us that trick in gym?"

Annie remembered. It was a basic self-defense mini-course that was mandatory for the girls in the school. They all called it anti-rape class because that was what it was. Annoyingly, while the girls were in that course, nobody was teaching a boys' course called *don't be a rapist.*

The trick was to put your keys in a closed fist so the sharp parts stick out between the knuckles. Then you punch an attacker's fleshy part.

"You stabbed him?"

"Yeah, like I told them" — them being the sheriff— "I got him in the thigh. But that didn't get him to let go either. I don't think he felt it any more than the mace."

"But then why'd he run off?"

"Honest, I think the screaming bugged him more than anything. I wouldn't say he let me go, though. He threw me against the car. I went down pretty hard. I'm gonna have a hell of a bump, I bet."

"You are indeed," the paramedic said. "But good for you for fighting him off."

Ed walked up. It looked like someone had dropped him in the

Connecticut River a few times. He was soaked through, and pulling his wet clothes tight to ward off the breeze, which had a tendency to cut through anything damp. Annie was just as wet, but wrapped in a blanket from the ambulance.

"How are you doing, Beth?" he asked.

"Super, Mr. Reporter." She gave him a thumbs-up.

"It's Ed."

"Thanks for coming to my rescue, Ed."

"Sure." He looked at Annie. "You want to go with her, or come back with me? Sheriff has some questions for us, but we can do that anytime."

"Do we get to ride in one of the cruisers, or will we have to walk to the station?"

"We can ride."

"Cool, let's do it."

⋮

The next hour was notable for the fact that all of the adults Annie spoke to appeared to have lost their minds.

First she sat down with Pete to talk about what she and Ed heard, saw and did, up to and following the attack. That went pretty well. Then Annie offered up what Beth told her, in as much detail as she could recall, omitting the identity of the attacker but nothing else. She even included the part about the mace not having an impact and the equal lack of response to the key stabbing. None of this caused so much as a skeptical grunt.

"Did she recognize her attacker?" Pete asked, looking up from her notes. She took notes longhand and didn't appear to have an interest in recording equipment. The sheriff's office was a small affair, though, with only two holding cells and nothing in the way of an interrogation room. They were talking in Pete's office.

"I don't know," Annie lied. Pete seemed to know it, too.

"I spoke to your . . . boss? Is that how this is?"

"You mean Ed? Coworker, how about?"

"Sure. He said she gave a name."

"She did. But she was mistaken."

"Annie, babe, give me the name and let me decide that."

She sighed. "Won't it, like, invalidate her testimony somehow? Like, when you catch the guy, if she named someone else . . ."

"The name, Annie."

"George Blake."

Pete nodded and slowly wrote George's name down on her pad of paper.

"And which direction did you say he ran?"

"I'm . . . sorry, what?"

Ed had his zombie theory, and it was a crazy theory. Sure, it appeared to be coming true right in front of Annie, but that didn't mean it was in any way a respectable theory.

"Direction?" Pete repeated.

"North. But, George Blake."

"Right, George Blake. I have that."

"He's been dead for five months."

"Almost six. I know that, too. Went to his funeral. Really pretty ceremony."

"Is this a prank?"

"Annie, I don't really believe it either, but until I can figure out which local is wearing the rubber Scooby-Doo villain masks, I'm taking these reports as they come."

"So maybe it *is* a prank."

"Sure, but I'm not in on it. Either someone's going to a lot of trouble, or zombies walk the earth."

"How *much* trouble?"

"Enough to dig up bodies in the cemetery. So, a lot. Unless they're digging themselves out. Can't rule that out."

"Sorry, Pete, but I'd really like to rule that out if it's okay by you."

"Whatever rocks your canoe. Did she say anything else you think might be pertinent?"

"Yeah, he said, 'Are you.'"

Pete nodded, and wrote it down.

"All right," she said. "I'm gonna talk to Ed for a few, why don't you help yourself to something hot before a chill sets in. That rain soaked everything, didn't it?"

⋮

The break room for the sheriff's department was just the office next to Pete's. The wall between them was glass, and the shutters that would ensure privacy were open, so while Annie couldn't hear any part of the conversation between Pete and Ed, she could see them, and it was clear this wasn't the first time they'd met.

"Well, that's perfect," she said.

She was cold, and tired, and more upset about Beth being attacked than she was prepared to acknowledge, so everything was annoying her, but of particularly special annoyance was the thought that Ed had continued his research without her around. That research obviously included befriending Pete and sharing notes on the local undead population.

It felt like the whole town was spinning out of control. Annie thought she knew everything about Sorrow Falls, and all of what she knew made perfect sense. But ever since Ed arrived, with his top-secret files he still hadn't shared, and his leading questions, and the sense she got that he had something really awful on his mind, it felt like her idea of the town was simply wrong. There was some dark consequence Edgar Somerville was afraid of, and he wouldn't share what that was, and zombies wasn't even that thing.

Or maybe she had to stop reading Lovecraft before bed.

"Is this little Annie Collins before me?"

Rick Horton was standing at the entrance to the room. Her instinct—as always when it came to Rick—was to put some distance between them, which was a challenge as he stood in front of the only way out. Then she remembered they were in the sheriff's office and she was probably okay.

Annie had known Rick most of her life, and had not, in that time, been able to pin down what it was about him that made her uncomfortable. It was just always so.

"Hello, Rick. You look sober today."

"Nice."

He shuffled out of the doorway to the coffee machine. On busy days at the diner, Annie brewed the coffee, so even though she didn't drink it herself, she knew what fresh coffee smelled like, and the stuff in the urn in the break room was pretty far away from fresh.

Rick threw some in a Styrofoam cup anyway. Annie sat down at the table and tried to look indifferent.

"You're with him, aren't you?" Rick said, nodding at Ed. "The man from the government."

"He's just a reporter."

"Sure. And you're just a cute little sixteen-year-old girl."

"I don't know what you mean."

"I mean you're more than that. And so's he. Everybody knows."

"Why are you here, Rick?"

"I am a charter member of the sheriff's youth rehabilitation out-reach program. I am, point-a-fact, the only member. It's a good deal. I empty out their trash every afternoon for the summer and avoid going to juvie for it. I also get to feel super rehabilitated. Have you told him?"

Annie sighed. "Have I told him what?"

He smiled. She'd always hated his smile. It was his most menac-ing expression.

"I never told anybody," he said. "Even when I thought . . . well."

"Look, Rick, it's been awesome catching up, but I have to get go-ing."

"Your friend is still in the office."

"He knows where he can find me."

She got up to walk out, but Rick stepped in the way.

"I'm sorry," he said. "I don't know why I say stuff like that. You don't gotta tell anyone. I haven't. Nobody'd believe me anyway."

"Please get out of my way."

"Just . . . listen, please. Did you see what I saw?"

She was taken aback by the question. "Well, I don't know. What did you see?"

"No, you didn't. You couldn't have, because if you had you'd be terrified. You'd be banging on the sheriff's door and telling your friend and he'd listen to you, because he would, because you're An-nie Collins, and people listen to Annie Collins."

"Rick. What did you see?"

"Everything. And it's all coming true."

He looked like he wanted to say more. There was a hollow, terrified look in his eyes she'd never seen before—or maybe she was never looking before. Maybe this was the Rick Horton that Rodney was always trying to talk to her about.

"What is?" she asked. "What's going to happen?"

Rick took a deep, trembling breath, sipped his burnt coffee, and calmed down a little.

"Forget it. I thought maybe you knew. This is probably all just in my head, you know, that's what they tell me. It's all in my head. I should go."

"Rick . . ."

"No, I have to go, really. It was good seeing you."

He shuffled out. And while she was always glad when Rick left, this time she nearly went after him.

Instead, she sat back down at the table and pulled out her cell phone.

She called Carol three times on Monday, and hadn't even tried once since, but after Beth's attack she thought this was a good time to hear her mother's voice.

Dear Mom, there are zombies, stay in Boston, she thought. *Everyone says hi.*

There was a notification on the open screen that took her by surprise.

Like just about everyone her age—and perhaps just about everyone in general—Annie had a habit of trying to do more things with her smartphone than the phone's memory was entirely comfortable with. In her case, that weakness had to do with photographs. It wasn't that she took a lot of them; it was that she never wanted to delete what she had. To deal with what had become—after three years of owning a smartphone—a large collection of images she didn't want to lose access to, she opened a cloud drive account. The space didn't cost anything, it had plenty of memory to deal with the pictures, and she could access them anytime without chewing up all the available memory on her phone.

The app on her phone also uploaded new pictures automatically, whenever her phone entered a recognized Wi-Fi spot with a strong enough signal. This was actually sort of a problem because dependable Wi-Fi in Sorrow Falls wasn't exactly commonplace. Her house didn't have it. Violet's did, but she never got on. Ed's car did, supposedly, but she hadn't tried to use it.

Typically, she relied on the library, the school during the year, or the diner. Joanne's Diner added Wi-Fi less than a year earlier in response to the Denny's up the street doing the same. It was probably their Wi-Fi that was responsible for the notification on her phone that a new picture had been uploaded to the cloud drive. The problem was, she couldn't remember taking any photos recently.

She tapped into the cloud server to access the photos and scrolled down to the most recent. It took a couple of seconds to realize what she was looking at.

Have you told him?

Rick's question still hung in the air. It was suddenly an incredibly important question.

"Hey, was that a friend of yours?"

Ed walked in and headed straight for the burnt coffee.

"Who?"

"Guy I saw you talking to. Looked about your age, right?"

"That was, um . . . sorry, I'm a little distracted, that was Rick Horton. I forgot to ask your zombie timing question, but you can probably still catch him."

"Oh." Ed looked like he was considering it. "No, it's okay. I should get you home."

"Actually . . . I think we should go someplace and talk. Maybe eat, but also talk."

"Okay. What do you want to talk about?"

"This, for starters." She held up her phone so he could see.

He went a little pale. This was kind of amazing as he was pretty pale to start with.

"How did you get that?"

"Like I said. I think we should talk."

⋮

There were many places to tie one on at night in Sorrow Falls. Annie wasn't terribly familiar with any of them, being a minor, but she'd been inside one or two on certain occasions, such as when her dad was back in town and wanted to take the family out for a meal.

The family dinner establishments were mostly outside the town, in places like Oakdale, Mount Hermon, and—in the other direction and somewhat farther—Brattleboro. But there were a few quasi-family places, i.e., places that served dinner and also alcohol, catering to adults but without anyone carding at the door or, if they were asking for ID, not before 10 p.m.

One such place was Jock & Jill's, a sports bar with a name that made it sound a tiny bit like an all-inclusive strip club. To get to it meant going from the diner parking lot (to which they were given a ride by one of the deputies) to the northern conclusion of Main and a dogleg left turn, up the hill on a road called Acorn, toward Durgin. Jock & Jill's rested atop a small hill at the corner of Durgin and Acorn.

Ed looked about as uncomfortable as he could when he realized the kind of place Annie directed him to.

"This is a bar," he said, pointing specifically to the onslaught of flashing neon.

"They have great appetizers here. And burgers. I hear good things about their drinks, too. The Martian Margarita's supposed to be top-notch."

"You can't go in here, can you? You don't have a . . . I mean . . ."

"What good would a fake I.D. do me, Ed? Practically everyone knows me. Don't worry, I can go in. The important thing is, the place is dark and loud."

They took up a booth in a corner in the back of the place, with the waitress—Annie didn't know her, but thought she looked familiar enough to be an older sibling of someone she did know—giving them the kind of uncomfortable glances people give when they think maybe, perhaps, possibly this older man is on a date with this young girl.

As soon as the waitress set them up with a couple of sodas—she was probably glad nobody at the table was drinking—Annie called up the photo on her phone and slid it to Ed.

"So tell me what I'm looking at here."

"It's a copy of a high-resolution photo that happens to be incredibly classified. How did it end up on your phone?"

"You didn't fully answer the question."

"You're right, I didn't."

"Ed, is this a handprint on the side of the spaceship?"

"It is. Keep your voice down."

They were being bombarded on one side by white-people classic rock, and on the other by the drone-speak of baseball announcers narrating two different games.

"I promise, nobody can hear us. I can barely hear us."

"How did you get this?"

"I took it. This is a little embarrassing, but do you remember the day . . ."

"When you got the text from your mother," he said, gasping. "I went to get my coat."

"The folder was open on your desk. I didn't even register what I was looking at. I just . . . I saw, and I . . . my phone was already in my hand. I didn't even remember this until an hour ago."

"Annie, you have to delete that immediately."

"Now, hold on. I think you owe me some answers."

"My answer's the same as it always was. It doesn't change just because you took a picture of something you shouldn't have."

"You do realize I'm a teenage girl with multiple social media profiles."

"Annie . . ."

"It would seriously take me about ten seconds to post the image, and it's no secret I live in Sorrow Falls. It'd probably go viral in a day, maybe two."

"Seriously, you can't."

"Do you think you'd get arrested as soon as I posted it, or would they wait a week or two?"

"I can't believe you'd do that to me."

"Dammit, Ed, just tell me. I can make it so it looks like you already did, so you may as well."

She was bluffing, and was about 80 percent sure he knew she was, but she also knew he was dying for an excuse to give up everything he had.

"All right, fine."

He took a long sip of his soda, which was amusing only because he clearly preferred for it to be something much stronger.

"Do you know what Cherenkov radiation is?"

"Sure. It's blue, right? It's when something travels through a medium at a speed faster than light through that medium."

Ed stared at her. "That's almost exactly right, how did you know that?"

She shrugged. "I just do. So go on."

"All right. A few weeks back, for less than a second, one of the sensors picked up Cherenkov radiation emanating from the ship."

"That's . . . interesting, but not really possible, is it? What was the medium? Air?"

"Air."

"Something was transmitted that reached the ship at a speed greater the speed of light through the atmosphere. That would be a technology . . . ohhhh. I understand. That's some alien technology going on."

"We still don't know whether the ship transmitted something into space or something out there sent something to the ship. In Washington, they're pretty split on which possibility is worse."

"You guys are always fixated on the worst idea imaginable when it comes to these things, aren't you?"

"I do risk assessments. It's my job to at least consider the worst-case scenarios."

"That's kind of a crap job. No offense."

He laughed. "You may be right."

186 · GENE DOUCETTE

"So what happened next?"

"There's a team of scientists attached to the spaceship project. There are twelve of them, and they're very smart, reasonable people who didn't deal well with this news. For a lot of reasons, I guess, one being that if it was Cherenkov radiation it should have killed some people around here and it didn't."

"How'd they detect it, then? If not radiation."

"Spectroscope, I guess. I don't really understand how they could tell the difference between a blue light and this, but they could. The upside was, they ordered a full rescan of the ship. That was conducted as quickly and as quietly as possible. An unmanned drone conducting an infrared scan of the hull picked up the handprint. By then I was already preparing to come here, so I missed the full-throated panic it had to have triggered.

"When I got here, my first job was to figure out if there was any observable change as a consequence of the . . . the message, or whatever was transmitted. The sensors are all pointed at the ship, basically, but nothing is pointed at the town. We needed to know if anyone here discovered something we were missing. But as soon as it was clear somebody actually touched the ship, the job got more complicated. That was how you ended up getting hired."

"I don't think I understand."

"We're pretty sure the handprint happened long before the Cherenkov effect, and we don't think they're connected. It's just that the print was missed before. But what it means is, someone in Sorrow Falls knows more than they're saying. I needed to find out who that person was. I still do, because right now the ship is creating zombies. I don't know why, and I don't know how, but I think whoever made that print does."

Annie sat back and considered that point.

"All right. So how do you know the ship is making zombies?"

"Who else? You think it's really likely the one place the dead are rising is the one place with a spaceship?"

"I agree; that's unlikely. How do you know there aren't other towns with a zombie problem?"

He smiled. "That's a really good point. First thing tomorrow, I'll call Washington and ask them for an update on zombies in other regions. Maybe something will come up."

"No, you won't."

"No, I won't, but that doesn't mean it isn't a good point."

The waitress arrived with their plates of greasy food. Discussions about the undead did nothing to dampen Annie's appetite, so she dug in.

"All right, assuming it's Shippie's fault."

"Shippie?"

"Sorry, that's what Violet and I always call it. Assuming the spaceship is doing it, how is it doing it? Shouldn't one of those government gadgets be catching this?"

"Sure, or your friends at the trailers. Although they didn't notice the drones, it sounds like, and nobody caught the Cherenkov radiation burst."

"They noticed the ship is breathing, that's something."

"Right." Ed rolled his eyes. He didn't consider the ship breathing a particularly respectable discovery. "But all of our gadgets are only good for things we know to test for. The ship was built by beings that mastered interstellar travel. They're bound to have a way to do something we can't detect."

"Magic, then."

"I definitely didn't say that."

"So why's it doing this? What possible use could a spaceship have for a bunch of zombies?"

"I have no idea. But I'm guessing the person who touched the ship knows something."

"Like what?"

"I don't know, Annie, I have to find them first. But I'm pretty sure they're the key to all of this. The sooner I figure out who they are the better off we're all going to be."

Annie threw a French fry at Ed's face. It glanced off the side of his head, causing no long-term damage.

"What was that for?"

"You still aren't telling me everything, Edgar. Why is all of this so very important right *now*? Stop dropping ominous hints all over the place, it's annoying."

"I don't have any particulars to share, but let's just say the government has a few plans for what to do with this town and that ship if the report I turn in makes them unhappy."

"Well, that's super. Then turn in a report that makes them happy."

"I can't really fabricate something here. There's too much at stake. Look, all I need to do is find out who made that handprint."

"Right, but you better have a backup plan is all I'm saying."

"I'm *sure* that person is still in this town somewhere, and somebody knows who it is."

"Yes, you're right about all of that, but I'm saying don't expect much from them."

"You know who it is."

She sighed grandly.

"I know they don't have the answers you're looking for, let's say."

"How can you know that? Let me talk to them and find out."

"You're talking to them now, Ed. I'm the one who touched the ship. Three years ago. And I have no answers for you."

THE NIGHT THE SKY FELL ON ANNIE

*A*nnie had been crying.

Her face was a mess. Her eyes were red-rimmed and her cheeks were all puffy, as if swollen after absorbing moisture from her tears. She sort of wondered what would happen if she pinched one of them: would water come out of the pores?

Anyone looking at her would know what she'd been doing, so it was a good thing she was alone in her bedroom, because it wasn't something she wanted anybody to know about. Not even her parents, not even when her parents knew why she was crying and that she was probably *supposed* to be crying. She refused to do it in front of them, even though it was their fault.

Not fair. Cancer isn't anyone's fault.

That wasn't always true, though. Some cancers really were the fault of someone. Like the tobacco industry. They could give people cancer. So maybe that was what it was: someone had given her mother cancer and they were the person Annie should be mad at.

Except according to Mom, it wasn't that kind of cancer. It wasn't because of the way her mom lived her life: not in anything she ate or drank or smoked or wore or breathed. It was just something happening in her mom's body, and that was who to blame. Not her mom; her mom's body.

This didn't work either.

Blaming her father showed a lot of promise, initially. He was away more and more, and if he'd been away less instead, he could have stopped the cancer from getting to Mom, like a rancher with a shotgun guarding cattle from poachers. It was an impossible thought, but these were impossible times. Annie had just learned she was going to be motherless by the time she turned twenty, and dammit if there weren't people who should be held responsible for that.

This isn't your fault, Annie was one of the things her mother said, so of course Annie had to at least consider blaming herself. She couldn't imagine how it could be her fault, and the entire line sounded more like something you said to your child after informing her of an impending divorce—which was honestly what she thought the *serious conversation* she'd been sat down for earlier was going to be about. But maybe there was only one playbook parents had for when they delivered bad news to their kids, and the line came from there. Either way, Annie couldn't imagine how it was her fault, couldn't conceive of any way in which she either caused cancer in her mother or stood aside as the cancer was allowed in. She could sort of imagine her mother standing bravely in front of Annie and shielding her from it, as if cancer were something fired from a gun, but that notion dissipated quickly.

She could blame God.

Annie left the mirror, which hung on the back of the door to her bedroom, to sit on the bed. The bed was near the window. From it she could see a good portion of the valley and a whole lot of sky, because there weren't any houses across the street and they lived on the crest of a bowl canyon that bottomed out at the river several miles down the hill. Her room was on the second floor directly above the front door/porch entrance, and the view from the window right over the porch roof was routinely spectacular. On nights in which she hadn't been notified of her future orphan status, she liked to sit on the roof and look at the stars. Sometimes she was especially lucky, and a clear night and a meteor shower would coincide. That happened the prior year with the Perseids, which were coming up again in a few days. She hoped to have another good view, and also hoped she cared enough to watch.

Annie didn't think she believed in God, or if she did, the idea she had of what God must be like didn't correspond with anyone else's. It was incredibly annoying in a time like this, because He (or She) would be an excellent being to pin the blame for her mother's cancer on. She could yell at Him for it instead, and then maybe go through the steps of doubting Him, wondering if He existed at all, working out for herself whether it was worth it to even continue using uppercase letters when thinking about Him. She had to believe in Him/Her (or him/her) before questioning that belief, though, and that seemed like a lot of effort.

Besides, it wasn't anybody's fault. It was just a thing that was now true. Her mother was dying, where yesterday she wasn't.

She opened the window and sat on the sill, her feet on the roof.

U awake?

The text was to Rodney, who probably wasn't. He'd just begun working at the shake place in the Oakdale Mall, which was weird for her because she didn't have any other friends who were holding down jobs, part-time or otherwise. He was her oldest friend, though—in terms of his actual age, not how long she'd known him—so it was appropriate he be the first to enter the work force.

He also lived right up the street, had a car of his own, and didn't have a problem using it to go places at odd hours. She tried to take advantage of that whenever she could: it was only a matter of time before he decided he didn't want to hang around with the little kid down the road any longer. Once he started dating girls his own age, she'd be a hindrance, surely.

Annie sort of wished she were older, because she sort of wanted to date him herself sometimes. Only sometimes, though. She had reached a peculiar age where about half the time the idea of having a boyfriend was the greatest thing in the world, and the other half of the time it was the most terrifying thing she could imagine considering. She decided that meant she wasn't ready to start dating anyone for real. Fake-dating, sure. She'd been fake-dating Dougie off and on for eight years, but that was just playing. They kissed once, but that was just playing too. Although he might have offered a contrary assessment of their relationship if pressed.

No, I'm not. Sound asleep.

Me too. Good stars tonight.

Neither she nor Rodney knew more than a couple of constellations, and exactly zero star names (she wasn't counting the sun, because it was the sun and because she couldn't see it at night anyway), so they made up names. It was another one of those things she expected him to grow tired of, especially on nights when he had an early milkshake shift to get up for.

A meteor came streaking along the horizon. Her first thought was it was an early sign of the Perseid shower, but she knew from the previous year which direction to expect those from, and it wasn't coming from that direction. (The constellation Perseus was one of the ones she could identify, specifically because of the Perseids.)

I should wish upon a star, she thought. *Would that work?*

Jiminy Cricket was now singing in her head, and that was unfortunate.

Meteors flamed out pretty fast when they hit the upper atmosphere. This one didn't, which made it a compelling surprise for about ten seconds, until it occurred to Annie that a meteor that made it all the way to the surface could cause a lot of damage, and this one was headed right for Sorrow Falls.

Or so it seemed. It was hard to judge real distance when looking up in the sky.

Just like every other kid—she assumed—when she reached a certain age she went through a UFO phase. Hers lasted maybe a year, which was long enough to absorb a few ideas on the matter of objects that flew in the night sky but could not be readily identified by the observer. One idea was that it was incredibly hard to distinguish between small and nearby, versus large and far away. Something a few hundred feet in the air and tiny, if misapprehended as something a mile in the air and large, could look like a vessel moving faster than a commercial airliner instead of, say, a firefly caught in a breeze.

She was pretty positive the thing in the sky at this moment was actually falling from outer space, but the illusion of it bearing down on Sorrow Falls specifically was probably just that: an illusion.

It was hard to shake, though. From her angle it hadn't moved left or right, but it had gone from high in the sky to lower in the sky, and it had gotten brighter. That really did give the impression it was coming her way.

Look out the window.

It held position for another three-count, then zigged to Annie's left, which is to say its descent angle clarified itself by heading northward. It was now traversing the sky from her two o'clock to her ten o'clock.

What for?

Just do it, quickly.

It wasn't going to come near Sorrow Falls. It was headed for Vermont or Canada.

O cool.

Meteor gonna wreck Toronto prob.

It was still coming down fast, though, which she was calculating based on how bright it was.

It was at this moment Annie realized she was looking at something other than a meteor. First, there was the thought:

I shouldn't still be able to see this.

If it was a meteor, it should have flamed out or been slowed down enough by friction to stop causing the air around it to catch fire, which was what made them glow in the first place. This one was still glowing, somehow.

Second, and far more important, it turned.

She nearly fell out of the window when this happened. It was on its right-to-left trajectory, going down at about a fifteen-degree angle, when it *maneuvered* into a descent that was straight down. It did that for five seconds.

Her phone rang.

"Did you see that?" Rodney asked. "Holy crap, what is it?"

"I saw. And . . . I think it stopped moving?"

It looked like it stopped, but it was still getting brighter somehow.

"It didn't stop, it's heading straight for us."

"Yeah, it is."

"Annie, that's a spaceship. It has to be."

She didn't know what to say. Rodney was right, but he couldn't be right.

For about five seconds, Annie thought the ship had plans to land right on her house, which would have been something of a capper for the way the evening had gone so far. It did come close, but once it was about two hundred feet up (probably?) the trajectory clarified again.

It was looking for a place to land. It was an alien spaceship and it was looking for a place to land.

The ship reached a spot down the road to her right, stopped dead in the air, and disappeared from view.

"Rodney, how soon can you be here?"

"We should call the sheriff."

"We should get in your car and go meet the aliens. Then we can call the sheriff."

"I'll be outside in ten."

⋮

Annie snuck out of her house on a semi-regular basis, either to go on a walk by herself or to drive somewhere with Rodney and whoever else he had tagging along. Getting out was easy enough, because the drop from the porch roof was only about ten feet.

Getting back in was a little harder. If she wanted to use the bedroom window she had to climb onto the roof, either by using the trellis on the side of the house or the tiny tree growing beside the porch. Neither of those things was built to support her, nor were they very good at it. More than once she ended up dangling from the edge of the roof and wishing she had sufficient upper-body strength to pull herself up from that position. Twice, she succeeded in swinging her legs around and up, but it wasn't a super pleasant experience because the roof tiles were like sandpaper.

Most times, she just snuck in the front door.

She hopped down from the roof and walked up the street to the standard meeting point, a large tree with a big enough trunk to hide a thirteen-year-old girl behind. This was so Rodney wasn't picking her up right in front of the house. Her parents probably knew she snuck out and were implicitly okay with it, but there was no point in treating them like idiots.

It was twenty minutes before Rodney pulled up, headlights off and rolling slow to keep the noise down.

She jumped in on the passenger side.

"What took you so long?" she asked.

Rodney pointed his thumb to the back seat.

"Hey, Annie," Rick Horton said.

"Jesus . . . hi, Rick."

Annie shot Rodney a look he chose to ignore.

"He called as soon as we hung up, for the same reason. He was on the way."

Rick was, in Annie's estimation, a creep, but he was a creep Rodney called friend, and she couldn't do much about that. He was also only *on the way* to Annie's house if Rodney took a roundabout way to get to her, which was contrary to the urgency she felt was required when it came to first contact with aliens, and she didn't like *at all* the idea that Rick would be one of the humans they would meet, either initially or at any subsequent point in their stay on Earth.

But, it was Rodney's car.

"What do you guys think it was?" Rick asked. He was unbelted, leaning forward and talking through the gap in the front bucket seats. It was a totally creeper move because his face was next to Annie's left shoulder and his eyes could look right down her shirt. There wasn't much to look at down there, so far, but there wasn't nothing. Rick's understanding of personal space was discomfiting. Also, he had alcohol on his breath.

"I think it was an alien ship," Annie said. "I watched it park."

"Me too! This is the balls!"

"Sit your ass back," Rodney said. "I don't want to brake and send you through the windshield. I like this windshield."

Rick sat back, and Rodney looked to Annie. "Where you thinking?"

"The Dewey farm, pretty sure."

The Dewey family farm was a couple of miles away, set back off Tunney Road a few hundred feet. Bob Dewey had ten acres across three fields. Pastureland was as good a place as any to set down a starship and the angle seemed about right from her perspective.

"Just look for the lights, yo," Rick said.

"It turned its lights off before touching down," Annie said. "I saw it happen."

"They gotta put out a porch light or something to see where they're walking. Imagine, you come from planet whatever, land here, and step in a cow chip right away. They'll probably blow the whole planet up for that."

"So they'll have lights, you're saying," Rodney said.

"I don't think they do," Annie said. "We'd see it through the trees."

Rodney took his Chevy down the dirt road leading to the Dewey farm, cut the lights, and rolled to a stop at their property fence. Only one of their fields was visible from this spot. The other two were hidden behind the homestead.

"I don't see anything," Rodney said. "You?"

"No, but it was right around here."

Annie got out and climbed onto the hood of the car, and when that didn't get her high enough she stepped to the roof.

Just barely, she could see the tree Rodney fetched her from. It obscured her bedroom window from view, but close enough. This was the line she'd looked down when the ship landed. The car was pointed right at it.

"What do you think, Magellan?" Rodney asked.

"Straight that way," she said, pointing in a direction that was, legally, trespassing. "We'll have to walk it, unless you want to take out that fence."

⋮

Stumbling through muddy cow pastures lit only by a half moon, with Rick Horton, wasn't anything close to Annie's idea of fun, but Rodney seemed aware enough of her discomfort to keep himself between them as they all stumbled along. Annie marked a tree as a destination point and kept that in front of her while they meandered, wishing she'd thought to bring a compass and a flashlight.

Rick would not shut up, and his volume control was wanting. He seemed to be a connoisseur of every movie involving aliens ever made, and was using this knowledge to draw conclusions regarding what they might find.

He was behaving like the kind of idiot nobody would seriously consider bringing along for an endeavor like this. Annie was still pissed at Rodney about it.

They reached the tree she targeted without discovering anything alien. On the other side of it were more trees.

"Keep going?" Rodney asked.

"It's around here somewhere," she said.

"KLAATU BARADA NIKTO!" Rick shouted.

"Shut the hell up, Rick," Rodney said.

"It'll bring 'em out."

"Seriously, man. I'm gonna make you wait in the car, you keep it up."

"How deep do you think these trees go?" Annie asked.

"Never been through here," Rodney said. "Couldn't say."

Annie was trying to pull up a map of the town in her head.

"Tunney loops, right? If we keep walking straight we'll hit it. There's gotta be a clearing or two between us and that."

"You sure it came down anywhere around here at all?"

"As sure as I can be. Let's keep walking. We could spread out a little."

"Good way to get lost."

"Or eaten," Rick said.

"Shut up, Rick."

⋮

They decided on a plan that kept them ten feet apart, as a means to cover more ground while not being eaten by predatory aliens.

Every few feet they'd do a call-and-response ("Marco!" "Polo!") to keep from getting too spread out. They walked through the woods like this for about twenty minutes.

Then they found it.

Rick was the first to the scene. He was on the left-most flank of their search perimeter, and the ship had come down in a field to his left.

"Guys . . ." was all he said at first. It was the most subdued thing to come out of his mouth all evening, so Rodney and Annie knew right away something was different.

They reached the clearing in a couple of minutes. Rick hardly moved in that time.

"I can't believe it," he said. "I was kidding around, but it's here."

The squat black ship was sitting in a ring of crisped grass. The ground was still smoking a little. There was no impact crater.

"I kind of can't believe it either," Rodney said. "What should we do now?"

Annie was equally dumbfounded. It was one thing to actively pursue something like this, but another entirely to actually discover it. She hadn't been thinking about the consequences of their quest because she was too caught up in its execution.

"I don't know," she said. "I didn't think this far."

Rick cupped his hands around his mouth. "Hello?" he said.

"Hey, c'mon," Rodney said.

"What? It's what we're here for, right? We come this far."

Rodney looked at Annie, who shrugged.

"Hello?" Rick said again. "Maybe they're in cryo-sleep or something. We should just go up and knock."

"It'll be hot," Annie said. "From re-entry."

"Doesn't feel hot to me," Rick said, holding his hands out. He was about twenty feet away.

"Hot to the touch, dumb-ass," Rodney said.

"No, he has a point," Annie said. "He should be able to feel it from there. We all should."

"See? Come on, let's go knock. Maybe we can open it up."

"That seems like a super-bad idea," Rodney said. "Someone more qualified and, like, with a Geiger counter should do that."

"Rod, there's *nobody else here*. We're the first, so man up and let's do this."

Rodney looked dubious, but Annie had to agree with Rick. There was really no turning back at this point. If it was radioactive, they'd already been exposed.

"I'm with him, Rodney," she said.

He sighed.

"All right, together. We do it together. Agreed?"

"Agreed," Annie said.

"Agreed," Rick said. "C'mon."

He waved them forward, and then they walked, slowly, in a matching pace, in the same order they'd walked through the woods: Rick, Rodney, Annie, left to right.

"Should we hold hands?" Rick asked. "Red rover, red rover, send E.T. on over."

"Cut it out," Rodney said.

They were ten feet out and standing on smoking earth, when Rick lost it.

It was subtle at first. Annie was preoccupied, because at around that same point she began thinking about her mother again, and she'd been trying very hard to bury those thoughts. The ship was probably the best distraction the universe could have shunted her way, and yet, ten feet from it, she was dwelling on the cancer again.

There was no telling what was going through Rick's mind.

"Hey, guys?"

"What is it?" Rodney asked. His expression made it clear he was wrestling with his own issues in that moment.

"I just . . . I . . . are you seeing . . . ?"

"You all right?" Annie asked.

"No. No." Rick was trembling. "I gotta go. I gotta . . ."

Then he turned around and ran off into the woods as fast as he could.

Rodney looked at Annie and shrugged.

"Bathroom?"

"I don't think so," she said. "Leave him be. He's probably not our best ambassador anyway."

They continued forward another three paces.

Rodney made a sound somewhere between a gasp and a choke.

"Hey, you good?" Annie asked him.

"I think I have to check on something."

"Right now?"

"Right now. It's really important."

"My mother's dying."

"What? What?"

"I said my mother is dying. Of cancer."

"That's terrible, Annie, that's . . . I'm sorry, I have to go. I'll wait for you at the car or I'll come back or . . . I have to go."

There were tears streaming down his face. Something awful had just happened to him, or he was remembering something awful, or something awful was about to happen and he had to go prevent it. *Awful* was definitely a part of what was upsetting him, one way or another.

"Okay, but . . ."

She didn't get to finish the sentence. He spun around and ran hard for the tree line. In only a second, she was alone.

Annie looked at the ship.

"Well, then. Just you and me now. So, hi, I'm Annie? If there's anyone inside, come on out, let's talk or something."

She was maybe five paces away.

Clearly, the others encountered some sort of defense mechanism. That was the only thing that could possibly explain Rodney acting so strangely, because he would never have left her alone, here, in this moment, for any reason other than that he was compelled to somehow. (Rick, on the other hand, was behaving like Rick always behaved, and this was no surprise. She would never understand why anyone liked hanging out with him.)

"Okay, so I'm next, what do you have for me?" she asked the ship. The ship didn't answer in any direct way.

Maybe it targets the most likely threats first, she thought.

Another two steps forward, and she was thinking about her mother again. They were the same thoughts she'd been working through an hour earlier, only so very much worse.

I killed her, she thought. *It was me. She's dying because she'd rather do that than stay, because of me.*

It was an absurd notion. She was positive it was completely true. It was followed by the idea that she still had time to fix it. She could go back, right now, and hug Carol and tell her she loved her and it was okay, and she didn't *have* to have cancer.

She just had to deal with this spaceship first.

Two more steps.

Mom's going to die tonight.

"I won't even get to say goodbye," she said aloud. She emitted something like a sob when she spoke, and realized she'd been crying this whole time, which was how she was before she saw the ship in the first place. She didn't want to be back in that place, where cancer was taking away her idea of what the future was supposed to be. She didn't want that. She didn't want to cry.

It was the ship that was doing this to her.

"STOP IT!"

She took another step forward, now in reach of the hull, and just like that the grief went away.

"That wasn't nice, Shippie," she said, naming it on the spot. "I'm just a little girl. I shouldn't have to deal with this."

Silence.

She reached out and put her hand on the side of the ship.

It was warm, but not hot to the touch. Her understanding of physics, while somewhat entry-level, was sufficient to convince her there was no way this should have been possible, not for something that was in the upper atmosphere less than an hour ago.

"You absorbed the heat, didn't you? That's clever." She took her hand back. "Is there anyone in there?"

Then the ship *did* respond. It wasn't verbal, it was visual. More exactly, a series of images appeared in Annie's head. Images from space—nebulae and neutron stars and patterns of light and gas she had no names for.

"I don't understand," she said. "I don't speak this language."

The images stopped.

It was waiting for her to respond in kind, but she didn't know how.

"Use words."

New images popped in her head: bolts of electricity, and rips in space, and impossible geometric patterns.

"No, I don't understand."

The images stopped again.

More silence. She could hear her own breathing, a few cicadas, and that was all.

Then the ship started to scream.

It was a high-pitched squeal, barely noticeable at first, but rapidly growing in volume, until Annie had to cover her ears.

"NO STOP IT HURTS!" she shouted, but this time the ship wasn't listening to her. She told it to use words, and this was the word it was choosing: EEEEEEEEEEE!

Annie didn't remember running away from the ship. The sound was so painful it wasn't likely a decision she made consciously at all. Her feet decided it on their own, more or less. And the sound stopped once she made it to the trees, so it was probably the right call.

Then she was alone in the woods with the greatest discovery in human history, uncertain as to how to proceed.

Call the sheriff, she thought. *Call him and wait here.*

But when she pulled out her phone she saw it was dead. Either the battery ran out or the ship killed it (it would turn out to be the latter, as the cell phone never worked again). She couldn't tell anyone, and her ride was gone.

She decided to push through the woods in the direction of the car. Rodney would be waiting. Of course he would be.

17

LONG DAY'S JOURNEY INTO NIGHTMARE

*S*o nobody saw you?" Ed asked.

Her first reaction was that Ed thought she made up the story, but she could tell by the look on his face that wasn't an issue.

"They never came back. I waited at the edge of the clearing for—I don't know how long, a little while, I guess. But when the ship didn't do anything new and Rodney didn't show up I headed to where we left the car. It was gone, though, so I just walked home from there. By the time I made it back it was something like four in the morning. Billy found the ship about an hour later. I think I was probably asleep."

What she didn't add was that Rodney couldn't look her in the eye for nearly a year, and their friendship never entirely recovered. Given their age difference, it had a shelf life anyway, but it fell apart pretty fast. She thought he would probably always feel bad about abandoning her, but they'd never spoken one word about that night so it was hard to tell.

Rick, meanwhile, went from problem child to full-blown disaster inside of a year. He was the real first contact, not her or Rodney or Billy Pederson. She often wondered if what he experienced that night was worse than what happened to anyone else.

"Anyway," she continued, "I touched the ship, but I obviously don't know anything more about what's going on now than you do, so you're going to have to come up with another idea."

"No, you're wrong, this is a big deal. It means the ship tried to communicate. Maybe it's still trying. We just don't understand what it's saying. What can you tell me about the pictures it showed you?"

"Hardly anything. I don't remember much, it was . . . it was a lot of information and it came at me too fast."

"I wonder, if we hypnotized you, maybe we could get more."

Annie laughed.

"And that is exactly why I didn't tell anyone. I don't want somebody poking around in my head looking for the alien. Plus I'm not one of those people who can be hypnotized."

"That's really why you didn't tell anyone?"

"Well, no. Nobody would have believed me, either. Like half the town came forward with stories once Billy went global and it was clear there was money to be had. If you and I had this conversation three years ago you would have been like, sure, little girl, whatever you say."

"You're probably right. What did it feel like?"

"What did what feel like? The pictures in my head?"

"No, the side of the ship. You wouldn't believe how much back-and-forth I've read debating that one question."

"Oh. Well, I guess it was sorta weird. I had so many other things going on I didn't give it a lot of thought. It was slick, though, like it was wet only it wasn't wet. Warm, too, but not, like, frying-pan hot, which I'd have expected. It was probably stupid of me to touch it at all, since it was clearly metal and had just been surrounded by fire in the upper atmosphere, but it wasn't giving off heat like it should have."

"Some kind of low-friction material with low heat retention."

"Maybe, yeah. I think it was absorbing the heat. Like in fuel cells or something. Dobbs thinks the whole thing is a big solar power collector. So what difference does it make if it was trying to communicate?"

"I don't know yet, I have to think about it. But it's more than we ever knew before about the ship. I wish we'd known this three years ago."

"Sorry."

"The zombies, too."

"I'm not following."

"Like I said, it could still be trying to communicate. The reports I've gotten indicate a few of them have been speaking. Really basic, but maybe we shouldn't treat the zombies as threats, but as crude efforts at contact."

"Great. You go look for one to talk to, but leave me out of it."

Ed's phone, resting on the edge of the table, thrummed with a new text. He checked the screen.

"It's from Pete. Looks like they're going to move Beth to Saint Mary's."

"Oh no!"

"I'm sure it's just a precaution."

"When are they moving her?"

"She doesn't say. You want me to ask?"

"Yeah, can we head back, I want to see her before she goes."

Ed checked his watch, surprised. "Wow, it's past nine."

"Crap, I was supposed to call Carol. She's out by now. She'd want to know about Beth, too."

"Maybe I should just take you back to Violet's. We can drive to the hospital to visit her tomorrow, if you want."

"What, are you worried about my bedtime?"

"I feel like I'm supposed to be. I'm pretty sure I'm violating some sort of labor laws."

Annie got up. "I'm not on the clock. C'mon, it'll take the ambulance another hour to get to the clinic, we can beat it there."

⋮

Bobby and Lu-Lu Weld were in the clinic lobby with Sheriff Pete when Annie and Ed came in. The place was otherwise empty, as Sorrow Falls was not known for having a long list of unexpected emergency situations on Tuesday nights. This was just as well as the clinic's waiting area was too small to provide any privacy. The Welds were having a quiet conversation with Pete that ended as soon as they saw Annie, whom they both hugged extensively and at length.

Annie liked the Welds a lot. They had a habit of adopting everyone who worked for them (even their unofficial under-the-table employees, like Annie) as if they were part of the Weld clan itself.

Bobby shook hands with Ed.

"Pete here says you and Annie here saved Elizabeth from this man. Thank you so much."

"Thank you, sir, but I think Pete may be giving us more credit than we deserve. Beth did all her own rescuing. We didn't get there until after she chased him off. You should be proud, she's got a lot of spirit."

"That she does. And so does this one." He rubbed the top of Annie's head affectionately. The Welds were basically parents straight from the 1950s.

"How is she doing?" Annie asked.

"They sedated her," Lu-Lu said. Her real name was Lucy, but Annie didn't know a single person who called her that. "We wanted to take her home, but the doctor thinks she could use a more monitored overnight, just in case, so we're just waiting on the ambulance."

Ed locked eyes with Pete and gave her a little nod, the universal signal for *can I talk to you?* Annie wasn't sure who was updating whom, but if she could guess, Ed was about to ask Pete for help in locating a zombie for a "take us to your leader" kind of conversation. Hopefully not involving brain eating.

"Excuse me for just a minute," Ed said. "It was a pleasure meeting you both."

"The pleasure's ours," Bobby said. Ed and Pete stepped out the front door.

"Can I go see her?" Annie asked. "Before the ambulance gets here?"

"Sure, sweetie," Lu-Lu said, "but she is lights-out right now. I'm sure she won't even know you're there."

"Go on in," Bobby said. "It's the first door on the left."

⋮

Annie had been past the lobby of the clinic only once, meaning she was actually less familiar with it than she was with the emergency room at Harbridge Memorial, despite the clinic's relative proximity to her on any given day.

There were three small private rooms with examination tables and cots. The rest of the space was pretty open, with a long counter for a nurse or a local volunteer. The area beyond the desk was an unknown. She imagined there were offices for doctors, X-ray machines, and so on. Down at the far end of the corridor was a set of double doors. An ambulance dock, probably. When Ed parked behind the clinic she'd seen one there.

A woman was standing behind the counter, sorting through paperwork in front of a lit computer screen. She looked up at Annie and smiled. They had a silent conversation whereby Annie asked to enter Beth's room and the nurse/doctor/random woman doing paperwork gave her permission.

Annie's one trip past the lobby was as a patient, the previous summer. She'd made the mistake of over-stuffing Bart with dishes, and was in too much of a rush to notice exactly what she was doing. The way the Hobart dishwasher worked was that a tray of dishes was slid in on a rack, and a handle was pulled to lower two side panels to seal a chimney-shaped compartment. Once the sides were completely shut, the machine automatically began the thirty-second wash cycle. If the tray was over-full, sometimes a piece of silver or a precariously balanced cup would interfere with the inside hinge of the sliding panel. The correct way to fix this was to pull the tray back out and either rearrange the things on it or remove some of those things and try again. The incorrect way was to reach into the machine and try to shove whatever was getting in the way *out* of the way.

Annie did it the incorrect way all the time, up until the day the thing that was in the way turned out to be a steak knife.

The cut was deep enough to need stitches, and she still had a tiny scar from it on the palm of her right hand. She could remember almost nothing about that day, other than what it was like to be in the back of the clinic, and that Beth was there with her. Beth was the one who wrapped up her hand at the diner and who walked her over and stayed until she was sure Annie was okay.

It wasn't even a big deal. Annie certainly would have done the same thing for Beth in that situation. But it suddenly felt like a big deal.

The clinic had made a few improvements in a year. The room was as small as ever, but the bed looked a little more bed-like than the temporary cot she last saw. Beth was asleep—given a mild sedative, as Lu-Lu said—with a fresh bandage on her head and her left arm in a sling. She wasn't strung up in the way one might expect of a person in a hospital, but this wasn't a full hospital. She had an IV, but no vital sign monitors. Annie imagined if her friend's injuries were life threatening, there would be someone in the room until the ambulance got there.

Annie sat in a chair on the right side of the bed and took Beth's free hand.

"Hi, honey," Annie said. "You probably can't hear me, but . . ."

Oh my god, this is so stupid.

"But anyway. Zombies, huh? I feel kind of bad about that. I mean, I don't know why I should, but I feel . . . I dunno, responsible, kinda. Weird, huh? I mean, it's not my fault. Sure, I didn't tell anyone about the ship, but, like, I'm not the one making zombies and sending them out to attack people."

Beth inhaled sharply, which startled Annie. Her friend appeared to be having a nightmare: her eyes were darting around under the eyelids and she kept twitching.

"Hey, it's okay, I'm here. It's all right."

Beth's fingers started twitching. Annie wondered if she should call someone in.

Normal? Not normal?

"Should I call someone?"

Beth, appropriately, didn't answer. But the twitching stopped and whatever was going on behind her eyelids quelled.

"I'll take that as a no. Anyway. I don't even know why I'm here, honey. I mean, if it were me looking at someone else here, right now, talking to an unconscious friend in an almost-hospital room, I'd say that someone else was here because her mom is in Boston in a real hospital right now. I mean, obviously, right? I'm probably feeling guilty about not going, and now zombies equals cancer in my head and wow, I should probably go get some sleep, huh?"

Definitely overtired, she wrote in her imaginary sociology notebook.

"Unnhhhh," Beth grunted. Then her eyes snapped open.

"Oh, hi!" Annie said. "They said you were sedated, but how are you? I just came in to say hello before I headed home. Your parents are out in the hall, you want me to get them?"

"Are . . . you?"

"Dude, that's not even funny. Lemme go and . . ."

"Are . . . you?" Beth repeated.

Annie let go of Beth's hand, but Beth responded by grabbing Annie by the wrist.

"Aaoow, Beth, honey, let go of me! Come on, I'm serious."

Annie was using her free hand to try to pull apart Beth's fingers, but it felt like she was going to have to break them to get loose.

"Your grip is too tight, you're hurting me, Beth. Cut it out!"

What the hell is going on?

"Are . . . you . . ."

"I heard you and it isn't funny!"

". . . her?"

"What did you say?"

She looked into Beth's eyes and realized something terrible: Beth wasn't in there.

"HELP!" she called. She didn't know how many staff were in the building or if sound could travel far enough to reach the waiting room and make any kind of difference.

"Are you her?" Beth repeated. She was trying to use her left arm to reach for Annie, apparently not aware it was in a sling.

"Beth, let go of me." She got two fingers loose. "HELP!"

A doctor she never met before—older man, new to the clinic clearly or she'd have known his face—burst in, quickly assessed the situation, and took Beth by the shoulders. He was trying to push her down into a prone position.

"Beth, you need to calm down," he said, in slightly accented English.

"Help me get free, she's hurting me," Annie said.

The woman from the desk came in next, followed by the Welds, and then Ed and Pete. Ed, seeing what the doctor was doing, went to *him* first, because nobody, it appeared, cared that Annie was about to lose her damn wrist.

"Do *not* try and wake her up!" Ed said.

"Excuse me, sir?" the doctor said.

"I've seen this, and I'm telling you, if you force her awake it may kill her."

"Oh my God," Lu-Lu cried.

"WILL SOMEONE PLEASE HELP ME?" Annie shouted.

"Sorry, sorry," Ed said. He knelt down to work on Beth's grip. "God, she's really got you."

"No kidding!"

"Beth, sweetie, calm down," Lu-Lu said from the door. She and Bobby looked afraid to jump into the middle of anything.

"Almost got her loose," Ed said. "Little help, Doctor?"

He was checking Beth's vitals, though, and not sure about respecting Ed's advice. Pete knelt down to help instead.

"She's too strong," Pete said. She was looking at Ed when she said it. "She was asleep, right?"

"Her heart rate is soaring," the doctor said, almost to himself.

"*You are,*" Beth said. "*You are. You are.*"

"What did she say?" Annie asked. "Ed . . ."

"YOU ARE."

All at once, Beth collapsed back in the bed and her grip went slack. Ed pulled Annie away from the bed immediately. Annie felt her feet go out from under her as he scooped her off the ground.

"Are you all right?" he asked. "Are you okay?"

"She said, 'Are you her,' Ed. 'Are you her?' That was their question."

Annie started to cry, and hated herself for it, while Ed held her. In the bed behind them, Beth Weld started to convulse.

⋮

In the aftermath of Corporal Vogel's death, all the men involved in the incident were pulled from their rotations. This was explained as a temporary thing to give them an opportunity to *get your heads right*, which was an army tough-love way of saying *perhaps you should speak to the base's psychiatrist before we put a gun in your hand again*.

Not one of the guys thought that was the real reason, though. As far as Sam—and by extension the other five—were concerned, they were pulled until everyone was cool with what happened. It was in the army's best interest to make sure this was a situation where one soldier went nuts, tried to kill another soldier, and then died because something was wrong with his head, rather than what it *looked* like: six men ganging up to murder a seventh.

The frustrating thing for Sam was that being pulled from his normal rotation made it look like he *had* done something wrong. There was no way around it. Everyone knew Vogel was dead, and Sam and his bunkmates were sitting on top of the man when he died. Having them taken out of duty just made it all look worse.

It helped that this was Sorrow Falls. Any other place, Sam's story sounded a lot more suspect, but in this town, the ever-present specter of the space flu lingered in the back of everyone's minds and made this sort of thing possible.

Another source of frustration was, after he declined to speak to Dr. Davidian about his emotional state, and after the inquest exonerated him and the others, someone decided to shuffle the rotation.

Again, he could see the reasoning: *let's make sure these six men aren't all guarding the spaceship at around the same time, just in case we have this wrong*. He would have made the same call.

It didn't mean he liked the outcome. His new team was (a) on a nighttime rotation with the spaceship, and (b) filled with men who'd come in with Vogel.

Sam had been in Sorrow Falls for fourteen months, which was longer than most of the men assigned to the base, but not as long as Vogel and his guys. They called themselves "lifers," and they'd been there for a little over two years. There were only ten of them—nine now—five of whom made up Sam's new team.

Two years didn't seem like a long time to be at a base that saw no combat, but as far as lifers were concerned they were owed some sort of special respect, which was annoying since they all carried the same rank as Sam and two were younger than he was. It was all very high school, but Sam could learn to deal with it.

Much more disconcerting was the extremely cavalier attitude they all seemed to have about their assignment. They collectively developed a disturbingly nihilistic perspective on the ship and the importance of their duties in regard to it.

Sam could understand this too. It was easy to fall into a late-night security guard sort of mentality around a thing that was supposed to be the most dangerous object on the planet but that continued to refuse to fulfill that responsibility.

On the other hand, nobody wants to hear *it won't matter, we'll all die anyway* from the soldier sharing his foxhole, whether or not it was true.

This was Sam's second night shift with this team, and the second night they told him to cover the front (street side) of the perimeter and to not worry about checking in unless he saw something important happen or had to take a leak. The first hour of the first night, he thought they were being generous in giving him the gate, because there were fewer bugs out front, and a few more things to look at. The back of the perimeter was nothing but a lot of trees and a squirrel or two, in contrast. But then Sam tried to check in at the hour—they were supposed to have hourly checks—and half the team didn't answer. He was about to escalate it (which would have meant a backup team driving down the hill from the base) when he was told the three guys in back were napping and to leave them alone.

So that was the first night, which was dry. On this, the second, it had already rained a ton and the ground was muddy, so Sam didn't see any way for a nap to be feasible without there being immediate and obvious evidence of said nap.

Just the same, when he tried to check in he was told to mind his own business.

He wondered if maybe they had hammocks hidden in the trees.

It was at exactly twenty-two-seventeen that the end of the world began. Sam always expected to have a front-row seat to it, but knew every other soldier at the base felt the same way. Even the lifers felt that way, although their expression of this sentiment was more tied up in concepts relating to fate and inevitability and passiveness, whereas everyone else tended to game-plan the scenario with a mixture of excitement and dread.

Either way, it was Sam who was at the gate at the beginning of the end. And the beginning of the end was startling indeed.

First, there was the heavy thump of a shock wave that traveled along the ground and knocked Sam over. He ended up on his butt. Across the street, the trailers rocked. He heard exclamations of surprise.

Sam scrambled to his feet and reached for his radio—still clipped to his belt—and his rifle, which he'd dropped. He opened a channel.

"SS1 to Base, we have something happening down here. Felt like an earthquake, but I think the ship did it, over."

Static.

Did they hear me?

The radios were susceptible to atmospheric interference from time to time, and this was the kind of night where such a thing was possible. That was why they kept a field phone attached to a landline near the gate. (This was, if nothing else, ironic, as field phones were designed to be portable communicators in an age before cell phones. Now, it was a hardwired alternative to wireless.) Sam oriented himself, located the phone, and started running for it.

"Hey!" someone shouted from the trailer. "Something's happening, huh?"

Sam knew the guy—it was the weird nerdy guy Annie knew. Dobie or something. It wasn't a great time for a chat, so Sam just waved and continued for the phone.

Then he saw the light, out of the corner of his eye, and he stopped moving to stare at it.

The light was Bunsen burner blue, and it was being emitted from a part of the spaceship most people likened to an antenna array. It was only glowing faintly, but glowing nonetheless, which was more life than the ship had shown at any point in the past three years, excluding thirty seconds ago.

"Holy crap!" the guy on the trailer shouted.

Go back inside, Sam was supposed to be saying. *Protect yourself, drive for the hills, get behind me. You want me on that wall.*

He didn't say any of that; he didn't have time. The light brightened and then there was . . . something like an explosion.

The sound it made was a lot more like an *implosion,* or maybe just the noise an explosion would make if played backwards. It happened in time with a tremendous wave of melancholy. When it passed through Sam his knees buckled and he gasped and nearly began to cry. It was weaponized depression; there was no other way to describe it. Mercifully, it lasted less than a second, or he might have put a gun in his mouth.

The light on the top of the ship glowed brighter still, and then a thin beam shot out of the top, visible only because of the mist still in the air from the earlier precipitation. It went straight up into the lower atmosphere until reaching something like a wall or an upper bound, at which point it spread out in all directions, like the cascade at the top of a geyser.

Sam fingered the channel on his radio again and only heard more static. Behind him, the trailer nutsos were collectively springing to life. Doors were opening and people were coming out. If any of them tried to rush the gate, Sam was going to have a tough decision to make.

But first, the phone. He reached the field phone and clicked open the line, which was all that was required to dial up the base as the phone had no other purpose and wasn't tied to any public lines. It ran along the same underground cable as the instruments surrounding the ship.

"SS1 to Base, this is Corning, over."

Silence. Sam thought about those instruments on the ground inside the fence. They were calibrated to detect the tiniest of changes, so what just happened probably caused every sensor to wet itself. There was undoubtedly a packet of exciting information being uploaded to the science team at this very moment, which meant even if Sam didn't get through there were people in the world—far away from Sorrow Falls—who were aware that this was happening. Whatever it was.

Not getting through to the base wasn't an expected outcome, yet nobody was responding. He didn't know where the phone terminated, but assumed a human being was in charge of anticipating a call. Perhaps that human was sleeping, like the men sharing his perimeter detail.

Then someone picked up the phone.

"Who's this?"

"This is Corning, at the ship. We've got something going on down here, I need . . ."

"Hold position, Soldier, we're locking down."

"Yes . . . yes sir, it's just . . ."

"Conserve ammo, shoot to wound if possible, and hold position!"

The line went dead.

Sam stared at the phone for a few seconds, not sure if he was ready to believe what he'd just heard. There were the orders, which were alarming enough, but that wasn't all.

On the other end of the line, in the background, he could swear he heard screaming.

⋮

Dill felt the earthquake and knew.

His new duty assignment was base perimeter, a job that had him guarding a bunch of men with guns in a town of hick farmers, which was about the dumbest job on the base next to latrine duty, which thank God they hired someone to do because *no thanks*.

Anyway it was a plebe job, and he hated everyone sharing it with him and thought everyone probably blamed him for Vogel for some reason even though *he* was the one getting choked to death in all that mess.

Unlike SS1 duty, perimeter guard at the base meant standing *inside* the fence and making sure nobody came at it from outside. This was — again — a base in a town in America and not the Green Zone in Iraq. He had to worry about the kid staring back at him from the farmhouse porch on one side, and that was it. There wasn't anybody else nearby. And again, he was guarding a bunch of guys who had their own guns.

Then the ground thumped.

Dill was from a part of the country that didn't do that. They had to worry about hurricanes every year, but you could see a hurricane coming. Earthquakes didn't creep across the ocean, they just struck without warning, and that was a kind of uncertainty that made him deeply uncomfortable.

It felt unnatural, which was why he was ready to attribute it to the ship instead, and also why Corporal Wen laughed at him for doing it. Wen was from San Francisco.

"You never been through a quake before? Calm yourself."

"That felt bad."

"The bad ones last long enough so you think they're not going to stop. That was a little thing."

"Can you even get earthquakes in Massachusetts?"

"Sure can. You can get them anywhere. Now we do what everyone does after a quake: we wait for someone to tell us the Richter and brag about having felt it."

Wen — who hadn't fallen over — helped Dill to his feet.

"You can call home tomorrow," he said, "and tell the family all about it. Come on, we should keep walking."

"We have to make sure the fence is intact," Dill said.

Wen laughed. "It wasn't that bad! Oh my."

They had started walking when Dill was hit with a wave of nausea and the odd notion that it would have been better for everyone if Hank Vogel had crushed his throat.

"Oh," Wen said quietly. "Did you feel that?"

"That's not normal for earthquakes, huh?"

Wen shot him a dirty look. "I think I want to call home now, not wait for morning."

"Yeah, I feel the same way."

He saw movement outside the fence.

"Hey, look," Wen said.

It looked like someone was walking toward them from across the field. It was hard to tell for sure because the perimeter lighting didn't extend more than a few yards on the other side and it was a dark, rainy night.

Dill stepped closer to the fence and squinted.

"There's definitely someone out there. You got a light?"

"What's over there?" he asked. "Where are they coming from?"

"They?"

"Your eyes are bad, I make at least three people." He stepped to the edge of the fence. "HELLO?"

No response. Dill could see them now. At least three leading the way, and maybe five or six more trailing behind.

"No flashlight?" Dill asked.

"Never needed one. What's over there? Do you know?"

Dill had been at the base for only two months longer than Wen, but he had reviewed the layout only the day before, at around the same time he got his new orders. But in the map in his head, there was just a void in that direction. A field, and then . . . *what is over there?*

The group was closing in. When they got to the edge of the spotlights they would reach a point where Dill and Wen had the authority to shoot.

"Army property, y'all," he said, his Cajun leaking out in times of stress. "Please disperse."

He took his rifle off his shoulder.

"What are you doing?" Wen asked.

"Just for show."

Wen followed suit. He looked about as nervous as Dill felt.

It wasn't an earthquake, he thought. It was the first thing that came to mind when it happened, but he'd allowed himself to get talked out of it by his San Franciscan partner. Then there was that wave of emotion that followed. What the hell could that be, if they felt it at the same time?

It had to be the ship.

The trio leading the pack of what was clearly now a group of at least a dozen started to come into focus. They were . . . dirty, which was weird. A light cloud of dirt came into the light ahead of them, falling from their clothes.

"Oh no," Dill said.

"What is it?"

"I just remembered what's on the other side of the field."

The first one to reach the light was in a dark suit and a tie, and half of his face was missing. His jaw swung left and right as he lumbered along in the muddy grass, connected to the rest of his face by visible tendons. The skin over his skull looked loose.

"What?"

"The cemetery."

Wen saw.

"Pickles, is that a zombie?"

"Yeah. You wanna start shooting?"

"I think maybe yes."

That was when the shouting *behind* them got loud enough to notice. There were men and women running around the base for reasons that went beyond the very real concern that the base was under attack from the deceased population of Sorrow Falls.

Wen readied his rifle. "Now?" he asked.

Dill looked over his shoulder and saw the large, familiar figure of Hank Vogel walking slowly across the basketball court.

The sirens started going off.

"Yes," he said. "Now."

⋮

When Beth started seizing, Annie decided it was time to completely freak the hell out.

She was way overdue. Between the ship, the any-day-now-ness of her mother's cancer, and the possibility of actual zombies, she already had way too much to cope with. Watching Beth, her de facto big sister, possibly dying right in front of her was quite enough.

She wanted her mother, and she wanted her dad, and she wanted to go home and rewind to the day before the spaceship landed, when the most important question in her life was whether she'd hit puberty in time for Rodney to think of her as something more than a kid.

If she couldn't have that, she wanted a fast-forward button instead, so she could skip ahead to the part where she was grown up and didn't have to worry about an adult giving her permission to be alone. She could leave Sorrow Falls and go to college somewhere. Home-schooled Violet could come with her. They would live in Paris, and date men with accents, and never talk about this town again.

With no fast-forward or rewind or even a pause, she couldn't do a whole lot for a while except cry on Ed's shoulder in the lobby.

"It's all right, it's all right, it's all right," he said over and over. "Just take a breath, Beth is going to be okay."

"The zombies," Annie said. They were the first words she'd been able to put together between the sobs.

"Don't worry about that either."

He sat her down on one of the chairs and pulled back, as it was clear she no longer absolutely required his shoulder. "Look, Beth is going to be okay. We don't know what happened yet. We also don't know if any of this zombie stuff . . . you know what? Let's stop calling them that. Zombies are made up, right? Until we see one, let's just . . . we'll skip it. Until we know what we're really dealing with, we'll skip it."

"Beth was a zombie."

"No, Beth was sedated and zombies are reanimated dead people."

"Well, okay." Annie wiped her eyes and her nose, and decided she must look a mess. "Something that wasn't Beth looked at me through Beth's eyes and said *Are you her?* and then *You are.* So basically, if you don't want to call them zombies that's fine. Call them dinglehoppers or something. Either way, I'm pretty sure I just started the dinglehopper apocalypse."

"You're overreacting."

"I'm allowed."

"Yes, you are. But I think we should go. The doctor is dealing with Beth. We can check on her in the morning. I don't think we should be in the way."

"I don't want to leave her."

"I insist. At least step outside for some air. I need to call the base."

"What for?"

"Did you feel the ground shake?"

"No. Did we have an earthquake?"

Annie remembered a quake when she was nine. It felt like a truck drove past, and that was what she thought it was until everyone was talking about it like it was a big deal and then she decided it was a big deal too, except it really wasn't.

"Must have been. Plus, there was . . . something else kind of weird. You were already upset, you probably didn't notice."

"What?"

Ed stopped and stared at her strangely for a couple of seconds.

"What is it?" she asked.

"Nothing, I just realized something. Hey, let's go outside."

It was approaching 10:30 p.m., which was just about the upper limit for Annie as far as being on Main was concerned. She was usually at least in the vicinity of her house by that time most nights, especially since the mall closed at 10.

The street seemed pretty deserted. It was still just as much of a Tuesday as it began the day as, so that was unsurprising.

Ed took out his cell phone and tried a call.

"Huh," he said, after three tries. "I can't get through."

"We can try mine."

He took her phone and punched in the number.

"Nope, that's no good either."

"Something wrong with the base? Try another number."

They were standing on the front steps of the clinic, which was on the northern half of Main, on the side of the street that looked down at the river valley. On the far left was the city hall and on the far right the library. On the near right, across the street, was the diner. All the storefront lights were out. Main was lit by streetlamps—they were quaint-looking lights designed to look like nineteenth-century gas lamps, even though the town never had such things—which gave it a sort of spooky feel in the late-night mist.

Hang on.

It wasn't as deserted as she thought. For starters, the army had begun manning all their checkpoints a couple of weeks earlier, and that appeared to be a twenty-four-hour mandate, so there were men at the checkpoint booth two blocks past the diner on the right. The soldiers appeared to be in a state of agitation, which is to say even from a few blocks away Annie could tell they had their guns out.

For another, there were pedestrians.

They weren't acting like pedestrians, which made it difficult to spot them at first. Pedestrians understood what sidewalks and streets were. These people were wandering in and out of the street-light arcs in a way that implied they were unsure as to their destination.

Ed had a business card in his hand and was dialing the number from it.

"I'm trying Hollis," he explained.

"Yes, he'll want to know about the dinglehopper apocalypse too."

"Stop that. And I can't get through to him either. Here." He handed back her phone. "Try your mother."

"It's a little late, I don't want to wake her."

"Then call someone else outside of Sorrow Falls. I'm going to call my apartment in Washington."

Annie tried her dad's number. He was either in Canada or on the road between there and Massachusetts, both of which qualified as being outside of the town.

The phone didn't ring. It paused for a while and then told her it couldn't make the connection.

"I have full bars," she said.

"Me too, and I can't get anyone."

She opened up the phone's web browser and hit a *page cannot load* message.

"No Internet either."

"Hey."

Ed wasn't looking at his phone anymore; he was looking at the street.

"Yeah, lot of people out tonight," Annie said, but on looking at the road she appreciated immediately how inadequate that description was. There were a *lot* of people out, coming up the hill from the row houses and reaching Main in groups of five and six at every intersection in both directions. They were all walking in that same disorganized way, but they were beginning to develop a sort of general directionality. One or two might drift left for a while or right for a time, but if the entire slow-developing mob was to be reviewed as a unit, it might be said that it was collectively converging upon the clinic.

"Does it seem like they're all coming this way?"

"A little bit, yes."

Then sirens began going off.

"Okay," Ed said. "Now we can start calling it a zombie apocalypse."

18

THE SLEEPWALKING DEAD

*I*t was Oona's idea to start operating in shifts.

She suggested it right after Annie brought her friend Edgar over to pretend to be a journalist and ask pointed questions about something that obviously happened recently. Whether that something was the "breathing" they were picking up or not, self-evidently the government had an idea that the ship was manifesting a new risk. The low-key poke-around of the "government operative posing as reporter" was very nearly polite and respectful, as dishonest as it happened to be at its core, so Laura mostly didn't mind, and Oona only minded because everything irritated her.

Working in shifts meant hardly spending any time together, because there were only two of them. With three or four, some overlap would have been acceptable, but Oona didn't want to pair up with any of the other campers because she trusted nobody aside from herself and Laura.

There was still a *little* overlap. Information had to be exchanged and developments discussed and theories hatched. Also, there were certain gun-cleaning rituals, which needed to be maintained. They didn't want to come out of this discovering they'd both been cleaning the same five guns for a month.

Laura had just begun her shift when the ground shook. It nearly rocked the trailer onto its side. It *did* knock Oona out of bed. Laura heard it from the roof.

"You okay, babe?" Laura asked. She was taken out of her lawn chair, and failed to fall over the side only because of the high wall. Their computer equipment—bolted to tables that were bolted to the roof—fared better.

Oona cursed for fifteen straight seconds, then climbed up the center ladder and poked her head out of the hatch.

"What in the name of baby Jesus was that?"

"Dunno. I think the ship stomped on the ground."

Laura got to her feet (her left elbow, which broke her fall, was going to have a monster bruise in the morning, she could tell already) and looked across the street at their Mount Doom.

"There's a light," she said.

"Lemme see."

Oona scrambled up. She was still dressed for bed, which meant floral flannels that were so far removed from her end-of-the-world leather chic she looked like a different person.

She saw the light, scrambled for binoculars, found them, looked at the light again.

"Definitely the ship."

"What else would it be?"

"Someone behind it with a blowtorch. Same color."

"It would only look right from this angle if that were true."

"Yes, darling, but what I'm telling you is it's not that, and we can rule that out, and it's actually the ship. Don't bust my balls."

To their right, Dobbs was shouting stuff at soldier boy across the street. Only a couple of the other rooftop residents were even awake, it looked like.

Three years and they're going to sleep through the Moment, she thought. What a shame that was.

"You were right," Laura said. "Keeping shifts was a good idea."

"'Course it was." Oona sat in her chair and started fiddling with the equipment. "I only have good ideas. Light me a smoke, would you?"

Right then the depression grenade hit. When it was over—and it was over almost instantly, thank goodness—Laura was lying on the trailer on her back and Oona was actively crying.

"Well, that was horrible," Oona said. "Get up and light me that smoke."

"Later."

Lighting a smoke actually involved rolling a cigarette, because it was cheaper to buy tobacco in bulk and there were fewer government-sanctioned chemicals. It was a process, anyway, and she wanted to pay attention. "What does the equipment say?"

"Says the anthill blew up." This was a reference to an in-joke, that their equipment was sensitive enough to detect an ant fart from a hundred feet.

Oona tapped out a few things. "Pretty sure that thing is emitting something."

"I see it." A laser-narrow light was pointed skyward, reaching a termination point that was probably a mile or two up.

It gave Laura an idea.

"Hey, I think I know what's happening."

"Art? Hey, Art!"

Dobbs was yelling from his own roof, because Art Shoeman was walking slowly along the side of the road.

She looked at Dobbs. "What's he doing?" she shouted.

"I don't know!"

He wasn't the only one. Mika and Morrie, Zeno and Johnny Nguyen were also out there. And Earl Pleasant. And Joy Chen. They had all exited their campers to begin a slow trek down the street.

"Art!" Laura yelled. "ART SHOEMAN."

Art stopped, and looked up at her. It was creepily slow and deliberate.

"You are not," he said. Then he turned and continued walking.

"What the hell."

"What did he say?" Oona asked.

"He said I'm not."

"Not what?"

"No idea."

Dobbs, meanwhile, climbed down from his roof to catch up with Art.

"Hey, hey, Art, where are you going? The ship, man, it's what we've been waiting for."

"Are you?"

"That isn't funny, man, come on!"

"Dobbs, maybe you should leave him," Laura called down.

"No, this is bull."

He grabbed Shoeman's elbow to try to get the older man to stop walking. Art's response was dramatic: he pulled back his arm and unleashed a wicked backhand that knocked Dobbs onto his ass in the brambles on the side of the road.

He wasn't done. As disconnected as Art Shoeman appeared to be to the world, he knew how to respond to a threat, and in a way that seemed impossible for a person of his age and general demeanor.

Art stepped forward and raised his leg to stomp on Dobbs, who was still stunned and largely defenseless.

Then soldier boy showed up. He must have heard the shouting and decided to involve himself, when he probably had more important things to do. He grabbed Art from behind, spun, and threw the old man into the street.

This had an undesired effect.

Everyone stumbling down the side of the road stopped, turned, and headed for the threat, which was now both the soldier and Dobbs. This wouldn't have been all too terrible because these were not people known for their physical well-being—except for the five army guys in their company—but there were a lot of them.

"Oh no," Laura said.

She spun around and flipped open the hatch.

"Where you going?" Oona asked. "What is it?"

There was no time to explain. Laura slid down the ladder to the main cabin, and out the door.

She got to Dobbs first. He was only twenty feet away, stuck in the brush.

"Get up, Dobbs," she said, grabbing his arm. "Hurry, get off your fat ass and move."

"What's wrong with him?" he asked. "Did you see Art?"

"I saw."

"What's going on?"

"The world's ending. Now c'mon, I'm not going to drag you!"

Dobbs pulled himself up.

He wouldn't be going back to his own camper because the route was cut off. Suddenly there were people everywhere, most of them weren't from the trailer community, and only a few had on army fatigues.

"Back to my camper. Hurry."

"Okay." He turned and ran.

"Hey, soldier boy!" Laura shouted. "Let's go!"

The kid already had his handgun out, and looked like he was deciding whom to use it on first.

"Where?" he asked.

"Trailer, straight back to my right."

"Get yourself there and hold the door, I'll be right behind you."

Just then, a siren sounded. It was an air raid siren, the kind people too young for the Second World War only ever heard in old movies. There was essentially no way this was a good sign.

"That's bad, right?" Laura asked.

"Yep, real bad. Get to that door."

Dobbs was little and round, and still woozy from the slap in the head, but he could run pretty well when his life appeared to depend on it, so he beat Laura to the door handily, and then waited for her.

"Get in," she said, "and don't touch anything."

She turned around. "We're clear!"

The soldier, perhaps unwisely, had begun engaging one of the other soldiers in hand-to-hand. Unwisely, because the other soldier didn't seem to have any pain receptors, and the rest were closing in. The non-zombie soldier—Laura couldn't think of any better word than "zombie" for what she was seeing—couldn't get free. Every time he tried to turn around and get away the larger man opposite him grabbed a wrist or a piece of his clothing and pulled him back in.

Suddenly, a shot rang out, and the zombie soldier's head disappeared in a red cloud.

"Dammit, no!" soldier boy shouted. "Shoot to wound, shoot to wound!"

"You're welcome," Oona said from the roof.

The soldier scrambled away from his dead compatriot and reached the door just ahead of the throng. Laura let him in and started applying the deadbolts, of which there were several.

"Don't . . . don't shoot to kill," the soldier said.

"I'm Laura. Welcome aboard."

"Sam. Thanks for the assist. Tell your friend up top to be careful."

"I will, but between you and me she may not care."

⋮

"What are the sirens for?" Annie asked.

"It's a lockdown. Containment strategy. They installed sirens all over the perimeter in the event conventional communications went out."

"I didn't know this."

"It wasn't public knowledge. A lot of things weren't."

"Like what?"

"We have to get to the car."

"Not until you answer my question."

"Annie! Look around. We have to get to the car."

He was right. Main Street was quickly turning into a pedestrian walkway. It was nearly impassable in both directions.

"Inside," Annie said. "Through the back."

They retreated into the lobby, and nearly ran over Pete.

"What's going on out there? Is the Luftwaffe bombing?"

"What?" Ed asked.

"The sirens."

"You wouldn't believe us," Annie said.

"Oh yeah?"

Pete opened the door, looked outside for a half second, and closed it again.

"Okay, I don't believe you," she said.

"We never said anything."

"I don't believe myself, then. What do we do?"

"You need to stay here," Ed said. "Lock the doors, keep them out."

"I don't think that's a good long-term solution."

"It doesn't have to be. As soon as Annie and I get to the car, nobody out there is going to be interested in coming in."

"Why's that?"

"They're looking for me," Annie said. "We're pretty sure."

"Now hang on, I can't —"

"Pete," Ed interrupted, "we really don't have the time to argue. Hold the doors, keep everyone in here safe, and try not to shoot any of the zombies."

Ed grabbed Annie's arm and the two of them sprinted away from a dumbfounded sheriff, past Beth's room, and down the hall. As Annie hoped, the doors in the back led to the ambulance bay, and from there the back parking lot.

It was empty. The zombies weren't smart enough to surround the building.

Ed was unlocking the car when they heard the amplified voice of one of the soldiers at the checkpoint.

"PLEASE RETURN TO YOUR HOMES. MARTIAL LAW IS IN EFFECT."

"Yeah, that's not gonna help," Ed said.

There was a loud pop Annie was pretty sure was a gunshot. She climbed into the car.

"This is going to go badly, isn't it?" she asked.

"I think probably. If it's like this down here I can't imagine what the base is like."

He pulled out of the space and turned the corner, which was when it became clear the only way out of the lot was to run people over.

"I hate to say this, but can we just go through them?" Annie asked.

"I'm nearly positive these people aren't actually dead and I don't think this car can take more than a couple of direct impacts. Town cars aren't really designed to plow into traffic and keep going."

"What is?"

"The army has a few war zone vehicles that would do it. Or one of those black SUVs you talked me out of using."

"That was solid advice at the time."

She looked through the rear window and thought about where they were.

"How do you feel about driving through yards?"

"Surprisingly good."

"Excellent. Turn us around."

Ed backed up and performed a hairpin in reverse that was actually a little cool. For a half second Annie felt like she was in an action movie.

She pointed to a spot between two trees.

"If you can get through there I think it's pretty flat right to Mrs. Evanov's yard. She used to have a wood fence but it's mostly fallen apart so hopefully we'll be okay. On the other side is Yucca."

"That's it?"

"That's it. Oh, but you'll have to gun it. There's a lip along the edge of the lot."

What happened next was somewhat less than Hollywood awesome. Ed gunned the engine and aimed for the spot, but the lip of which Annie spoke was eight inches and squared off, so there was no ramping up and over it. There was only a hard bump, which raised the car and its occupants into the air and down again, inelegantly, and awkwardly off-course. Ed was able to wrestle the vehicle sufficiently to maneuver it between the target trees rather than into one of them, but lost enough speed that the wood fence Annie insisted was barely there became a significant obstacle.

The horizontal support post ended up across the hood. Ed had to stop the car and remove fence parts before continuing through Mrs. Evanov's yard.

"The road's just there," Annie said, pointing ahead. Ed steered through the yard.

Halfway around the side of the house, a figure lurched in front of them. Ed swerved, but a soft-but-distinctive thud indicated he had failed to miss completely.

"Oh God, what was that?" Annie asked.

"Just a guess, but that was probably Mrs. Evanov."

Past the side of the house, he skidded onto Yucca Way. It wasn't entirely zombie-free, but it wasn't nearly as bad as Main.

"Okay, now what?" he asked.

"Depends. Where are we going? If you want to head for the ship you're facing the wrong way."

"I want to hook up with the end of Main, then the bridge."

"That's not near anything."

"That's the point. I'm getting you out of town before I do anything else."

"Ed . . ."

"This isn't open to debate. I promised to look after you, and the best way I know to do that is to get you as far away from here as possible. Now get me to the bridge."

⋮

"Someone said that to me before," Dobbs said.

Dobbs, Sam thought. *No wonder I couldn't get it right, what kind of name is that?*

"Who?" Laura asked.

The three of them were still down in the main cabin of the trailer, while the fourth occupant—someone named Oona—marched around on the roof with what looked like a high-powered sniper rifle. The rifle was probably meant for him or someone like him.

She was pacing up there, not using the gun. Sam took this to mean the mob resumed its slow stagger down the hill and was leaving them alone. He would have used a side window to verify this, but their windows were all shuttered with steel panels.

"I don't know who. He came up to me in the woods."

"You were on your poop run?"

"How did you know about that?"

Laura laughed.

"Everyone knows about it, Dobbs. We were all wondering why you stopped."

Sam thought Laura had a really pleasant laugh and a nice demeanor, and she looked really cute. He wasn't sure if he felt that way about her specifically because she and her friend up top just saved his life or not. Then he decided there was no point speculating, because given the trappings of the room, this woman and the other one were romantically engaged.

Laura was wearing shorts and a basic blue T-shirt, which made her look far more normal than she appeared to actually be, based on what was hanging on the walls. It looked like they owned a small collection of leather armor. They also made their own bullets and rolled their own cigarettes, and collected *Penthouse* calendars. It looked like they were also keeping urine in jars in the back of the trailer, but he couldn't be positive.

"Some creeper walked up and asked me, he was like, 'Are you,' and I got the hell out of there rather than figure out what the answer was. I figured it was just some weird guy."

"How long ago was that?" Sam asked.

"Two, three weeks, probably. Hey, thanks for the save."

"No problem. I'm supposed to . . . I just realized I've abandoned my post. I should get back outside."

"Your *post?*" Laura said. "Your position was overrun, you can't go back out there."

"It didn't look like they were interested in anybody here. They were heading toward Main before he interrupted one of them."

"That was Art Shoeman," Dobbs said. "Not just *one of them.*"

"Yeah, well, it looks like my entire team is out there with him. More reason to get back, the fence is unguarded."

"I think the ship can take care of itself, Soldier," Laura said.

"It's Sam. And I have orders."

"Well, they're stupid orders given the current situation, Sam. You don't want to end up being a zombie like your buddies."

"I think I need to fall asleep for that to happen."

"Sure, or die."

There was a knock on the door.

"*Don't answer that,*" Oona said from above.

"What's going on?" Laura asked.

"Don't open the door and don't let the kid leave. Get up here."

There was a second and a third knock, and then it became clear these weren't knocks in any normal sense. Someone out there was banging on the sides of the camper.

I guess they haven't gone anywhere, Sam thought.

There was an interior ladder to the roof, which was about the best idea Sam had ever seen in terms of camper design given the current reality. These were a couple of survivalists, and they'd planned well. He appreciated that at any other time he'd have used the word *paranoid* to describe what he was seeing. That word was now *practical,* and it made him think he was exactly where he should be, regardless of his orders.

Then he got to the roof. Laura went up first, with Dobbs slow to follow. Sam got up there last and took one look at the arsenal of weaponry hanging on the reinforced low wall surrounding the rooftop, and a new word replaced *practical.* That word was *militia.* These ladies were a two-person militia, and this camper was definitely built to withstand an attack from other people with guns.

The army, in other words.

Oona was a husky woman in pajamas with kittens on them, still holding a high-powered rifle. The expression on her face made it plain that she was not happy to have him there.

"Look but don't touch," she said, referring to the guns. "Those ain't for you."

"I'm guessing the barrel end is," he said.

She smiled. "I don't think we gamed a single scenario where one of you ended up here with us, so you're not wrong."

"Any zombie scenarios?"

"Oh sure, a bunch. What did you mean about falling asleep?"

"Isn't it obvious? Those people down there aren't dead, they're sleeping."

"So more like they're possessed."

234 • GENE DOUCETTE

"If that works better for you, yes."

"Why don't we just wake them up?"

"I dealt with this once before. I'm pretty sure if you do that you'll kill them."

"Huh. Well, that leaves us with a hairy problem, Soldier."

"How so?"

The camper rocked lightly.

"That's how so. Have a look over the side."

Because of the high walls, Sam had to walk right to the lip.

There were at least fifty people out there, and half that number were closing on the camper.

"I didn't know there were this many people in Sorrow Falls," he said. "Where are they coming from?"

"Farmhouses," Laura said. "And the base up the hill."

Sam remembered the screaming he heard in the background when he called in. At this time of night, probably half the division would have been asleep.

"It's too soon," he said. "Unless the zombies are moving faster when we aren't looking."

"Or they learned how to drive," Dobbs offered.

"I'm not saying that's impossible, but if they could do that they would have driven past us. The ship isn't their destination. Something downtown is. The guys in fatigues must be from one of the outposts."

This piqued Oona's attention. "Come again?"

"The . . . outposts. We have ten or twelve of them set up in the hills. That's where the sirens you're hearing are all situated. It's for the cordon scenario."

The trailer rocked again. The people below were trying to knock it over.

"I don't understand why they're doing that," Dobbs said. "Like you said, they were on their way to Main."

"It's a threat response," Laura said. "They're acting like white blood cells."

"Because I killed one," Oona added. "That's why. What was the cordon scenario?"

"It's a containment directive, in the event of a contagion, or . . . well, or this, I guess. It's to keep all the weirdness contained within the town. The river's a natural border to the east, but anyone can walk out through the woods north, south, and west. The men at the outposts have orders to fan out and put a soldier at each passable point. It's not impenetrable, but it's better than nothing."

Bump. The camper rocked again.

"Nice to know you all had plans to trap us in here."

"We would have been trapped right with you. We have no jurisdiction outside the town line, so the perimeter had to be within it."

"Well, I disagree with you there, Soldier," Oona said. She stepped up to the edge of the roof and looked down at the crowd. "A man standing at the exit is the only one not trapped in the room. Now are you telling me all these people down there are alive?"

"I don't know if they all are. That woman there, for instance. She's probably not."

He pointed out a zombie in a nice dress with no nose and only one eye. The left side of her body was semi-crushed, so she was dragging herself mostly with a working right leg. She was about thirty feet away and heading for the camper, albeit slowly.

"All right, so we'll call those original recipe zombies."

Oona took aim with the rifle and fired once, a clean head shot that dropped the woman immediately.

"Dammit, Oona!" Laura yelled. "That's why they're attacking!"

"They're already attacking, and we had to know if the same thing that drops the free-range ones also takes out the original recipe."

"I think you're mixing your chicken metaphors."

"Shut up, Dobbs, the one with the gun does the naming."

"They all stopped when you fired," Sam said. "They learned what a gunshot means."

"How could they not know that?" Dobbs asked.

"I mean whoever is running things down there learned it."

The trailer rocked again.

"Okay, two things," Laura said. "First off, maybe we need to keep firing guns to get them to stop trying to push us over. Second, we could probably use an escape plan here. I don't want to know what they're planning to do to us in a breach, do you?"

"We can hang the outside ladder off the back and hit the field, head for the woods, maybe," Oona said. "The four of us can carry a lot of provisions and a lot of guns. I mean, as long as Dobbs's poop zombie isn't out there still."

Dobbs looked over the field side. "They're circling around now. We'd have to drop and run in the next minute to pull that off."

"Not enough time," Laura said. "We could start wounding them like Sam suggested. They can't chase us with a bullet in the leg."

"Shoot to kill and be done with it," Oona said. "Us or them."

"Guys," Sam said.

"Oona, it's not their fault!" Laura said.

"I appreciate that, but it's still us or them, and I like us better."

"*Guys.* Why don't we just drive away? This thing still runs, doesn't it?"

⋮

The headlights drew attention to the car, but they had little choice. Ed didn't know the roads well enough to navigate in the dark, and there were people to avoid besides.

It was also helpful when they discovered other cars on the road. This happened after they made it out of the tiny side streets and back onto Main, at the far northern end and away from the thickest part of the sleepwalking horde.

Annie and Ed decided, en route, to stop calling them zombies and start calling them sleepwalkers, since the latter was more accurate and less terrifying, and also self-justified the decision not to run them over without prejudice. Plus, *the sleepwalker apocalypse* sounded sort of cute.

It was not, alas, entirely accurate, because Annie kept spotting people she knew who happened to be dead.

The other cars were operated by residents who were either not asleep at the right time or were not susceptible for some other reason yet to be explained. The first car they came across nearly killed them, as the driver was obviously not dealing with the reality of the situation well. He cut across a lawn just before they made it to the Main Street intersection, coming within a mailbox or two of side-swiping their driver's side before swerving into the ninety-degree left-hand turn ahead.

By the time Ed got the car to the same point, the other car was already ahead by three blocks. Its taillights disappeared at the bridge.

"They have the same idea," Ed said.

"I hope he made it to the bridge and didn't skid off the side of it, he wasn't all that in control."

"Must be his first apocalypse."

The speeding car did make the bridge, but he didn't get a lot farther. They caught up at the end of a line of traffic.

The northern bridge was one of the more impressive parts of the town, even if few thought much of it outside of its functional use: connecting the northern tip of Sorrow Falls with the town of Mount Hermon by spanning the river. It was impressive, more for its hundred-foot drop than its three-football-field length, and certainly not for its two-lane width.

There was no traffic heading into Sorrow Falls at this time. Instead, both sides of the solid double-yellow line were filled with cars attempting to get out, and honking loudly to see if that helped somehow.

"What's going on up there?" Annie asked.

"The sirens. Dammit. I wasn't thinking."

"What?"

"The lockdown. The army closed the checkpoint."

"It's a wooden barrier. They can just run through it. Are they worried about their cars at a time like this?"

"No, but the men with the guns on the other side of the wooden barrier might be a concern."

"They *wouldn't*."

"Annie, that's what their orders are. C'mon."

He turned off the car and climbed out.

"You think we can sneak past?" she asked, getting out.

"No, but maybe I can talk them into letting you through."

238 • GENE DOUCETTE

"You just said—"

"I know, but I have to try. The . . . sleepwalkers think you're the person they want. Maybe getting you out of town will end this whole thing."

He took her by the hand and started along the narrow space between the cars and the guardrail. There was a nominal sidewalk on each side of the bridge that was really only wide enough for one person at a time. The railing was more impressive, with a fence on the other side of it that was suicide-prevention tall.

It was a lot cooler on the bridge. The wind along the river cut right across and reminded Annie that her clothes still weren't entirely dry from getting caught in the downpour earlier. That seemed like it happened ages ago, and to someone else.

Behind them, other people were starting to get out of their cars. They'd started a trend. She was pretty sure this wasn't a good kind of trend.

"What did you mean, they *think* I'm the person they want?" she asked.

"I believe they're mistaken."

"That's sweet, but what makes you say that?"

"Just a theory I'm working on."

"You're just saying that to make me feel better."

"No, I mean it."

As anticipated, the end of the traffic jam was the army checkpoint. The gates were down, and four men with M16A2's just like the one Sam carried stood at the ready on the other side of those gates.

"Do you know any of them?" Ed asked.

"We're not close enough yet. Think it'll make a difference?"

"No idea. I'm pretty sure I don't, though, and I was sort of hoping I'd have more than just my ID to stand on."

They were still four cars away from the front when the driver of the first vehicle decided he'd had enough. Him Annie recognized: it was Lew Stempel. He was one of Hollis's foremen. She went to school with his daughter, Winnie.

Lew had apparently been sitting at the gates for a while, no doubt leaning on his horn the entire time—as she remembered it, he wasn't known as a patient guy—before jumping out and walking right up to the first soldier at the barricade. Annie wasn't close enough to hear what he was saying over the intermittent honking and the wind on the bridge, which was perpetual and considerable. His gestures were pretty easy to read, though.

He threw his hands in the air, and pointed at the crowd behind his car, and banged on his chest. All the while he was walking closer to the army's perimeter.

Two of the soldiers had their barrels trained on him, but he kept walking.

I dare you to shoot me, he was saying. It didn't look like they were going to.

Like Ed said, the army had orders, and if those orders meant to shoot an American citizen on U.S. soil, they were supposed to do it. This was one of those questions that came up from time to time in polite media conversations about Sorrow Falls: could a soldier really do that, if they had to?

So far, it looked like the answer was no.

Lew stepped around the gate and began arguing with the first of the guards face-to-face. This got more and more heated, and looked like a volatile enough situation for Ed to stop when still a couple of cars away, and put his arm across Annie's shoulders in that protective sort of way adults did sometimes.

"This might get bad," he said.

Lew abruptly pushed past the corporal and sprinted down the Mount Hermon side of the bridge.

The second soldier, who had neither been shoved nor directly confronted, took aim and fired a warning shot above the head of the fleeing man, a clear indication that this time, they would not hold their fire, and the next shot would not miss its mark.

It was the closest Annie had ever been to gunfire. She ducked instinctively, and let out a little scream she was immediately embarrassed about.

Lew was surprised too, and stopped in his tracks, but not entirely because of the gunshot. He stopped because of what happened to the bullet that missed him.

They all heard it, even over the horns. It was the sound described by the sheriff of Sorrow Falls three years earlier, when he fired a handgun at the spaceship: a deep THUD that resonated with the bottom of the stomach and caused knees to buckle.

"The ship's barrier expanded," Ed said. "That was what that feeling was."

"You're saying the only thing between us and getting out of Sorrow Falls is a few feet of depressing thoughts?" Annie asked.

"Maybe?"

Lew Stempel decided to continue running, perhaps reasonably concluding that at a certain point the army's bullets wouldn't be able to reach him.

Unfortunately for him, the nature of the defensive barrier changed. Instead of slowing down, becoming sad, and reversing course, Mr. Stempel reached a point where he could no longer move. It was like he was stuck in an invisible membrane, as perhaps he was. That membrane was flexible, like an elastic band, and also like an elastic band it didn't store energy for long.

Lew shot backwards. He was airborne for the first ten feet, and then rolled another five or six before bouncing to a stop.

Ed looked at Annie.

"Back to the car," he said. "Before we're trapped on this bridge."

⋮

It was to Oona's and Laura's immense credit that the trailer, which hadn't moved in over a year, started up immediately. There was gas in the tank, the engine was clean and the fluids filled, and the tires were fully inflated. This was as much a part of their monthly maintenance cycle as gun-cleaning, toilet-cleaning, and bullet-making.

At the same time, they'd been parked for so long, the idea of driving away was as odd to them as it would be if this were a real fortress instead of a tricked-out family camper.

"All right, she's started," Oona said from the driver's seat. It took ten minutes just to dig out the seat, which had been storing dirty laundry and unused Mason jars.

"Start driving," Sam suggested from the passenger seat.

"Where, and how?"

There was a sea of zombies in front of the vehicle. Half of them were ignoring the camper and walking downhill, but that didn't mean they weren't in the way.

"We can head to Main, maybe see what they're so interested in down there. If we don't like it, it's just a quick right over the bridge and out of town."

"Thought you said the soldiers were buttoning up."

"This thing's bullet-proof, isn't it?"

She laughed. "Most of it is. Windshield's not. Too expensive. We didn't plan to drive into gunfire, to be honest. Thought you were all about staying at your post."

"I was. But now I'm thinking it would be best if someone made it out of here to report on what's going on *in* here. I don't think signals are making it out."

"Plus you want to live through the night."

"I had that thought."

"So how do you want to get rid of all them?"

"I can start shooting at their feet, I guess. If I need to. They have a self-preservation instinct or they wouldn't freeze at the sound of a gunshot, so if you start rolling they may get out of your way."

Once they started moving, the zombies intent on tipping the trailer either lost interest or were engaged in extremely slow pursuit; it was basically impossible to tell the difference. Sam took up a position on the roof, using his own M16 to warn off any zombies about to wander into the path of the trailer, while Oona drove. Laura helped Sam using a rifle of her own. She wasn't properly trained on its use, exactly, so Sam had to spend a few minutes discussing the finer points of suppression and crowd-control fire.

It was slow going initially, with a lot of bumping to convince people to get out of the way, but it eventually worked well enough to get the trailer out of the dirt and onto the road.

"Hey, did you guys get a chance to analyze any of this?" Dobbs

242 · GENE DOUCETTE

asked. He was inexperienced with guns and showed no interest in learning, so while Sam and Laura patrolled the roof, Dobbs sat down with the electronics to see what was what.

"Oona will shoot you in the face if you touch any of that," Laura said.

"Nah she won't. This is pretty cool, what you've got going on here. These archives? How come you never shared any of this?"

Laura looked over his shoulder.

"These are under password, how the hell did you get in?"

"She left it open, I swear."

"I repeat, she'll shoot you when she finds out."

"Aw, c'mon, Laura, the world's already ending, this is no time to be guarding secrets."

Laura sighed and went back to her position at the edge of the roof.

"You guys captured a new audio signal before we started driving, did you know?" Dobbs asked.

"No. Play it."

He tapped a few commands, and the audio file played over the speakers.

"That's someone breathing," Sam said.

"We've been getting that for a month," Laura said. "It's too constant to be a person, though."

"Are you sure?" Sam asked. "Some of the guys were sleeping behind the ship at night. Not me, but some of the guys."

"Unless one of them was asleep for the entire month, it's not that."

The breathing accelerated drastically, and got louder. It sounded like the wind of a man in a sprint.

"Well, that's new," she said.

"If that was really coming from the ship, I'm sure we would have known about it," Sam said.

Dobbs laughed. "You think they'd tell you?"

"I think if the spaceship started breathing, yes, someone would tip us off."

"But it's not the ship . . . oh, hah! That's brilliant."

"What?" Laura asked.

"You know, I bet the government's scientists never even heard this. You met with that guy, right? Annie's friend, the guy *writing an article?*"

He put the last words in air quotes to point out how little he believed this.

"We did, yes."

"Did you show him this? What did he think?"

"I don't think he took it seriously."

"But it was news to him, wasn't it?"

"I think it was."

"Betcha the government's audio sensors had a filter in place. Something that excluded known sources of sound. It'd be the right choice if you want to pick up a small sound hiding beneath the crickets and the traffic and all that. The better the program the worse it would be for them."

"That makes sense," Laura said. "The ship listened to the sounds in the field, and then when it needed to do something that made a noise it mimicked the native sounds. The government filtered it out because it thought it was manmade."

"Why did it need to make a noise?" Sam asked.

"That's the best part," Dobbs said. "If this timeline is correct, I'm pretty sure you guys captured the zombie communications channel."

⋮

The car was blocked from behind by the time they reached it, but there was room to conduct a three-point turn using the left lane, which wasn't yet full of cars driven by people thinking they could escape the presumption of carnage only a zombie apocalypse can deliver.

The road leading off the bridge was about as narrow as the bridge itself, but only went about two hundred feet before connecting with Main. Annie wasn't sure where Ed intended to take her next. There were plenty of other ways out of Sorrow Falls that didn't involve bridges, and more than a few that also didn't involve

244 • GENE DOUCETTE

army checkpoints, but if what they just saw held true in all directions they were stuck within a containment field being maintained by the spaceship itself. If that were the case, there wasn't going to be anyplace he could take Annie safely. Half the town was zombies (the *sleepwalker* thing just wasn't going to stick) and she saw no reason to expect them to stop until they had what they wanted.

Or, in this case, *who* they wanted.

The zombies, last seen amassing at the clinic, had adjusted their route and were heading down the street toward the bridge, and there was no real explanation for why they were doing that other than that Annie had moved from the clinic to the bridge, and they wanted Annie. Or Ed, theoretically, since he was with her at both locations. It seemed unlikely, but the possibility existed.

"How did they find us so quickly?" she asked.

"Don't know, but I'm not happy about it."

They were closing off the end of the road.

"You may have to plow through a few zombies if you want to get us out of here," Annie said.

"Maybe not."

He gunned the engine right up to the edge of the horde, and then slowed abruptly, nearly to a complete stop. The people in front of him showed no predilection for getting out of his way when it looked like he was going to barrel through them, and were no more willing to step aside when he slowed.

"Duck down," he said.

"What are you going to do?"

"Just do it!"

She slid down until her head wasn't visible through the window.

Ed started rolling the car forward at a pace no faster than five miles an hour. She could hear the front of the car brushing up against people. It sounded like they were going through a dry car wash.

"If I can just . . . nudge them . . ."

The car kept rolling. Every now and then it would slow until he surged the engine to get a little more power behind it, and then the stubborn obstacle before him either gave way or fell over.

"Is it working?"

"I think so. We're almost to Main . . . uh-oh."

He was looking in the rearview mirror.

"What is it?"

"They stopped walking to the bridge. They're circling back."

"Back to where?"

The rear windshield shattered from a heavy blow. It didn't explode in pieces, because car glass was good like that. Instead, it fell down into the back seat as a single sheet.

Annie screamed.

"Dammit," Ed muttered. Then he punched it.

The engine screamed, and the car lurched forward, then up, then forward again. Annie was practically on the floor of the car, and could feel every bump and thud through the undercarriage. Without question, they were running over people.

Meanwhile, someone was trying to crawl into the car through the space left by the shattered rear window. It was a woman Annie didn't recognize, clinging onto the side of the opening and bleeding from the pieces of glass stuck in the frame. She was probably on the lower side of her forties, this woman. Maybe she was a mother of one of the younger kids in town. She could be someone who liked antiquing, and ice cream, and Sunday choir. Now she was running the risk of losing a finger as her vacant eyes searched the car for Annie.

Ed hit a rough patch in the road and started to fishtail. Annie could feel them losing control.

"Slow down before we end up in the river," Annie shouted.

"You are . . ." the woman in the window said.

"If I slow down we're stuck. I'm . . . dragging at least three people. Hold on tight."

"To what?"

"Um, okay, sit up, get your seat belt on."

She pulled herself back up into the bucket seat and strapped in. The woman clinging to the rear appreciated this, clearly, as she started saying "You are" even louder.

The hood of the car had a passenger too, a confused-looking

young man Annie recognized as a customer of the diner. His expression seemed to indicate that he had no more idea than anyone else why he was riding the outside of a moving car.

Ahead of them, townspeople were converging on a point just ahead of the hood of the car. There was no way anything short of a tank was going to make it through all of them.

"What are you going to do?" she asked.

"Look left."

She did. There were more zombies, but on the other side was an empty space for about ten feet, beyond which was Main.

"No, no, no, don't do that."

"Why not, it's clear."

"It's clear because the grass is hiding a crevasse."

"You're exaggerating."

"I'm dead serious. There's a crease right there."

"A crease? I can jump a crease."

"Ed . . ."

There was no more discussion, because then Ed jerked the wheel to the left and floored the gas, and committed to the move.

The space he was aiming for actually had a name, and that name was Charlie's Pocket. It was well established long before the early demise of one Charles Dane Fincus that it was possible, if not paying attention, to miss the turn for the bridge, but Charlie performed the feat so spectacularly that he was the one everyone talked about when they talked about the pocket at all.

Building the bridge meant extending the land from the level of Main Street to the edge of the river. The process left a little lip of space at the corner, on both sides, where Main dropped off but before the land build-up for the bridge commenced. Most parts of the year, the void was invisible, either due to the naturally growing long grasses that came up from the riverfront, or snowdrifts.

One night some years prior, Charlie Fincus took the turn for the bridge at a speed estimated after the fact to be somewhere in the range of seventy miles per hour. He missed the road, and hit the pocket instead. At that speed, the pocket turned into a slalom course that carried his car straight down on its side until it rammed into the edge of the river, flipped up, and landed upside down in the water.

Charlie wasn't wearing his seat belt, so he didn't make it all the way to the river in the car. Instead, he was flung like a rock from a sling when his Chevy went hood over tailpipe. He landed on the riverbank, but what made the story so memorable was that the bank he landed on was on the other side of the river. He died on impact, thankfully.

Annie knew the legend of Charlie's Pocket, but didn't think she had enough time to convey it to Ed, who wasn't working with a ton of options anyway. She was just glad the town hadn't gotten around to putting up the necessary guardrails yet, a rare instance of bureaucracy working in someone's favor.

The car hit the curb at an angle, the left tire bouncing up before the right, turning them a little bit too even with the edge of the bridge. Their momentum corrected for it in time, though — barely — so they hit the pocket with a little speed.

The good news was that when they went airborne they lost the people (or parts of them) that were being dragged. The bad news was that they weren't airborne nearly long enough to clear the jump. The weight of the engine block pulled the nose right down to the ground, and far too soon. Ed hit the gas as soon as the front tires were down, but by then the car was already facing a twenty-degree angle. In other words, while the car's nose was pointed at Main, it wasn't heading in that direction. It was sliding into the pocket.

"Annie, you're going to have to jump from the car," Ed said, way more calmly than such a statement warranted.

"What?"

"I mean it, right now. Unbuckle, open the door, and jump as far as you can."

"What about you?"

"I have to hold my foot on the gas so you can get free. Soon as you're out, I'll join you."

"C'mon, that's what people say right before they die in a ball of—"

"Annie, please!"

"Right, but I better see you in a minute."

"You will, I promise."

She unbuckled, pushed open the door, and jumped clear, into tall grass that hid an unanticipated steepness.

As soon as she was out, the car gave in to gravity. It slid past her and caught the deep part of Charlie's Pocket. It didn't stop until it reached the river.

She didn't see Ed get clear.

"Dammit, Ed, now what am I supposed to do?"

It seemed unreasonably quiet, lying there in the tall grass. She could hear her own breathing, and the car grinding to a stop at the riverbank, but she was beneath the bridge and the road, and so insulated from the sound coming from those places. It was oddly peaceful, and staying right there was tempting. Maybe the zombies wouldn't find her there, and if they did, it was possible every one of them would slide into the pocket and never get near her.

It wasn't a terrible plan, and she couldn't think of anywhere else to go.

"You are . . ."

The woman from the back of the car made it out okay, it looked like. She was halfway down the hill and climbing in Annie's direction. It made for a compelling reason *not* to stay where she was.

Violet's. I could go there.

She would need to find a car, or find someone with a car.

Just break into a house and find the car key, that's all.

It wouldn't have been all that difficult, not with everyone in town on the streets. Zombies weren't driving, and there were twelve blocks of row house residences less than a mile to her left. Sure, driving the car anywhere was going to end up being a serious challenge, but one thing at a time. Annie couldn't stay where she was, so even if stealing a car wasn't really a viable long-term plan, it was at least a plan.

She got up and started climbing. Main was pretty close, and she was a fast runner, and none of these people were moving all that quickly. She could do it.

When she reached the edge of the ravine and got to her feet, she realized with some measure of horror how mistaken she'd been.

Every single zombie from the edge of bridge road to the corner of Main was looking right at her.

"Oh," she said. "Hello, everyone."

Someone came up from behind and grabbed her arm. She screamed.

"It's me, it's me," Ed said.

"Jesus Christ!" She slapped him in the chest. "I thought you were dead, don't do that to me!"

"I'm sorry, I thought you saw me! I landed on the other side of the ravine. I waved."

"You *waved?*"

"I didn't want to shout."

Annie pointed at the crowd. "Like that would have mattered."

"Well, I know that now. So, um . . . what's our plan?"

"Learn to fly."

"Any other ideas?"

"Why aren't they moving?" she asked.

"I think they're waiting for you to move. They have you cornered."

"Not really."

She nodded to their left.

The last building on the eastern side of Main was a gas station. South of the station, the land between the river and the road opened up to allow for the row house neighborhoods, but on the back side of the gas station itself was nothing but open space leading to the river. Directly behind the garage was a flat area wide enough for a person but not a car. There weren't any zombies standing on that ground.

"Run behind the station, cut right to Main, steal a car, win the game. What do you think?" she asked.

"Sounds good to me. Except I've never stolen a car."

"Neither have I."

"I mean I don't know how to hot-wire one."

"Ed . . . one thing at a time. We run on three. Ready?"

19
WHERE THE SIDEWALK ENDS

*T*hings got worse the closer they got to Main. The zombies—both kinds—were more common, creating a real jam on the road. This was not at all helped by the people who were awake and still in full possession of their faculties. Those folks were basically freaking out all over the place.

Aside from their catchphrase, the zombies were mostly silent, and once they concluded the person in front of them wasn't the person or thing they were looking for, they were content to leave them alone. The problem was with the living/awake, because they were seeing friends and family stumble around and act collectively weird, and that was a little terrifying. The impulse was to do the same thing Dobbs did when Art Shoeman first stumbled down the road: stop, grab, confront.

This was perceived as a threat. As lumbering and seemingly mindless and aimless as the horde was, when there was a threat, they acted in concert as well as any army Sam had ever seen or heard of. They were a formidable opponent, or would be if they mastered tools and moved a little faster.

Every minute or two Sam heard someone scream, shout, or beg for help, and knew he was hearing a citizen discover the consequence of threatening a zombie.

He also knew he couldn't do anything about it.

"This is terrible," Sam said, as the latest piercing cry turned into a strangled gurgle.

"End of the world, Soldier," Laura said.

They were still at their post at the head of the camper roof, looking for targets, but it had been a while since a shot was required. They'd reached some sort of unspoken mutual understanding with the zombies: the camper wouldn't run them over if they didn't get in the way. It meant they were essentially traveling at the same speed as a tired jogger, but at least they were moving.

"Where's the rest of your boys?" Laura asked. "I thought the military was here for just this situation."

"Yeah, I don't know. My last communication with the base . . . it sounded like they were under attack. I have to wonder if anyone even made it out."

"Under attack from whom?"

"Well, themselves. The ones who were sleeping. If I were the spaceship controlling these guys, I'd give the soldier zombies a different agenda, wouldn't you? At least the ones on the base."

"Take out the biggest threat in the area."

"Exactly. But, you know, I'm just guessing. All radio communication is down. The sirens and the landlines are the only things working."

"Internet's down," Dobbs said. "I think the ship is cutting us off from the rest of the world too, not just each other." He looked up. "Like a dome over the town."

"That happened early, I saw it," Laura said. "Are you having any luck with the signal?"

Dobbs had been typing furiously for a while, to the eternal annoyance of Oona, who kept shouting expletives through the floor regarding "nerd-boy" ruining her data.

"No. I think there's a signal embedded in the audio you picked up, but the equipment may not have captured all of it."

"It's pretty precise equipment."

"Sure, but this signal was designed to be picked up by a different kind of receiver, and if you *had* recorded all of it I'm not sure I'd want to listen."

"What kind of receiver?" Sam asked.

"A human brain."

"Oh."

"I do have an idea, though. We know the ship is using some kind of subsonic radio frequency to deliver instructions. Maybe it's enough to know the brains of these people are susceptible to that kind of information packet."

"I don't understand," Sam said.

"I do," Laura said. "You want to go up the scale, see if anything resonates?"

"Worth a shot."

Laura turned to Sam. "He's going to try using sound as a weapon."

"Because their brains are . . . never mind," Sam said. "If it makes sense to you guys, go for it. Maybe you can use that, to make it louder."

He pointed to the microphone array above the electronics table.

"That's for receiving," Dobbs said. "This isn't like thrusters in *Star Trek*, we can't just reverse them and turn a microphone into an amplifier."

"I know that. But those microphones are embedded in a parabolic shell. You can use the shell to amplify the sound from those external speakers on the computer."

". . . Oh. Yes, good idea. We can do that."

⋮

The seismic event recorded at 10:17 p.m. EST was captured by most of the sensors sharing the field with the Sorrow Falls spaceship, and also by the usual USGS systems some distance from Massachusetts.

Given that the epicenter was quickly identified as being Sorrow Falls itself, it was of no particular surprise to anyone when the USGS reported that this was not a true earthquake. The cause was not a tectonic plate shift, but a source of tremendous energy on the surface. It was likened to the effect of a large object striking the Earth's crust from space, only without applying brakes first.

When the sensors in the field captured data relating to the quake, that data was conveyed along the ground cable leading from the field up to the base, where it was dumped to an extremely well-guarded cloud drive. There was a tremendous amount of data in that drive, but very little information. In essence, if one of the sensors measured something about the ship, that measurement could be taken a million times, creating a million data points, but if it was the *same* measurement—if the numbers never changed—no new *information* was being obtained. The best that could be said about most of this data was that it could be proven, microscopically, that the ship wasn't different in any appreciable way than it had been three years earlier.

This wasn't true of every sensor, but it was pretty close to true.

The cloud drive capturing the input data was built with certain alarms. If any one of those millions of data points happened to diverge significantly, a program established to monitor the input would blast a text to a discrete number of people around the world. (That discrete number, at 10:17 p.m. EST, was twelve. No other people on the planet had access to the cloud drive data.)

Twenty-two such text blasts were sent in a span of two seconds, which was enough to get all of those twelve scientists logged into the drive by 10:20 p.m. EST.

Exactly one minute later, all contact with Sorrow Falls was severed.

There were really only two pinch points in the communications channel: either the cable to the base was severed—which would have required an explosive, or an axe and a good deal of dedication—or the wireless tether between the army base and the drive was interrupted.

Dr. Louisa Sark, the first of the twelve, administrator of the cloud drive and one of only three members on the team who did *not* have a Nobel Prize, followed protocol. First, she reached out to the tech room at the Sorrow Falls base. The phone rang, but nobody picked up. Second—and this wasn't strictly protocol—she called the cell phone of one of the base's technicians with whom she was friendly. The call couldn't be completed. This, she decided, was a strong indication that the connection between the base and the drive was the problem. It also convinced her something serious was happening in Sorrow Falls.

The third call was to the Pentagon.

Dr. Sark had misgivings about this part, but in addition to being an astrophysicist, she was an employee of the government, and one of her responsibilities was to report information regarding their extraterrestrial visitor to the military. Most of the time, the reports she filed were unspectacular, but she was perfectly aware of the consequences of a spectacular report, because she knew exactly what the Pentagon's contingency plans looked like. She'd consulted on them.

She knew that by making the third phone call, there was a very good chance she was sentencing the entire town of Sorrow Falls to death.

At 11:03 p.m. EST, two fighter jets and a bomber were scrambled from Hanscom Air Force Base. At the same time, a contingent of army soldiers were dispatched from Fort Devens, and the police departments of Oakdale, Mount Hermon, Harbridge, and Brattleboro, plus the Massachusetts, Vermont, and New Hampshire state police, were all put on alert. Everyone had the same orders: find out what the hell was happening in Sorrow Falls.

At 11:17 p.m. EST, a Massachusetts state trooper named Gellman tried to approach the town from the south, across the bridge connecting the bottom of Main with Oakdale. He failed to get his car more than halfway across the bridge before it stalled, and refused to restart.

Trooper Gellman encountered a Sorrow Falls resident named Rodney Delindo, who claimed to have been trying to get home across the same bridge for the past fifteen minutes, unsuccessfully. Mr. Delindo reported that there was a force preventing him from crossing on foot, and that same force appeared to be disabling autos.

Gellman could see cars attempting to cross from Sorrow Falls into Oakdale. Army men stood at their sentry point post and appeared to be barking orders at the cars, and then firing shots above their heads, but he could hear neither the orders nor the gunshots. Mr. Delindo reported that in the few minutes he'd been standing on the bridge he had seen persons wandering on the Main Street side in a manner he described as "zombie-like."

At 11:22 p.m. EST, the report submitted orally by Gellman became the first confirmation that Sorrow Falls had been compromised in some unknown way. It was also the first report of zombies, but most considered that portion little more than poetic hyperbole.

Similar reports came in from other parts of the surrounding area.

The points at which the inbound roads became impassible were not perfectly in sync with the town property lines: some points were well outside the town line, and a few were over a hundred feet inside of it. At roughly 11:45 p.m. EST, an intrepid individual in the war room at the Pentagon—for this was where the next decision logically had to be made—mapped the points and connected them. The line he drew formed a circle.

At the center of that circle was the spaceship.

The president was awoken at 11:56 p.m. EST, briefed from 11:59 until 12:17, and then presented with the considered opinion of his army chief of staff.

At 12:23 a.m. EST, for the first time in history, the president of the United States ordered the military bombing of a domestic target.

There was already a bomber in the sky above Sorrow Falls. At 12:27, the order came through, the crew of four said a quiet prayer for the population beneath them, and then they released two thermobaric bombs.

Thermobaric explosives were the obvious choice, for being by far the most destructive non-nuclear option available. According to everyone's understanding of physics, one of these bombs would destroy the spaceship and everything else in a three-mile radius. Two such devices were frankly considered overkill.

As it turned out, the spaceship disagreed with the planetary consensus regarding the laws of physics as they pertained to explosive blasts and shock waves.

The bombs never reached the surface. It was the considered opinion of all who watched this happen that the devices did in fact explode, but the devastation that should have followed an airborne detonation failed to happen as well.

There was a bright flash, but that was all. What should have followed—even with an airborne detonation—was a concussive wave, and that wave should have taken out the bomber and both fighter jets, everyone in Sorrow Falls, and a whole lot of the people in the surrounding towns.

None of that happened. Instead, something above the town swallowed all the energy from the bombs.

It was, in its own way, the most terrifying show of force anyone had ever seen. It led to possibly a much more important question: if that was the ship's defense, what did its offense look like?

⋮

There were only about five or six legitimately famous people left in Sorrow Falls. For the most part, the people lucky enough to be involved in some verifiable way with the events surrounding the arrival of the spaceship had cashed out and moved to a wealthier zip code. Billy Pederson was one of the few who hadn't.

From everything Ed knew about Billy, he considered staying put something to be boastful about, and mentioned it in all interviews. A cynic or a professional analyst (Ed was both) would say Billy wanted to remain in the public eye and knew enough about his own brand to appreciate that without a constant, direct association with the ship and the town, he was distinctively un-famous.

In a way, this approach worked, because people still put him on television now and then. He had a handsome face and an easygoing style in front of the camera that made him perfect for anything from a fifteen-second spot to a two-minute piece. Any longer than that and his appeal ran aground, which was why his efforts to turn himself into—in order—an actor, a television commentator, and a reality TV star all failed.

Still, most everybody knew who Billy Pederson was and could identify him easily. Ed was able to do this even when encountering Billy in the dark behind the Yarn Palace while hitting him in the head with a baseball bat.

Ed had actually planned to speak to Billy while in Sorrow Falls. It was going to be for appearances, mainly, because Ed was thinking it would be easy to fool people into thinking he was a journalist, and a real journalist would of course speak to Billy Pederson. But their free times never quite lined up, and once it was clear nobody really believed Ed was writing a magazine article, he stopped trying so hard to make the appointment. None of that factored into the moment when he clubbed Billy with a stick, but it did lead to Ed feeling a little bit worse for having done it, for reasons he couldn't fully explain.

This was perhaps forty-five minutes after Ed and Annie fled the scene at Charlie's Pocket. They'd run down the line behind the Main Street businesses for a block, until the area behind the shops widened into the row house neighborhoods. This, at first, seemed like a good thing, because the bigger the territory, the more places there were to hide. A lot of people lived in those blocks, though, so there were a whole lot of zombies wandering around. It was quickly apparent that they could make up for their slowness afoot with high volumes and coordinated movement.

Ed and Annie barely made it back up the hill to the shops again. On three occasions one of the townspeople got close enough to grab and hold down Annie, so Ed had to learn very quickly what was involved in getting them to let go. It seemed to be a combination of her screaming and him whacking them in the head with whatever was available. A shriek at the right pitch appeared to confuse them somehow—something Beth commented on earlier in the day—and the blow to the cranium stunned the zombies enough for Annie to wriggle loose.

By the time Billy grabbed ahold of her behind the Yarn Palace, they'd gotten pretty good at it, and Ed stopped thinking of the people whose skulls he was damaging as people at all. Then he recognized whom he'd just clubbed and felt terrible about it.

It was another fifteen minutes of hiding and sprinting and hiding before they made it to the back of the diner.

Annie had a key.

"Not that I know who to call, but the landlines are down too, in case you were wondering," Annie said, emerging from the kitchen. She had a first aid kit and a look of concern. The latter probably had to do with the lump above Ed's left eye.

He was sitting at one of the counter stools, which was just a mistake. The chair had no back to it, and without the constant fear of death his adrenaline was dropping.

This is when people faint.

"Okay, let me have a look at that," Annie said. She opened the kit on the counter. Ed took off his glasses and let her have a look.

"Gonna leave a mark?" he asked.

"Probably. It's just a lump, though, no cut. Don't know what I was thinking with this kit, you need some ice."

She disappeared in back again.

"You could have called the president," Ed said. He reached into the first aid kit and pulled out a couple of bandages, which he decided he probably needed too. His body was starting to notify him of a variety of trouble areas on his person that might in fact be bleeding. Scratches, mostly. He was glad zombie-ism wasn't contagious in Sorrow Falls like it was in the movies.

Annie re-emerged with a dishtowel wrapped around ice cubes.

"I don't know his number."

He took the ice, removed his glasses, and pressed the towel to the lump. He was a little alarmed by how large the bump felt.

"I do."

"Ooh. So what would we even say? 'Mr. President, Sorrow Falls is overrun by zombies?' He'd think we were pranking him."

"Prank calls don't make it to the Oval Office. But I think I'd tell him not to bomb us."

"Not to . . . why would they do that?"

"It's one of the contingency plans."

"That's a really crummy plan."

"That's the nature of contingency plans. They tend to be awful, but they exist to stop something even more awful from happening."

"What kind of bomb, Ed?"

Ed didn't answer, which was an answer unto itself.

"Jesus Christ, how is *that* a better option?"

Ed laughed.

"You don't really realize what you've been next to all this time. I don't think anyone in this town does. You know, we tried to move it once? The plan was hatched after the first year. We became convinced that thing was just a large piece of abandoned tech. So we got the idea to just scoop up the entire field and roll it out of town. Heavy earth-moving equipment was requisitioned and everything."

"I don't believe you. I would have seen the diggers."

"They never made it into town. Things kept happening en route. Trucks would stall, engines would blow, and steering columns would lock up. Nothing made it all the way. And that's the problem. That ship is plugged into our communications in a way we can't even understand, and it can affect mechanical equipment at a distance that extends far beyond the immediate area."

"Wow."

"Yes, wow. And it gets worse. The next plan after that was to install failsafe explosives around the ship. That way, if things went wonky someone would just push a button and blow up half of Sorrow Falls. Remember that munitions explosion last year?"

"Yeah, that was a terrorist thing."

"That was the story, certainly."

"But that was in Delaware or something."

"Yes. It was. The devices that failed were the exact ones scheduled for installation in Sorrow Falls, down to the last serial number. The message wasn't subtle."

"Message?"

"It can hurt us anywhere, anytime, and more important, it

doesn't want to move. Most people assume it landed in Sorrow Falls at random, but that's not the case at all. It wants to be right here, in this town. And after three years, we still don't know why. We do know how to destroy an entire town, though, if we have to. We're pretty good at that."

Annie stepped away from the counter, to the front window. The curtains were closed, or they'd have zombies trying to break in already. By his estimation, they had maybe ten minutes before the group collectively figured out exactly where he and Annie were, and then it would be over, because as much as it was to their benefit short-term to find a place to hole up and rest, in the long term, they were cornered.

Annie peeked around one of the curtains.

"We know it wants me," she said.

"We don't know that."

"All right, it thinks it wants me. What's the difference?"

"We don't know what it wants you *for*. Maybe it's just mad you screwed up the paint job on the hull."

"Funny."

"I'm serious, what's happening out there doesn't even make sense. If the goal was to get you to the ship, the zombies would be giving us free access to the southern half of Main, but they aren't."

"You mean they would be herding us there."

"That's exactly what I mean."

"Well, what we're doing isn't working, is it?"

"We're on the wrong side of the town is all. We just need to get across Main somehow."

"They're lined up out front. I don't think we'd make it."

She closed the curtain.

"What if I went alone?" she asked. "Like, what if they aren't herding us to the ship because you're with me and I'm supposed to go by myself."

"And what if they want to find you so they can tear you apart? I can't let you do that."

"Like you could stop me?"

"Annie . . ."

"Well, what other choices do we have? Surrender's the only thing we haven't tried, and maybe if I do it you'll make it out alive."

None of us are making it out alive tonight, he thought.

"I'm not about to let a sixteen-year-old sacrifice herself for me."

"Not just for you. The whole town."

"Well, that's very noble of you, but we need a better option."

"Like what?"

"I don't know, but . . . Annie, they don't want you to bring you back to their planet and make you a princess. This isn't a movie. This is a malevolent force fixated on you, and we have to assume the worst because we've been given no indication to think otherwise."

"And yet no better options are forthcoming. Like you said about contingency plans, if all we have left are bad options, isn't this the least bad option?"

"I'm not ready to—"

"Wait."

"What?"

"Shh. Do you hear that?"

"Do I hear what?"

Annie opened the curtain and looked down the southern end of Main.

"I don't believe it," she said. Then she was out the front door before Ed could even ask what was happening.

He stumbled to his feet, a whole lot more dizzy than he probably should have been prior to facing off a zombie horde. He grabbed the baseball bat that had only recently brained a local celebrity and staggered to the front, wishing he had time to grab a butcher's knife or something. Not that he knew what to do with one in a combat situation.

He was at the door when he heard what sounded like a woman screaming. It wasn't Annie. It sounded a little like Beth, but it wasn't her either.

He stepped outside. Joanne's Diner had one of those old-fashioned front porches, with wood benches for people to sit at and watch the town drive by. It was a quaint touch that almost demanded the road in front of it be composed of dirt and only used by horse-drawn carriages.

Annie was standing at the edge of the steps leading to the sidewalk that ran along Main. A modest horde of zombies was amassed along the curb in neat double rows, ready for her to make a move.

She was ignoring them, because up the road a camper was creeping toward them. The screaming sound was coming from the camper.

"Who is that?" Ed asked.

"Not sure, but look."

She was pointing to the townspeople closest to the camper. They were stumbling about like drunken zombies, no longer fully in control of their limbs.

"That's brilliant," Ed said. "They found a frequency that disrupts the zombies somehow. This could give us an opening."

"An opening? How about a ride?"

She took her first step off the porch. The zombies in line ahead of them took a counteraction, meaning to surround her. But then their synchrony came apart like a loose string pulled out of a sweater, as the trailer reached the front of the diner.

Ed was about to say all sorts of things about how they didn't even know who was driving or whether they were friendly when Annie spotted someone she recognized on the roof.

"HEY, CORPORAL!" she shouted. "CAN A GIRL GET A LIFT?"

⋮

It was no longer possible to tell who was a zombie and who wasn't.

At first, it was pretty easy. There were the zombies on the other side of the fence, who were clearly undead creatures who recently unburied themselves from the cemetery over the hill. They responded well to head shots, and stayed down without a fuss. Dill could have dealt with their kind all night.

The soldier-zombies were an entirely different matter, but even then—at first—it wasn't too hard to draw the line. The "dead" was made up of soldiers who had recently been sleeping in the barracks, just like Vogel was. And also like Vogel, they carried themselves with a singular determination to kill.

Dill ended up reflecting on this particular point during a quiet moment. Hank only went murder-happy after being interrupted in his task—whatever the hell that was—while on this night everyone hopped out of bed and went bonkers immediately. No weird *are you?* questions from these guys.

The implication was obvious. *The ship's coming after us,* he thought.

The best way to tell the men under the control of the ship apart from the ones who weren't was to see who had a gun and who didn't, because it turned out weapons training wasn't a part of the zombie combat manual. This should have made it a whole lot easier to resolve the attack as quickly as Dill and Wen had at the fence. But no matter how well you train a person, for the most part they're not going to be ready to shoot down half of everyone they know, whether those people are technically already dead or not.

This was another thing Dill spent a lot of time wondering during the free moments when it made more sense to hide and be quiet and hold his breath. Were they dead or not? If there was a way to make the ship *stop* doing whatever it was doing to them—and there wasn't even a second when anybody reviewing this situation considered it the fault of anything other than the spaceship—would the men just . . . wake up and be okay?

It was both a compelling and a terrible question, because every armed soldier, at one point or another, shot a zombie in self-defense. It was nice to think the blame for the death rested squarely with the aliens (or whatever was in the ship) but it was still the bullet that did the damage.

Soldiers weren't supposed to think like that. But when the enemy was the same guy you just played poker with the day before, or ate with that evening, or shot hoops with last week . . . there wasn't any kind of training to prep you for that. A guy would have to be psycho to be ready to dive into that kind of situation feet first, and the army was supposed to keep an eye out for that kind of crazy.

This was how things got out of hand so fast. The guys with the guns hesitated in using them too often, and ended up overrun. That was only the second-worst thing about it. The worst was, unless they were torn apart completely, they ended up as the more traditionally deceased kind of zombie, just adding to the army of the enemy.

By the time Dill found a corner near the motor pool in which to hide, it was literally impossible to tell who was who. Everyone had on fatigues, and the guy you were standing next to a minute earlier might be the dead version of that same guy, and you wouldn't know until he came at you.

He could still hear the occasional gunshot, shouted command, and cry for help. There were small pockets of living soldiers out there in the night—the base's lights had been out for an hour—but Dill was about as likely to hook up with one of those pockets as he was to learn how to fly.

It made a lot more sense to grab one of the armored Humvees and drive out.

He'd been watching mini-hordes of zombies stumble through the motor yard for twenty minutes. They didn't seem to distinguish the vehicle from the buildings, or the buildings for trees. Their ability to identify a moving person as a threat was about the best they could do, and the upshot was that none of them appeared to care that there was a car just sitting there and waiting for someone to take it.

Swallowing every bit of courage he had left, Dill slipped his rifle under the jacket beneath his left arm, and stood.

Running to the Humvee would have been a mistake. It was only twenty yards, but the zombies reacted to running. Instead, he walked, slowly, his arm dangling to conceal the gun, his breathing as slow as he could make it without blacking out.

There were at least a dozen of them in the open space. He assumed they were communicating with each other silently somehow—their attacks were coordinated yet they never spoke—so if one got close he would probably recognize Dill as not being One of Them. He tried to meander in such a way as to prevent that from happening.

It was just about the most terrifying thing he'd done on a night full of pretty terrifying things. Probably the worst part was when he realized he was looking at Corporal Wen from twenty feet away. Wen was clearly deceased because living people didn't tend to walk like that with a broken collarbone. Just as clearly, the dead didn't retain any memories the living held, because Wen looked right past him.

When he got to the door of the Humvee he stood motionless for about fifteen seconds before slowly . . . slowly . . . trying the door latch. It was unlocked. This was, in truth, only a minor bit of good fortune because the window was down. More important was the question of where the ignition key was.

Normally, keys were left in the vehicles parked in the pool, which was just good practice on a base where any one of them might need to commission a vehicle. But just because that was the practice didn't mean that in this instance the key was actually there. On a day when the world wasn't ending, this would've meant only a temporary inconvenience, because there were more Humvees at the other end of the yard to choose from. But that was pretty far away in the zombie base world, and once he opened the door he'd be letting everyone around know he wasn't one of them, so sprinting the yard wasn't going to end well.

After steeling himself for what was to come, he opened the door, threw his rifle in the passenger seat, and climbed in. The door he pulled closed as slowly as possible, just short of slamming it shut and engaging the lock. First, he had to check for the key . . .

. . . it wasn't there.

"Dammit," he muttered.

Directly in front of him, about thirty feet, one of the zombies adopted a pose Dill was familiar with. It meant *something's not right over there.*

He was about to grab the rifle and reopen the door for his final death-sprint when he felt something cold touch his neck.

"Are you one of them?"

It was a voice he didn't recognize, and it was too high for an adult. He thought maybe it belonged to a kid. The gun barrel against his neck didn't much care who was holding the other end, though.

"I can talk, and I can drive, so no I ain't."

"No telling, maybe they learned how to do those things."

"Well they didn't. Or if they did, I'm not one of 'em anyway. Do you have the keys? 'Cuz they're coming, and if you don't you may as well pull the trigger and then use that on yourself because they're gonna do worse."

"I want you to take me to a friend in this, can you do that?"

"I can drive you to Nebraska if you wanna go, but I need the keys."

"Not Nebraska, just up the road. I want to make sure she's okay."

"Sure, fine."

The kid—it was definitely a kid—held the keys out next to Dill's face. He snatched them out of the air, slammed the door closed, and started the engine.

This got everyone's attention.

He raised the windows and flipped on the headlights.

"You better put that gun down and belt yourself in, son, this is gonna be real unpleasant."

He snuck a peek in the mirror at his hijacker.

"You're the kid from the farmhouse on the other side of the fence," Dill said. "What are you even doing here?"

"I sneak on the base all the time," he said.

"You picked about the worst time to try tonight, didn't you?"

"Are you gonna drive?"

"Sure am."

Dill found a gear and stomped on the gas pedal.

The gate leading to the street was straight ahead through a guarded checkpoint with a lowered yellow crossbar, and an unknown number of zombies. The guards were gone and the bar was made of wood, but the people jumping in the way were going to slow them down. Fortunately, a military Humvee was essentially designed to drive over people.

"Tell me again what you're doing here?" Dill asked.

"I heard the gunshots," the kid said. "I was worried she might be here."

"Who's that?"

"My friend Annie. I saw her here before."

"Oh sure," Dill said. He aimed straight for a drill sergeant named Keith and tried not to feel guilty about enjoying the experience of running him over. Then he heard the sound the man made as his body went under the wheels and decided there was nothing about this to enjoy at all.

"Do you know her?"

"My buddy Sam does," Dill said. "I met her once. She's a real sweetheart."

The boy tensed up. "I want to make sure she's all right is all."

"Don't worry, she wasn't at the base. I'd'a known. She's probably fine. I bet your parents are worried, though, huh?"

"My parents are zombies. I think the whole town is."

"Right. Well, my friend Sam was on duty at the ship. That's where I was headed."

And maybe to figure out how to stop the zombies at the source, he thought.

"You promised," the kid said.

"Yeah, we'll check on your girlfriend first, just tell me where we're going. Then we'll go check on my friend. Okay?"

"Okay. But she isn't my girlfriend."

⋮

Oona stopped the camper long enough to let Annie on, but almost refused to let Ed aboard.

"Uh-uh, nope, that son of a bitch knew this was gonna happen, he can join the zombies."

"Oona, be serious," Annie said.

"I'm serious, kiddo."

"Why would I keep something like this to myself?" he asked.

"Don't know. You're the one working for the government; this is probably all one big-ass experiment. I should shoot you is what I should do."

"Oona, technically I work for the government. Let him on," Annie said. They were both at the edge of the door, so the handgun the angry lesbian in the driver's seat was pointing at Ed was also pointed at Annie.

There was stomping on the roof.

"*Oona, you let him board!*" Laura said through the ceiling.

Oona sighed, looked up, and put the gun away.

"You're lucky she's nicer than me. Get in."

Sam slid down the ladder from above as Oona put the camper in gear and the screaming vehicle got underway.

"Annie!" he said. "You're okay!"

They hugged. She felt her face go flush and hoped the fact that she was blushing wasn't too terribly obvious.

"Looks like you hitched with the right crew," she said as he released her. "How'd this happen?"

"Really long story. How did you end up here?"

"That's also a long story."

"Where are you heading?" Ed asked.

"We already tried the south bridge, sir," Sam said.

Annie almost giggled when she heard him refer to Edgar Somerville as *sir*.

Laura climbed down the ladder behind Sam.

"So now what?" Ed asked.

"Well, the bridge was all choked up with cars, so we figured we'd head along here and maybe see what the zombies were looking for at the same time."

"Looking for?"

"They were all headed this way. Can't figure it out, though. They're just milling about along here."

"Oh my goodness, look at you," Laura said, speaking to Ed. "Hey, sit down, let's take a look at that eye."

"I'm fine," he said.

"You're not fine. What happened to you guys?"

"He was protecting me," Annie said. "I'm who they're looking for."

Sam laughed. "They're going after anyone they think's a threat, we've been seeing it all night." To Ed, he said, "I think if you hadn't fought back, they may have just left you alone and gone on looking."

"No, Sam, I mean it. I'm who they're looking for. That's why they're wandering around right now. It's because I'm nearby."

Sam looked at Ed, who was wincing because Laura was applying an antibiotic to an open cut on his arm. Ed gave him a little half-nod.

"Seriously?" Sam asked. "But why?"

There was a stomp on the ceiling.

"Crap, what was that?" Annie asked. "Is someone else here, or . . ."

"They can't get on the roof, that's just Dobbs," Laura said.

"Dobbs made it? That's great, what about . . ." But Annie didn't finish the sentence. Based on Laura's expression, she didn't need to.

"Pretty sure we're the only ones who got out," Oona said. "Everyone else is either one of them or . . . well, or one of them the other way. Coming up on the bridge, we could use some shooters."

"The bridge is closed," Ed said from the couch.

"We'll see about that," Oona said.

"It was Dobbs that figured out they were sensitive to the sound," Laura said.

"Way to go, Dobbs!" Annie shouted through the ladder opening in the roof.

"He's got the headphones on, he can't hear," Sam said. "Tell me why they're after you, specifically."

"It's complicated."

"Hey, how long has he been doing that?" Ed asked. "With the screaming noise."

"I dunno," Laura said. "A little while."

"He should stop."

"What's wrong, Ed?" Annie asked.

"This is an intelligent force. If you give them too much exposure for too long, they'll figure out a patch, and then it won't work anymore. Which is a problem when you're surrounded by zombies."

"You have a point, Government," Oona said over her shoulder. "But we're getting out of town. Soon as we're in Mount Hermon, we'll do just that."

"I told you, the bridge is closed."

"Unless the bridge is *gone*, I'm driving over it. I don't care who's in my way."

"She won't be able to," Ed said to Laura. "The ship won't let anyone leave. You have to explain that to her."

Just then, they all heard something that sounded like thunder. Given that it was audible over the high-pitched screech coming out of the equipment on the roof, they were suitably impressed. Also, it probably wasn't thunder.

"Jesus, Mary, and Joseph," Oona said.

"*Hey, hey did anyone else see that?*" Dobbs shouted from the roof.

"What was it?" Annie asked.

"Well, I don't know," Oona said.

Dobbs's head appeared in the roof opening. "I think they bombed us," he said.

"They who?" Annie asked, although she knew the answer.

"The military. Just guessing."

"The whole sky lit up," Oona said. "But, in a, like a dome, like we were on the inside of a snow globe. Hey, Mr. Government. There's something keeping us in, huh?"

"It comes down about halfway across the bridge. Annie and I saw it happen earlier. You'll just bounce off if you can even get to it."

"It's true," she confirmed.

"Well, that's fantastic," Oona said. "It's Edgar, isn't it?"

"Ed. Yes."

"Edgar, if everything you two are saying is true . . . we can't get out of Sorrow Falls, nobody can get *in*, the sonic attack is gonna stop working any second, and we're riding around with what all the zombies are looking for, in a camper carrying less than a quarter tank of gas. Is that right?"

"Wait, what do the zombies want?" Dobbs asked.

"Later," Sam said.

"Yes," Ed said. "All of that's correct."

"Then we're gonna have to shoot everyone in town to survive this."

"Not necessarily. Do you have a map?"

⋮

A few minutes later, Ed was in the passenger seat of the camper looking at a map of Sorrow Falls, and Annie was sitting in the back. She was feeling a little lightheaded, a lot exhausted, and a tiny bit hungry. She also had to fight the urge to start crying, which really pissed her off. As much as she was aware that this was her body's normal post-stress reaction, and as much as nobody was going to hold it against the sixteen-year-old zombie catnip for freaking out a little, she didn't want to be *that* kind of sixteen-year-old. She wanted to be the kind that people thought was older than sixteen, who everyone knew, who was never out of her element. Annie spent a pretty long time cultivating the *girl who was always going to be okay*, and she didn't want a little thing like the world ending to screw with that image.

She also really, really wanted to call her mom. It probably wasn't a huge secret that something had gone awry in Sorrow Falls. Someone had to tell Carol her daughter was okay. The worry would just make her condition worse.

At the same time, she was glad her mother was in Boston. The thought of her cancer-riddled mom wandering around town in her slippers and bathrobe, trailing multicolored fabric wraps in her wake, was both comic and horrifying.

But Annie couldn't call anyone because of the ship, and since the ship closed off the town specifically to look for Annie, if the stress ended up killing Carol, *that* would end up being Annie's fault too.

The whole thing made her want to curl up in the loveseat in the back of the camper and sleep until it all went away.

She couldn't do that, though, because Sam wouldn't let her.

"What do you mean, you touched the ship?" he asked. Laura was there too, expressing more or less the same sentiment, but without the tone of betrayal. "When did you do this?"

"Sam . . ."

"Did you sneak past the guards or something? I know the back of the fence was vulnerable."

"It was three years ago, the night it landed."

He looked surprised, but a different kind now. "How could you not tell me?"

"I didn't tell *anyone*. I didn't even tell Ed until earlier tonight, and only after I found out half his gig was to figure out who touched Shippie."

"Shippie?" Laura asked.

"The . . . yeah, the spaceship, it's what I call it sometimes. Look, I just want a nap."

"You can't sleep. In fact, here." He handed her a small tablet. "It's a caffeine pill. We talked about it, and decided we can't risk sleeping until this is all over."

"Yeah, that makes sense."

She took the pill and gulped it down.

"Never had one of these before."

"They're fine," Sam said. "I've had three. So why would they be after you for touching the ship?"

"I don't know. I have no idea what's going on, which is the problem. The ship was cold and smooth, and that's all, have a nice day."

There was a thump, and a bump, and the sound of tree branches brushing up against the side of the camper. They were going off-road.

Dobbs came down from the roof. They'd been running silent since leaving Main Street, which was working out okay so far as Annie could tell from the back. According to Sam everyone in the hills had been heading down toward Main and the river all evening. It would take them a while to relocate Annie and follow.

"Looks like we're going to hide in the forest, or something," Dobbs said, heading back. "I've never seen this part of town."

"Does he think that'll make a difference?" Sam asked Annie.

"I don't know, I guess. He has a plan. I'm too tired to care."

She did peek out the window, though. She saw nothing but dense woods, and began to wonder for herself what Ed was up to.

Then she thought maybe she recognized where they were.

"Ed, where are we?" she called.

"Come on up here."

She got up with Sam's help, partly because the loveseat was particularly cushiony, partly because he was a gentleman.

Getting from end to end in a camper bouncing madly due to an unpaved road was a real treat, especially since this particular cabin was a museum of practical post-apocalyptic junk.

She got to the front in time to see Violet's house just as it was coming into view.

"You sure this is the place, champ?" Oona asked. "It ain't even on that map."

"Positive," Ed said.

Annie was ashamed to realize she'd hardly even thought about her best friend through the entire ordeal. Somehow she imagined Violet and her family would be okay, because it seemed like nothing that happened in the rest of the world had an impact on them.

Ed was perhaps thinking the same way, but for entirely different reasons.

"They're not going to be up," Annie said. "Not at this time of night."

But when the headlights hit the porch, there they were: Violet, Susan, and Todd, waiting there like this was the most normal thing in the world.

"Oh well, that's not creepy at all," Oona said.

She pulled over behind the family car, and Ed stepped out. Annie climbed over the passenger seat and out the same door.

"Evening," Ed greeted her.

"Hi," Violet said neutrally.

"So I'm not sure how to put this, but . . . take me to your leader?"

20
A SUPER-INTELLIGENT SHADE
OF THE COLOR BLUE

Ed's head hurt.

The wound above his eye was still swollen, though not as bad as it had been about an hour earlier, before Annie applied ice, and he had three other cuts on his arms that required disinfectant and bandages, and they were all throbbing in time with his heart.

Over the course of the evening, he'd managed to: throw himself out of a car moving downhill backwards—that the door didn't kill him was a miracle unto itself—onto a pile of rocks; club a woman over the head with a piece of rebar he found lying in a ditch behind the gas station; break the arm of a man who had been dead for at least twelve months; get nearly brained by a fence post when a zombie executed a surprisingly nimble maneuver and drove his face into it; and hit a celebrity with a bat.

Annie, thankfully, was mostly untouched and either unaware of how many times they'd almost gotten through Ed to get to her, or deliberately ignorant of it. If they survived this—his opinion on this possibility had only improved slightly in the past hour—she would be reliving a few things in therapy that she was currently pretending never happened.

He expected he would be doing the same.

"Ed, don't be weird," Annie said with a laugh at his somewhat unusual greeting. "Hi, I'm glad you're all up, it's been a crazy night."

She didn't understand yet.

Violet stepped off the porch. Her parents didn't move, they just smiled a little.

"I'm glad you're okay," Violet said.

"Are we safe here?" Ed asked.

"Yes."

Violet looked at Ed for a solid three or four seconds, in a creepy-mature sort of way even Annie could sense: she inhaled sharply, and he felt her body tense up through the hand he had on her shoulder. Violet knew exactly what Ed had figured out, and didn't see any point in denying it.

"They can't find me here," Violet said. "They won't come to the house. It's safe."

"But it isn't *you* they're looking for."

Violet looked at Annie, and back at Ed again. "No."

"I'm afraid so."

"You should all come inside. We have a lot to discuss."

"Ed," Annie muttered, as Violet and her family turned around and headed back into the house, "what the hell is going on?"

"I'm pretty sure your friend is an alien and her parents are zombies," he said. "Sorry to break it to you like this."

"Right. Well, I'm pretty sure *now* the day can't get any weirder."

⋮

The first indication Ed had that something was amiss with Violet and her family probably should have been when he met Susan for the first time, but it wasn't. He was able to look back on that conversation and see the signs, but she didn't set off any alarms in his head during the conversation itself. Instead, it came from the most mundane of tasks: property research.

After he dropped off Annie, he went back to the base and was continuing his research when it occurred to him he should probably record the name and address of the people she was staying with

276 · GENE DOUCETTE

in the documents he'd been given by the court. He was her legal guardian, after all; he didn't want anyone asking *where is she* and have to cough up such an incomplete answer as *she's staying with her friend Violet up the road.* He didn't know their address, and *Jones* was a pretty common surname.

He thought about calling Annie and asking—he'd also neglected to ask Susan for her phone number—but decided not to bother her with something he could just look up.

That was when it started to get strange. An Internet search gave no indication that there was an address associated with the dirt road leading to the house, and the road itself wasn't even identified on the maps. When he pulled up a satellite image of the area, the house wasn't visible from above.

On Monday, after meeting with Pete he went to City Hall and pulled up property records to match the approximate GPS location of Violet's home with historical ownership of the land in that area, and hit two problems. First, every electronic search for the coordinates he was inputting—a guess in the first place—ended up with a point on the map that was either too far north or too far west. Second, nobody claimed property ownership of *those* points either, for the past seventy years.

Records older than seventy years were archived in the library, so he went there next. The property archives of Sorrow Falls were perhaps more thorough and extensive than any he'd ever seen, but there was no private ownership of the land, and no maps which even recognized the space as existing, even though it clearly *had* to exist.

All it meant was the town owned it, and that was fine, except when he approached it from *that* angle, he also came up empty. There were no forestry records, hunting licenses, reports of fires, gypsy moth infestation summaries, soil sample surveys, leaf-peeping expeditions, bobcat spottings, wildlife conservation projects, or any other kind of indication, official or unofficial, that this part of town existed.

It was even possible to chart the missing territory mathematically. The total acreage of Sorrow Falls could be calculated as a whole, from border to border, or it could be calculated by adding up the total of the privately owned property with the total of the town-owned and state-owned property. The two sets of numbers should have been roughly equal. Instead, nearly twenty acres were missing from the second set.

It was deeply weird. He was still trying to put it together when he stopped by the diner for a late lunch. Beth waited on him, so he took the opportunity to ask her—in the most casual way he could—what she thought of Annie's friend Violet.

Beth had never heard of Violet. Ed thought that was a little surprising given how often Annie described them as the best of friends, and how Beth was like a big sister. It made him want to ask more of Annie's peers about Violet, but he didn't know any of Annie's peers.

Only then did he start to rethink his conversation with Susan, which was strange yet at the same time strangely familiar.

Susan answered questions with questions, offered generic sympathy, and repeated things said to her, and this went on right up until her daughter left the room. Ed had experienced that kind of interaction before, on a computer, *with* a computer.

Violet's mother was a living, breathing Turing test. She wasn't a person; she was someone pretending to be a person.

⋮

There were no versions of the conversation that needed to happen next that played out well in Ed's mind if it also involved notifying anyone from the camper about the aliens in their midst. Oona was angry and paranoid, Laura mostly followed her lead, Dobbs was terrified and paranoid, and Sam . . . Sam might have been okay, but he was over-protective of Annie, and Annie was going to be having a difficult time.

He explained to the others that they were safe *for the moment* and they were welcome to relax and stay in the camper or on the porch. Susan (or whatever she should have been called) offered to bring out coffee, and apologized for being unprepared for guests at one in the morning.

It was in their nature to assume Ed was wrong, and they were not safe at all, which was fine. It would keep them busy with their gadgets, looking for ways in which they were still in danger. It would keep them looking toward the woods at the zombies that were surely on their way instead of toward the house and the alien inside of it.

It freed up Ed and Annie for perhaps the most important conversation in human history. As was perhaps true for most important conversations, this one took place at the kitchen table.

"I don't know exactly where to begin," Violet said.

"You can begin by telling Ed he's crazy," Annie said, "and you're not some kind of freaky alien zombie lord."

Violet laughed.

"Zombie lord is a stretch. But I can't do that, because he's right. I'm sorry, I . . . I wanted to tell you *so* many times, especially after the ship landed."

"Tell me *what?* Come on, this is crazy."

Ed put his hand on Annie's arm to try to calm her.

"Why don't you start with explaining *what* you are," Ed said. "As long as we've dispensed with the idea that you're a sixteen-year-old girl."

"The body I'm wearing is biologically indistinguishable from that of a sixteen-year-old. I think she was seven when she died, about eighty years back. A respiratory ailment of some kind. The lungs are still imperfect."

"You've gotten older *with* me," Annie said. "We've been friends for six years, don't you think I would have noticed?"

"That's true. But before you and I met, she—I—was a ten-year-old girl for a very long time. Figuring out how to stop and restart the aging process was one of the first things I had to learn if I wanted to stay here."

"Here like on this planet? I'm losing my mind. Ed, help me, I'm losing my mind."

"Before this I was Susan for a long while," Violet continued. "She started out much younger. So did Todd. I'm sorry, Annie."

"How long have you been here?" Annie asked. "You've only been in Sorrow Falls for six years, but how long have you been on the planet?"

"That isn't really correct. The first memory I allowed you to have of me was six years ago, but I've been here for much longer."

"Allowed? Wait. Wait. *How* long? You were here before Sorrow, weren't you? You were when Oliver Hollis banged the drum."

". . . Yes. I was."

"Ed, I saw that happen, in my mind, when we were looking at the drum. I was there. Violet, what did you do to me?"

"I'll explain."

"Is this why they're after me?"

"Annie, calm down," Ed said. "C'mon, we're finally in the right place to get answers, so let's get them, huh?"

"Right." She nodded. "Right, sorry, it's just my best friend the undying alien set me up as zombie bait and I'm a little freaked out about that, my bad."

"It wasn't intentional!" Violet said. She reached across the table to take Annie's hand. Annie pulled back like there was a cobra at the end of the arm.

"I mean it," Violet said. "Until this minute it never occurred to me that I was putting you at risk. The ship should have gone away by now, I don't know why it didn't. It couldn't sense me. I don't know why this is happening at all."

"Let's go back to the first question," Ed said. "Tell us what you are."

"All right."

Violet leaned back in her chair and spoke only to Ed. Looking at Annie upset her, which Ed thought was interesting.

"I don't think there's an easy way to explain it, though, not to . . . not to a human."

"Do you have a body of your own?"

"Not in any sense you would recognize. I would say we're energy-based, but that's also reductive. More like . . . an idea. A self-aware idea."

"*We.* There are more?"

"Yes."

"Are you the only one of your kind here?"

"Not anymore, no. But for a long time, yes."

"The meteor in the painting," Annie said. "The one distracting Josiah. That was when you came here."

"That's not historically accurate. I put that there as a gag, although I was the only one who ever appreciated it properly."

"*You* did the painting?"

"Yes, as Susan. I was going through an artistic phase. It didn't last. I never met Josiah, so I made up the details of that day on the river. But you're right, I did meet Oliver. I also bore him children. That was in a different body, of course."

"You're saying the Hollis family is a half-alien race," Annie said levelly, as if with everything else she'd already heard, this one particular detail was straight-up ridiculous.

"Maybe in temperament. Biologically, no. I have no genetic material to pass along. But the entire drum ceremony has been depicted incorrectly. The land the Sorrowers found wasn't considered cursed. It was holy. The natives kept away out of respect and, yes, fear. When they came to the tree stump and used the drum, it was to call the other tribes together, but it was also to summon my attention. I resolved many of their disputes by fiat. By the time Oliver came upon the drum, I'd already grown weary of the arrangement, and was interested in a more immersive experience with humankind. But to answer the rest of the question, the ship that fell to earth in this region many centuries ago came down before Josiah Sorrow was even born. And I wasn't aboard that ship."

"Who was?" Ed asked.

"Nobody. It was an unmanned pod. It's beneath the house, if you'd like to examine it. I suspect we don't have a great deal of free time, though."

"You're going to have to explain that."

"It's really simple. As an intelligence without a physical form I can travel the universe at the speed of light—faster, if you'd like to discuss extra-dimensional travel, although I imagine we have no time for that either. But I need a place to *go*. If you think of me as a piece of information, I need to be transmitted and received, just like any other piece of information. Likewise, I can only interact with the physical world through physical things. If I want to see something, I need to find eyes, or reside in something with an optical interface."

"So the ship beneath us is a giant antenna array and memory bank."

"Essentially."

"Is it the same as the one up the road?"

"No. Same technology, different model. I have the equivalent of a roadside motel. Shippie is more like a tank or a battleship."

"Don't call it Shippie," Annie said.

"Why not?"

"That's something Violet and I called it, and I don't know who you are."

"Annie, I'm still Violet."

"Whatever, go on. Ed, go on, ask her something."

"Where did the technology come from?" Ed asked.

"Who built it, since we are beings without hands?"

"That's a good way to put it, yes."

"A very, very long time ago, one of my kind infected an advanced species of interstellar travelers with a new idea. That idea was the basis of a technology used to build a large number of probes and send them all over the galaxy, looking for planets that could support life. So far as the species was concerned, the probes were a long-term exploration plan employing inventive new ideas and bending space-time in ways nobody had ever thought of before. In truth, it was to create landing spots for us, so we could visit places that didn't have sufficient technology to suit our existential needs."

"Infect?"

"It's the best word choice out of a number of bad word choices. It would be just as fair to say that one of our sentient ideas took seed in the minds of technologically advanced beings in order to advance them further, so as to accommodate the goals of the sentient idea. They thought of the idea as theirs, when it was the other way around."

"I'm afraid to ask," Ed said, "but what happened to that species?"

"They destroyed themselves. Technology was introduced to them at a time when they were unprepared for it. An equivalent would be handing a nuclear weapon to a caveman."

"You destroyed a whole species to get those ships?" Annie asked.

"The death of a species was a consequence of the actions of one of my kind, yes. But entire species die all the time, often because of the poorly executed use of an idea. I find it hard to blame this entirely on the idea itself." She turned back to Ed. "Can I ask you a question?"

"Sure."

"Why do you think they're after Annie?"

"Honestly, we were *really* hoping you could answer that for us," Annie said.

"She touched the ship," he said.

"She . . . Annie, why didn't you tell me?"

Annie laughed. "Vi, in the game of *things we should have told each other*, I'm pretty sure you're gonna lose. I didn't tell anybody."

"The night it landed. The same night . . . oh, of course. I understand."

"Cool, explain it to us."

"The probes are designed to land on alien worlds and collect data, but the designers understood that some of those places might contain hostile lower life forms, so there are security countermeasures that have, what you would call an AI package."

"Something that learns," Ed said.

"Exactly. That package will analyze anything it considers a threat and look for ways to repel it with minimum environmental impact. The reason for this should be obvious: it can't get a clean understanding of a place if its existence manifestly alters that place."

"Well *that* didn't work well, did it?" Annie said.

"Not in this instance, but in a world where the most advanced life form was a squirrel or a stegosaurus it would have been sufficient. You know this defensive program exists because you've seen it in use."

"It convinced me to call my mother," Ed said. "It was very persuasive."

"Exactly. But a few hours after landing it would have only begun to calibrate to the environment. It would have defaulted to a generic blast of negative ideas. I'm surprised it didn't destroy your mind completely, Annie."

"Maybe it lowered the volume after wrecking Rick Horton."

"He was there?"

"Yes. I was the only one to touch the ship, though."

"That was the night your mother . . . that was the same night, wasn't it?"

"It was."

"I think the reason you made it past the countermeasures was that the thoughts it gave you were ones you'd already had independently, that same evening. It was showing you the worst thing you could imagine, but you were already coping with that actually happening. If you'd been there a day later, you would never have made it that far."

"Yay, me."

"What happened when you touched the ship?"

"It put a bunch of pictures in my head? I didn't understand what I was . . . well, seeing isn't the right word, but . . ."

"I understand. You reached the hull. The next logical conclusion would have been that you were a member of a higher life form, so it tried to communicate."

"Then it shrieked at me."

"Yes. I'm sorry, both of you, there's no polite way to put this. Humans aren't nearly advanced enough. It recognized this and concluded you'd breached the defense due to a programming error. Once again, I'm surprised you were able to walk away."

"More like run, but okay. So we're the squirrel and the stegosaurus in your eyes."

"Not in my eyes, no. To the ship, yes."

"Now it thinks she's you," Ed said. "Isn't that right?"

"That isn't exactly right. It's confused."

"Hold it, you need to back waaaay up, both of you," Annie said.

"Why is it looking for you, why does it think *I'm* you, and what is up with the zombies? Also, the ship has been here for three years. Why is this happening now?"

Violet sighed. "A lot of things went wrong here. I thought I planned for all of it, but . . ."

"Start with why it's looking for you," Ed suggested.

"I'm sort of a runaway. In the parlance of the times."

"Oh my God, you're hiding from your dad," Annie said. "The abusive crazy one you told me about."

"Yes. We don't really have genders, and don't require two parents. He's the one who thought of me originally."

Ed laughed. "That's your reproductive cycle?"

"It is. If one of us has an idea of a new version of ourselves, we can think that new idea into being. There's a complexity to it that I'm failing to account for, but that's the essence of the process. He thought of me, but as I matured I came into my own, as a fully formed being or, if we're sticking with this wording, I became my own idea. He responded poorly, so I ran. I used the probe outpost network to explore the universe until I found this place. I sent a pulse through the network to disable all the probes in this star cluster to cover my tracks. I knew that wouldn't dissuade him forever, because unlike humans when we say forever we mean *forever*. He's a stubborn idea as old as eternity with no reason to stop looking.

"I knew he'd send the warships, and that someday one would land here. I just had to make sure I was prepared when that day came. You were my only mistake, Annie."

"I don't understand what that means."

"Have you ever wondered why none of your friends seem to remember me?"

"Well, yeah, it's because you're you. Socially awkward you."

"I couldn't let anyone retain an idea of me. It's literally a piece of who I am. So when I was out of their sight, I was out of their minds too. If a ship landed and looked for me in the minds of other people, it wouldn't find me. All except for you. I've allowed you to carry me in your head for the past six years. We're in this mess because, as it happens, the one person in Sorrow Falls who absolutely should not have interacted directly with the spaceship is the one person who did."

"But . . . why?" Annie asked.

"Because I like you? I wanted a friend. It's why I've been growing old with you. I'm only *here* in the first place because this is the sort of thing I've learned to value: real connection with life. It's not something that's easy to come across, trust me. I'm older than your sun. It's rare."

"Oh. Well, that's sweet, Vi."

"I mean it. I didn't intend to get you into trouble. I've connected with others in the past and it was fine. Oliver, for instance. You aren't the only human who's retained an idea of me."

"Super, but the ship landed on my watch. And now the world's coming to an end because I seemed like a cool kid to hang out with. That's a weird responsibility."

"The world's not coming to an end," Ed said.

"I'm not sure that's up to you."

"It sounds to me like Violet has a say in it," he said. "She isn't interested in seeing the world end either."

Annie looked at her friend. "I don't know, she's let everything else happen, hasn't she?"

"I swear I didn't mean to," Violet said.

"You mentioned AI," Ed said. "In the ship. How advanced is it?"

"More advanced than anything mankind could develop."

"I appreciate that, but . . . is it advanced enough to, say, blow up a munitions depot in Delaware?"

"From the moment it landed it started burrowing into every communications network on the planet. By now I doubt there's anywhere outside of this kitchen that isn't being recorded somewhere inside the ship. But to answer your question, no. It's collecting information passively, for use as necessary. And it's looking for evidence of me. But that's all."

"And you know this because you have the same access to the same networks, only you aren't passive at all about it."

Violet looked away.

"I had to do it," she said, technically addressing the refrigerator. "If those bombs reached Sorrow Falls the ship would have simply detonated them as soon as it recognized the threat. That would have killed half the town, and it wouldn't have been harmed in the slightest. I did the same with the machines you planned to use to remove the ship from town. I knew it wouldn't have allowed that. Obviously, there were more consequences attached to the problem with the explosives."

"Jesus Christ," Annie said. "Violet, five people died."

"I realize that. A thousand times that many would have died otherwise."

"I appreciate that it must have been a difficult decision," Ed said.

"I was trying to keep everything as much the same as possible so the probe would be recalled without incident. It's why so little has changed here, Mr. Somerville."

Annie stood. "You know what? I need a minute. You guys keep on going, I think I've heard enough for a while."

Ed's instinct was to tell her she should stay put, because zombies. But he believed Violet when she said they couldn't find Annie as long as she stayed near the house, for the same reason no GPS signal could find the house and people had been misdrawing maps of the area for two hundred years.

"Are you okay?" he asked.

"I just need some air. This is . . . sorry, I mean, it's cool, she's an alien terrorist and her whole family is reanimated dead people, and I just need a minute with all of that. Before the next crazy thing comes up."

"Yeah, of course. Just don't go far."

"Nope."

Annie left without even looking at Violet.

"Sorry," he said.

"It's all right, she's . . . I feel terrible, she is literally the last person on this planet I meant to harm."

He decided to take that in the spirit in which it was intended, but his first thought was she didn't give a damn about him or anyone else, zombies or otherwise.

"I didn't forget about you," he realized. "That was intentional, I take it."

"It was. You dropped Annie off; I had to make sure you remembered where and with whom. I can't say I was surprised you figured this out. You came to Sorrow Falls looking for me at the outset, whether you realized it at first or not."

"Why did it take three years?" he asked. "For the ship to kick all this in?"

"The ship should have taken off shortly after arriving and failing to detect my presence in or around where the first probe landed. It didn't leave, I now know, because of Annie's interaction. That initiated a secondary program. As I said, it's been collecting information, and learning, and performing a risk assessment."

"Funny, that's why I'm here."

"That was the easy part. It probably finished within a few weeks. It wasn't that which took so long."

"What did?"

Violet looked over her shoulder at Todd. Then she raised her left arm. Todd raised his left arm as well. She lowered hers, he lowered his. Her right arm went up, and so did his. It was like a puppet routine.

"The ship had to learn how to make zombies?"

"It's only a matter of electrical systems and frequencies. It took me a couple of years to make a basic version that's like the ones wandering around town now. It was a century before they were advanced enough to fool a person, and even with that I've been relying on some of the equipment in the capsule in the basement. These guys wouldn't fool anyone outside of its signal reach. Finding people to use is also a challenge. For me, I mean. You have to find someone whose nervous system is still intact and with no missing body parts."

"But who's already dead, right? That appears to be a distinction lost on the spaceship."

"Yes, I never tried this on a living person, but I have a lot more respect for humans than any of the programming in Shippie would. You're all lower life forms, and it's using you to perform a search."

"Three years to learn how to make a zombie, then."

"No, even then, it probably had that figured out in less than three years. After that it was merely on standby."

"I'm going to hate myself for asking, but standby for what?"

"For his arrival."

"Your father."

"My creator. When I said I wasn't the only one of my kind here anymore, this is what I meant. The probe would have finished its review of the life forms on the planet and sent its report. I doubt that report stated anything so unsubtle as 'your daughter is here,' but it would have included enough interesting things to warrant a visit. I suspect it was only after his arrival that the data from Annie's mind was analyzed in enough detail to identify *me* within it."

"All right. Now we're caught up and I need to know how we can fix this. Do you have any idea how we can break this connection the ship has with the people without also killing them? The last time anyone tried to wake up a sleepwalking zombie, the man died of a brain aneurysm, so I'm looking for a better solution than that."

"I don't know, Mr. Somerville. I'm afraid even if I gave myself over to him, he'd see no reason to spare anyone. And I don't mean anyone in Sorrow Falls, I mean anyone at all. Old ideas can be vengeful and unforgiving. With him . . . you have to appreciate that the longer an idea is isolated, the more inflexible it becomes."

"Isolated how?"

"Ideas are meant to live inside minds. More than that, we're meant to interact with those minds. It's how we evolve, and grow, and adapt to whatever present we're engaging. I was a very different kind of idea when I came here than I am now, because of that interaction. If he does find me, he will barely recognize me. I'm not so certain he'll be happy with whom I've become. And inside that ship, he has the capability of destroying the world. He may do exactly that, just out of spite."

"Well, then, we need to come up with a plan to nullify that ship."

⋮

Ed and Violet emerged from the kitchen about twenty minutes later, having formulated something—if not a plan, at least a way to get to one.

The others hadn't drifted far from the camper.

"Hey, Government," Oona said from the roof. "I'm not saying you're right or wrong about being safe here, but all our instruments are going nuts. Where the hell are we?"

"Nuts how?" Ed asked.

Dobbs popped up. He and Oona were evidently working together on her electronics array, which was an improvement over any other time in the evening, from what Ed had been told.

"Like we're on a slab of magnetized iron, or a ley line," Dobbs said.

"Ley lines aren't real, you idiot," Oona said.

"That's under dispute."

"No it's *not*. You gonna read auras next? C'mon."

"Any zombies, though?" Ed asked.

Sam stood up. He had binoculars in his hands. "No sign that I can see. I was going to do a recon."

"Don't bother, Sam," Violet said. "There aren't any out there."

"I'd like to be sure . . ."

"Violet."

"Violet, right. Have we met?"

"A couple of times. I'm a friend of Annie's."

"The compass just spins," Dobbs said. He held one up to illustrate his point.

"I'm sorry," Violet said. "That's my fault. It's the capsule."

"What capsule? And who are you again?"

"I'm Violet, Dobbs. This is my house. We've met."

"Sorry, don't remember."

"It's okay."

"What capsule are you talking about?"

"The one under the house. It's protecting us right now. It's why you, Oona, needed Ed to tell you where to turn off the road, and why the zombies can't find us, and why all of your equipment thinks it's half a mile west of where it actually is, and why the compass thinks true north is down."

"Jesus," Oona said. She pulled her pistol and aimed it at Violet. "She's an alien, isn't she, Edgar?"

"Hold it, hold it. Calm down." Ed stepped in front of Violet, which was just a bad idea, but he didn't have any good ones. "Look, we have a lot to do and not a lot of time. Dobbs, you found the frequency the zombies were communicating on, right?"

"Yeah, but . . . dude, is she really an alien?"

"Focus, Dobbs."

"I did, but I can't translate it."

"I may be able to," Violet said.

"Right now, everyone out there is looking for someone," Ed said, "and the only way to make this end is to convince them they're looking in the wrong place."

"So, you want to send the zombies to where, Oakdale?" Dobbs asked.

"I mean wrong planet, not wrong town."

"I think you should get out of the way," Oona said.

"Oona, you're not going to shoot a little girl. We need her help."

The barrel quavered. "Aaahhh," she said, disgusted either with Ed or herself. She holstered the gun.

"The tech we need to leverage is in the root cellar," Violet said. "You're all welcome to come down and have a look."

Laura came from inside the camper.

"That doesn't sound at all inviting," she said. "But sure, I'll go."

"You're serious, there's an alien ship in the basement?" Dobbs said. "Can we touch it?"

"Yes, I'll disable the defenses."

"Hot damn, I'm in."

"Laura, can you get Annie?" Ed said. "I think she should see this too."

"What do you mean?"

"She's inside, right?"

"No? No, she was in the house with you."

"She went out the back," Ed said. "I just figured she came around here."

"She must still be back there," Violet said. "Hang on."

"Sam, can you see her from up there?"

"No, but it's dark. But where could she have gone? I mean, this is the only place she's safe."

Violet stiffened. "Oh no."

"What is it?"

"I just sent Todd in back to check. Annie's bike is gone."

21
SO THE ABYSS GAZES ALSO

*A*nnie was flying.

That was the thing nobody seemed to understand when asking about the bike. Under certain conditions, it was the closest she would ever get to actually taking flight. This was true even though she could feel every bump in the road, and even when she had to keep pedaling to maintain the takeoff speed.

It was dark, and Violet's road was made of packed dirt that was still damp from the rainfall, on top of which there were potholes from natural erosion, so riding down it at twenty miles an hour on a bike, without a helmet, was pretty reckless. Annie didn't particularly care, though. She had a headlight to help identify the dips — she knew where a lot of them were already, as this was hardly her first trip along the road — and she was a nimble and experienced cyclist. And as long as she was on the bike and riding as fast as she could, all the zombies and aliens and everything else that had taken up residence in her head were gone.

She just didn't know where she was going.

After exiting Violet's kitchen, she wandered out the back of the house and saw her bike sitting there, and without really thinking she began checking the tires and the gears the way she would if she were preparing for a trip. Then she just decided that was what was happening: she was going on a trip. *Where* was still up for debate.

Any trip would require getting past the camper undetected, though, because surely nobody there would understand, so she committed to a long loop around the front of the house, through the woods she'd caught Todd wandering around in. By the time that loop was completed she was at the elbow in the dirt road and out of Sam's rooftop view, and there was nothing between her and the rest of the world but open road. So she turned her light on and started pedaling.

It was glorious. The entire day just vanished into the humid late August nighttime air, and for about five minutes Annie was a six-teen-year-old girl with regular old sixteen-year-old girl problems that didn't include extra-dimensional thought monsters.

Then she reached Liberty Road.

There were zombies all over Liberty, because of course there were. Violet's alien mojo reached the end of the dirt road, so that was where the trail went cold. A whole bunch of sleepwalking townspeople were meandering aimlessly while whatever was controlling them tried to understand information that suggested Annie was assumed directly into heaven at around that spot.

The smart thing to do, as soon as she realized what she was heading into, was to turn around and escape back into Vi's protective bubble. But for that moment, Annie liked less what was behind her than what was in front. Plus, the zombies were kind of well spaced—much better than the shoulder-to-shoulder maneuvers she'd seen on Main Street—which made it seem like just another entertaining challenge for Annie and her cyclocross bike.

They're just slow-moving pedestrians, she thought.

She hit Liberty at speed, and committed to a tight right turn that pointed her uphill and in the direction of her house. This made a lot of sense, because she knew the zombie population only got denser the farther downhill (toward Main) she traveled, but that didn't mean it was a logic-driven decision, or even a decision at all. She just started heading that way.

She wasn't heading home, but that was also not an actively made decision, it was just what she knew she was doing.

⋮

The bike was a gift for her fourteenth birthday, and was the only expensive thing she owned. At first it was just a thing she used now and then, but once it was clear her mother wasn't going to be up to driving her down the hill *all* the time, it became indispensable.

Even in winter. It was only five miles to the school from Annie's front door, but it was a ferocious five miles when there was snow on the ground, regardless of the vehicle. However, it turned out there were only a handful of occasions in which there was (a) snow on the roads, and (b) not-canceled classes. Generally speaking, the roads were cleaned up pretty fast, partly because the army insisted on the state prioritizing the roads in Sorrow Falls when it came time to plow.

Annie fell in love with the cyclocross bike as soon as she saw it. Her father had to take her all the way to Brattleboro to find a decent shop, and the place was full of light carbon three-speed bikes designed specifically for short-travel commuting and priced to encourage people to get them. Annie wasn't interested. Whether because she'd already been riding the streets on the out-of-a-box Schwinn she was now too big for and understood the kind of conditions she had to deal with, or she was instinctively drawn to the sturdy one-of-a-kind machine in the corner, she knew right away that this one was for her.

The bike was pale yellow, aluminum but with a carbon fork. Heavier than the full carbons, it *felt* like something solid and dependable. Not quite a dirt bike and not exactly a touring bike either, it was designed for a sport where competitors threw themselves down hills on their bike and ran up other hills with the bike on their back.

People tended to look twice when they saw her on it. The A-frame design was flattened and stretched, so riding on it meant always being in a forward position. This lowered the center of gravity, kept her out of the wind, and made it easier to corner and maneuver in tight spots, but also made climbing hills a lot more difficult. It also probably looked a little odd.

⋮

At first, Annie tore past the zombies like they were standing still, because they almost were. It was a little harder than with regular pedestrians because normal people moved with intent in one direction and these guys were kind of drifting, but they were far enough apart for this to not be an impossible problem. It was just a new challenge. She enjoyed it perhaps more than was appropriate under the circumstances.

It only became clear how foolhardy she was being after about a mile of travel. That was when the zombies ahead of her started organizing, and focusing less on trying to grab her as she went by than on closing off her available routes of travel. It stopped being so much fun then, especially after she nearly ran over a seven-year-old girl.

Annie knew the child, sort of. She didn't know the girl's name, but she'd spotted her in the library a couple of times. Seeing her out at two in the morning, in her pajamas, stumbling around with the others and trying to catch Annie — or whatever their intentions were — was like a punch in the stomach. It was enough to remind Annie that her two a.m. bike ride wasn't putting just her at risk.

She decided to go over the shoulderless left side of the road. If the bike was meant to be thrown down hills, perhaps it was time to try it out on one.

Liberty, Patience, and Spaceship Road — and Annie's own street, a small spit of connective tissue between Liberty and Patience called Calabash Way — encircled a large land area consisting of private roads and farmland. The properties belonged to six different families. From her bedroom window, which was on the top floor of a house already at the top of a hill, she could see the checkerboard effect of their vegetable crops, smell the fertilizer, and hear the cows lowing on warm afternoons.

From a distance, the farmland looked flat. Annie didn't realize exactly how incorrect this was until she hit the first field off the roadside. The downhill wasn't all that bad. She nearly went over the handlebars thanks to a couple of ditches, but neither was deep enough to completely eat her front wheel, so she made it out. But once the area flattened into what should have been easy travel, it became much worse.

The soil was loose and muddy, and either terribly uneven or full of rows that stuck up like train tracks. Travel felt like one of those dreams where she was trying to run but couldn't move her legs fast enough to get anywhere, unless she was getting thrown from the bike, in which case it felt like one of those dreams where she was falling off a cliff.

She got thrown three times, thankfully to a soft landing each time. This was hardly guaranteed, as the fields had their share of sharp protrusions just waiting for someone to get impaled.

The good news was, the terrain slowed the zombies down too. She was going ten miles an hour or less depending on the size of the plants in her way, but the uneven surface was causing a lot of comic stumbling and falling behind her.

The bad news was, this detour was only a temporary solution. Since there were roads on all sides of the fields, and the zombies were all along those roads, she'd basically put herself in a position to be closed in on from all sides. Her hope was to punch through to the other side while there was still a gap to hit.

That was a solid plan right up until she hit Mac Tunney's cornfield.

It wasn't the field itself that was the problem. Actually, it was the smoothest ride she'd experienced up to that point. The rows were neat and wide and the ground between them was level and a lot more solid than she had a reason to expect. But the rows didn't head in the direction she wanted to go, and it was impossible to ride against the grain in a cornfield in August. The stalks were too high.

She had to stop five or six times to push diagonally through the rows before continuing the ride. This was a little terrifying, because off the bike she couldn't see over the stalks, and she knew there were people out there closing in on her. She could hear them.

Then she got the flat.

It wasn't easy to poke a hole through one of her tires. There was a thick layer of Kevlar between the tread and the inner tube that could redirect everything short of a nail driven dead straight through the middle. For that to happen, she either had to run over a nail positioned on the ground just so, or someone had to go after her tire with a hammer and a nail.

For whatever reason, there was a stray nail in Farmer Tunney's field. Maybe it fell from one of the combines or out of a hardware kit, or maybe the universe hated her personally. Somehow, in a two-acre field of corn, her rear tire found that nail.

She felt it right away, and knew exactly what it was, and kept riding anyway. One of the things about hitting a nail was that you could keep going for a little while so long as you didn't pull the nail out. It plugged the hole it made.

The seal was weak, though, so air escaped around it pretty quickly. She made it probably an extra quarter-mile on her dying tire, and then another forty feet on the flat before giving up. It just wasn't possible to continue; the rear wheel couldn't give her any traction at all, and her maneuverability was gone.

It was better at that point to continue on foot. Although *better* was a relative term. It was faster than the bike in its current state, but not much faster. And she was taller on the bike. She could see Calabash, and her bedroom window, on her right, and used that to help maintain the correct orientation, but there was no avoiding the zombies any longer. If they came up from the left or right, she wouldn't know until they had her.

Maybe that's okay, she thought. *Maybe I should just let them catch me.*

⋮

After only ten minutes of running, Annie was too winded to continue. She felt like this was something she should have been embarrassed about, until she remembered how late it was and how much of the past twelve hours she'd spent fleeing. Perhaps simply running was easier on her head, because it kept her mind from dwelling on all horrors great and small, but it was hell on her legs and lungs. She had scratches all over those legs—she was in shorts—and her lungs didn't seem to know how to get enough oxygen anymore. Her heart was racing at an alarming pace; she could feel it thumping all the way up her shoulder and along her left arm.

So she stopped, and listened. And determined two things.

First, they were all around her. She could hear corn stalks rustling in every direction. There was hardly any wind so it couldn't have been anything else.

Second, something big was coming. Something with an engine.

It wasn't on the road; that was obvious from the bumping and crunching sounds. Somebody was driving something through the corn stalks. Since as far as she knew, zombies didn't drive cars, she headed toward that noise.

She got close enough to see the headlights bouncing in her approximate direction (as opposed to taillights heading away from her) when a hand grabbed her ankle.

The dirt came up fast, swatting her in the side of her face and knocking her a little loopy. It was a second before she understood that the ground was where it had always been, she'd just fallen onto it. Her head was next to a big rock that would have probably cracked her skull if she'd fallen a little to the right.

She picked the rock up in her fist and rolled onto her back.

An old woman had her ankle. She kicked loose, then threw the rock at the woman's face before she had to hear another iteration of *arrre yooooou*. As the lady fell backwards, Annie climbed to her knees and then her feet, and then stopped, because a much larger person was now blocking her route.

She'd never seen him before, but he was enormous. He looked like the kind of zombie a rock to the face would only slightly inconvenience.

Then she heard the car again.

"I'M OVER HERE!" she shouted. "HELP ME!"

There was shuffling in the row behind her, and rustling to her left and right.

Nowhere to go.

The engine's roar was the first indication that all was not lost. The headlights were the second. Then the army Humvee exploded onto the scene with the kind of cinematic drama one just didn't see all that often around Sorrow Falls. The front fender connected with the huge zombie barring her path and sent him flying, and then skidded to a stop with the back door aligned with the corn row. The door flew open. Annie half expected to hear an orchestral swell.

"Get in, girl," the driver said. It was an army guy; she thought she knew him. "Hurry up!"

She ran. It was only twenty feet but she could hear them closing in on her so it was a terrifying twenty feet. She dove into the back seat and landed squarely on top of Doug Kozinsky.

"Dougie??"

"Hey, Annie," he said.

She pushed off him and reached back to close the door as the driver floored it.

"Pickles, right?" she said.

"Corporal Dill Louboutin at your service."

"How'd you guys even *find* me?"

The Humvee fishtailed a little, trying to execute a turn to get back up onto the road, so Dill had to concentrate for a few seconds. Annie peeked behind them. The field was crawling with zombies. It was a wonder they hadn't gotten her.

"You can thank your boyfriend there," Dill said.

"I'm not . . . Sorry, I've been telling him . . ." Even in the dark, she knew Dougie was blushing.

"I broke out of the base with a gun to my head," Dill said, "so this young man could ride off to your rescue instead of just getting the hell out of town like any sane person. We drove to your house, but nobody was home. Looked like you're missing some floor in that place, too. Dunno if the zombies did that or what, but . . . well, then we spotted the bike light from the porch. It seemed clear there were a number of zombie folks interested in converging on a moving target in the middle of the field. Mr. Kozinsky imputed that this moving target was you, and we're both a little surprised he was right."

"I recognized your bike," Dougie said.

"From up the hill?" Dill asked. "It wasn't anything more than a light."

"Yeah, but I *knew*."

"Well, thank you, both of you," she said. "They almost had me."

The Humvee made it out of the corn. Rather than crest the road—it was steep from that angle—Dill kept to a route on the space between the lip of the street and the edge of the field.

"So what did they want you for?" Dill asked.

"I think they want to take me to the ship."

"Oh. How come?"

"I'm not sure."

"Okay. Well, I'm gonna hook up with the road up here and do everything I can to get you two kids out of town, all right?"

"There *is* no out of town," Annie said.

"What's that mean?"

"Nobody can get in or out. We're all trapped here."

He laughed. It had a tinge of hysteria in it, like that was the piece of news that finally sent him over the edge.

"Well, all right, where do you want to go?"

"Can you take me to the spaceship?"

"I thought that's what the zombies wanted to do."

"It is."

"But you're going anyway."

"Yes. I'd just rather do it under my own power. Less bruising that way."

"Well, all right. I was on my way there after as it was. Plus these villager zombies ain't trying to kill me like the army ones are. Should be fun."

⋮

It wasn't fun.

Dill seemed to enjoy it all right. He'd reached a sort of dissonance over what he was doing, which was running over people.

He was good at it. In a video game he'd be leveling up. In the real world, he was having a psychotic episode.

There were sick thuds and crunches, and the Humvee kept lifting off the ground unevenly, and she knew what each one of those sounds meant. She kept her eyes closed and tried to resist telling him to slow down and go around, because that was the wrong advice.

"It's going to be okay, Annie," Dougie said. He'd been clutching her hand since she landed on top of him, thinking perhaps that this was comforting. She didn't find it comforting, but he probably did. Plus, he rescued her. That was worth at least a little hand-holding.

"There's a lot going on you don't understand, Doug. But thanks. I appreciate you thinking of me."

"Of course."

"So Dill, why were you going to the ship?" she asked.

"Seemed like the place to go," he said. "Spaceship makes zombies, go to the ship to stop the zombies, right? Plus, my boy's there."

"Sam?"

"You know it. Woo, look out!"

He swerved into a guy in a polo shirt and knocked him sideways off the street.

"Ten points."

"Sam's not there," Annie said. "I left him a little while ago."

"Why'd you do that?"

"There are a lot of long stories, Pickles, I don't have time to tell you any of them."

"Yeah, okay, but don't call me that. So he's all right?"

"He was when I left him."

"That's one thing I don't have to worry about, then, girl, thanks. I didn't want to run down my buddy. Glad he's not one of these dead-eyes."

"The soldier zombies are bad," Dougie said. "We had to go through a lot of them to get off the base."

"What were you even doing *on* the base?"

"Mom and Dad are out here somewhere, so . . . Once I figured out what was going on I found Dad's revolver and snuck on. I do it all the time; they don't even check the fences below the field grass. I saw something was up with the soldiers and thought, you know. I know you were there before."

Annie realized he'd risked his life looking for her, and added it to the list of things she was already feeling bad about. It wasn't as consequential as possibly triggering a zombie apocalypse that was slowly killing the town, but it was right up there.

"Comin' up," Dill said.

Annie took a look through the windshield. The grounds around the ship remained lit up by spotlights, but there wasn't a lot to see. The campers looked abandoned, and there were hardly any zombies.

"Do you have a key to the gate?" Annie asked.

"No, but I can just . . . uh-oh."

"What?"

The answer was coming up the hill. Army soldiers zombie-walking in something like a coordinated fashion, at a slightly faster clip than the civilian ones had exhibited. They were headed for the gates as well.

"Behind us too," Dougie said, looking out the back window.

"They're converging on the ship," Dill said.

"To keep us out?" Dougie said. "Cuz we're gonna beat them there."

"Keep us out or keep us in," Annie said. "Look, I don't want you two to get hurt. If you want to drop me off, I can get in there on my own."

"How are you going to get in?" Dill asked. "There's barbed wire over the top, you know that. Why do you even want to *get* in?"

"To put a stop to all this, same as you."

"Well, that's heroic, but you're just a little girl. Now sit back and belt yourself in, I'm gonna get us through those gates."

She leaned back, and buckled in, and hoped the car didn't end up damaged enough so it couldn't drive back out again, because they were going to be cornered otherwise.

With a loud *yahoo* that made Dill sound entirely too cliché, he reached the edge of the dirt in front of the gates and stomped on the gas. The Humvee reared up like a horse about to execute a monstrous leap, then rocketed forward.

The fence was never all that imposing. From the time it went up, it was clear the functional intent was to formalize the line behind which someone in an army uniform would shoot. It was never meant to repel an assault from a motorized vehicle. Conversely, the low-to-the-ground military Humvee was built to do exactly what it did to the fence.

They blew right through the gates. It did a little damage to the Humvee, but it was the kind of damage that only seemed important in a world without zombies. By the time they ground to a halt, they were fifteen feet inside the circumference.

"Now what?" Dill asked. "Have to admit, I didn't think this far ahead. Should we shoot it or something?"

"I've thought this far ahead. You and Doug should turn around and get out of here."

"I already said . . ."

"Then stay here. But the whole army base is on its way so you won't have a lot of time to escape."

She hopped out of the car and started toward the ship. She could hear lovesick Dougie shouting from the back seat, and Dill shouting from the front. Undead and unconscious men in fatigues were amassing at the hole they'd just made in the fence, and behind them an entire town was being driven in the same direction.

Enough was enough.

"HEY," she shouted. "ANYBODY INSIDE? I AM HER."

One of the "eyeball" holes in the ship lit up—half a million people on the Internet who had been arguing over the function of this particular recess for the past three years would have been thrilled to see it serve a function—and directed a light at her face.

She squinted, and waved, which seemed like the polite thing to do. Then came a hiss: beneath the eyeball the side of the ship was opening. It wasn't a welcoming sort of opening, not in the way a ladder or a staircase might be considered an offer to enter: the side of the hull split, and two pieces flapped apart like a set of double doors. A faint bluish light shone from inside.

It was impossible to tell what was inside the ship with all the light, but what was clear already was that nobody was going to be emerging from inside. There was no E.T. casting a shadow.

Annie looked back. The army soldiers had all stopped moving. Dougie was shouting something at her, but she couldn't understand what he was saying. It didn't matter, anyway. There was only one direction to go.

She walked toward the light, and climbed inside the spaceship.

22
ANNIE'S IDEA OF ALIENS

*T*he best way to describe what happened—upon the discovery that Annie had run off—was *coordinated panic.*

Sam had to be restrained, which was a challenge as there was nobody there physically capable of really restraining him. Ed estimated a half an hour passed from when Annie left the kitchen to when he discovered her absence, which was easily enough time to collect her bike, loop around the camper, and pedal down the road to a point beyond where it was safe to be without an adequate zombie defense, such as a large RV. Sam wanted to chase her down on foot, if need be.

Meanwhile, Dobbs had a million questions for Violet, but he was asking them so rapidly she didn't have time to answer, and didn't appear to have much of an inclination to either. She was too busy blaming herself for Annie having run off, which in Ed's opinion was probably a bit justified. Oona, who was struggling with the question of whether or not shooting Violet constituted an intelligent choice, may have also been a distraction.

They were a team of capable individuals, one of whom was an apparently immortal alien being wearing the body of a young girl. They needed to decide what the matter at hand was, and come up with a plan to fix it.

"Violet," Ed said, "can the technology keeping this house invisible travel?"

She looked at him without speaking as she ran through the implications of the question. In their conversation, he'd become used to the sense of wrongness she gave off when not actively trying to behave like a sixteen-year-old. There was maturity in there that was not unlike the sort of imitative adultness Annie exhibited, except in Violet it was more extreme, and decidedly unnatural. It was what Ed felt meeting a vampire would be like.

Provided vampires were real, of course.

"It can," she said. "But it also can't. The act of travel would make it visible, like a bubble in water. We would be detected by the absence we would create."

"My GPS puts me in another spot," Dobbs said, "so why wouldn't that keep working if we move?"

"The reason it works is this place hasn't existed in any physical or electronic survey of the land since the country was born. You'd have driven past if Ed wasn't navigating, and Ed would never have found it if Annie hadn't showed him. But everything south of us has existed for some time." She looked at Ed. "He would notice."

"He who?" Oona asked. She was going between helping Laura keep Sam from bolting down the road and fingering the handle of a revolver tucked into her waistband.

"We can explain later," Ed said. "Violet, what happens if a zombie wanders down the road?"

"Nothing, because that's impossible."

"Fine, pretend it isn't impossible, what would happen?"

"The commands from the host would stop making sense. It would be similar to receiving driving directions from a GPS that thought you were in a different place, only a zombie wouldn't have the presence of mind to recognize incorrect instructions. But it would only be temporary. The host would recognize the anomaly and we'd be detected."

"Good enough. Dobbs, if we get near the ship, can you pick the signal up again?"

"I dunno, probably. I think their equipment can. Oona would know . . . it's her stuff."

"We can do it, but why?" she asked.

"Later. Violet? If it's mobile, we need it. Oona, Laura, does this thing have enough gas left to get us across town?"

"Yeah, barely," Oona said.

Laura pointed to Violet's family car. "We can drain that tank, maybe. It's not a diesel rig."

"Good idea."

"So we're going to get Annie now?" Sam asked.

"We're going to the ship," Ed said. "That's where she's going."

"Why the hell would she be going there?"

"There's no place else to go."

"And if she's not there?"

"One thing at a time, Sam."

⋮

The light faded to a soft blue that was just sufficient to allow Annie to differentiate between when her eyes were open and when they were closed. It came from no particular location and illuminated no details on the ship's interior. There was something that could be construed as a video screen in front of her, except it wasn't made of glass and had a depth to it that was absent in a standard television set. That she even thought of it as a screen suggested this information was coming from a font of experience that didn't belong to her.

It felt a little like being on the inside of a chicken egg. And, like a chicken egg, it was fully enclosed.

"Hello?" Her voice came back with a metallic echo. "I'm going to need air."

There was nothing in the way of a response . . . and then there was.

Images: vibrant, colorful, frightening images of collapsing stars and nebulae and black hole event horizons. There was light viewed from the perspective of a point in space, and a point in space from the perspective of a beam of light; a thing that looked like an amoeba pulsing in a sea of heavy gas; a hailstorm of aluminum riddling a carbon-dense planet; a civilization of squat humanoids developing tools on a huge planet with tremendous gravitational force; another civilization, of light-limbed hermaphrodites dying in a conflagration on a planet that had previously never known fire.

"I don't understand any of this," Annie said.

A centipede-like creature the size of a commuter train roared expletives from a circular mouth full of needle-sharp teeth, at an airborne slug with gossamer wings. Annie could smell the ammonia-rich air and feel the rage of the giant centipede, and understand its anger. But she didn't know what she was supposed to *do* with this understanding.

"Air. I'm going to suffocate."

She was already running out, but whoever was operating this picture show couldn't understand what she was saying. So instead, she started *thinking* about suffocation.

The centipede and the airborne slug began to choke, and then the picture changed to the humanoids on the gravitationally intense planet grabbing their throat areas and gasping. Then a human man appeared. He was a white human with light brown hair and a shiny white smile, in a blue polo shirt. The most generic rendition of the species imaginable—provided television was the source—this man appeared to have emerged directly from a toothpaste commercial, as perhaps he had.

Annie hoped he was a construct and not a real person who existed out in the world somewhere, because as she focused on him, he began to choke as well. He gasped and pawed at the generic room he stood inside of, clutching the back of the generic chair and stumbling over a generic cat to the generic floor. He twitched and screamed silently, and continued to do so until he stopped breathing.

"This shell . . . requires."

The voice came from all around her, in the same way the faint blue light did. It wasn't so much that there was no specific source; it was that whatever the source was, she was on the inside of it.

"Air," she said.

"This shell requires atmosphere."

"Yes."

A new hiss sounded, an indication of a valve or pipe opening or unlatching or releasing, and then she could breathe again.

"Intake atmosphere exhaust waste."

"Thank you, yes."

Annie realized she'd arrived at this point with a certain number of preset expectations about this experience. The first was that there would be a presence in the spaceship, and the second was that this presence was Violet's father. (Or, more exactly, "father.") Given all she'd been told regarding how terrifying he was supposed to be, that she was not at that moment afraid meant either she had become very brave recently, or she was just too exhausted to be frightened.

Another assumption was that the alien she would be speaking to would have a deep, ominous-sounding voice. That expectation was colored by the movies, which were no doubt themselves influenced by humankind's historic depiction of both authority figures in general and deities more specifically. Zeus on high, making sonorous declarations to cowering mortals at the foot of Mount Olympus, was always expected to speak in a voice as deep as thunder, and so on.

The voice she heard inside the ship was a man's voice, certainly, but it wasn't the kind of voice that commanded awe. It was the kind that was trying to sell her something. It was what she would expect the suffocated white man from the toothpaste commercial to sound like if he'd managed to get a word out.

At least he has a voice now, she thought.

The picture show was interesting, except that it wasn't really a picture show so much as an immersive experience. The longer it went on the more her other senses kicked in and she began *experiencing* what was happening instead of looking at it through a camera lens. These were memories, and they were being added to her mind. It was a peculiar way to communicate. It was faster, perhaps, than words, but had none of the nuance.

"You are not her," the alien said, in his peppy sales voice. If it weren't quite so life-or-death, she might find it funny. *But if you buy this detergent you can be her.*

"I am her," she said. "I am the one you were looking for."

"You are the one and you are not her. She is of you, you are not her."

"What's the difference?"

"You have . . . her smell."

"Her smell? That doesn't make sense."

"Your words are so small. Her scent is in your mind."

"You can read my mind?"

"I can taste your . . . yes. Your ideas. I can taste your ideas."

"I understand. She is not me, but the idea of her is a part of me."

"Yes."

She was trying to pinpoint a source of the voice, so she knew which direction to face when talking.

"How are you speaking? Like, do you have a mouth?"

"I do not eat."

"Mouths in humans are also for speaking. If you have a visual . . . I mean if you can see me, look, my mouth is moving."

There was a terrible moment, just after she said this, when the thought came that perhaps her mouth wasn't moving at all. She could *feel* it moving, but this was uncharted experiential territory, and she couldn't discount the notion that everything happening to her was internal. She could be projecting a version of herself in her own mind that was speaking and looking, just like the way she thought she could smell the atmospheric ammonia of an alien landscape. Her senses weren't necessarily trustworthy.

"I see, yes," the alien said. "The sound of my voice is rendered from the archives collected in this . . . outpost. Mouth is an inefficient speech requirement. I would not mimic an inefficiency."

"But so, you can't read my mind. I'm really here, in the ship, talking out loud right now, and this isn't just happening in my head."

"Your ideas leak into this ship, but thoughts are . . . thoughts are . . . The words are crude. Thoughts are pieces. Fragments of unconnected . . . What is this?"

The picture show kicked in again. The alien had plucked an image of a cloth hanging from Annie's own memory.

"That's a tapestry. It's from a medieval castle. I saw it when I was eight, when we went on a field trip to the Museum of Fine Arts in Boston."

She remembered liking the tapestry for reasons she still couldn't explain. She spent a half an hour looking closely at it, until Mrs. Parris dragged her away.

The image zoomed in on a corner of the tapestry that was eye level to an eight-year-old. It was a frayed edge. The indirect lighting of the room reflected off the glass case protecting the ancient cloth.

"These parts."

"Threads. Those are threads."

"Thoughts are this."

The image jumped back to the full picture. It showed men on horseback in a tournament in the foreground with a castle in the background. Annie remembered liking the horses in particular.

"Ideas are this. Ideas are full things, contained. Endless but bounded, as a sphere. Ideas can *be*. Thoughts cannot. Even simple thoughts in a crude mind are threads."

"So, no, then."

"I cannot read your mind. I can exist in your mind but not read it. Only you can know your own mind."

"But you can exist in my mind," she repeated. "As an idea. I don't like how that sounds."

"That's irrelevant."

"Maybe to you."

"I can exist as an idea in your mind, but not in my entirety, no more than this device in which you sit holds my entirety. I can be shared, and I can exist independently elsewhere. I am endless but bounded. Now you will tell me where the one I seek is."

"I don't know. Who are you looking for?"

"You are attempting evasion. You have her scent."

He began pulling images from her mind and displaying them, as if to show exactly how easy it was.

"She travels," he observed. "Tell me where."

"Please stop pulling those images out of my head."

"You are a crude life form, you should accept your limitations."

"Well, it's rude."

The images continued to play, possibly more so Annie could understand how much the alien was extracting of her idea of Violet. He wasn't showing her anything she didn't already know, certainly.

"I have examined the records and cannot find this place," he said. "It is on no maps."

Annie laughed.

"Yes, it's a funny little place."

"She travels with strange beings . . . I do not understand. You."

"Annie. People call me Annie."

"Annie, I will call you. You will help me find her."

"I don't really think I have any incentive to do that."

"I do not understand."

"Sure you do. She's my friend, and I don't think she wants to go anywhere with you, so I don't know why I would lead you to her."

"This warship can eliminate the planet if I choose."

"Well, that's a good incentive. Can it really?"

A series of images flooded her mind. It was a much more aggressive sharing of information than before, possibly because she was seeing into the idea of another idea. It was something like a schematic of the spacecraft, but despite using scientific principles nobody on the planet had ever been exposed to, she felt like she understood. This either meant the alien was getting better at communicating with her, or she was getting better at receiving this style of communication. When it was finished, she understood the ship's workings alarmingly well, as if the schematics had been saved off in her head. It made her want to ask the alien if he could also put Spanish in there so she didn't have to take it next year.

"Well, you definitely *can* destroy the planet with this," she said.

"You understand."

"Sure. But if you do that . . . I mean, wouldn't she die with it?"

"Ideas can never die."

"Fine. Weird, but fine."

"You will tell me how to find her."

"Okay, but I have some questions for you first."

There was a long pause. She imagined him in another part of

the spaceship (although it had no other parts) pacing furiously and cursing her in some alien language.

"I will answer questions."

"Great!"

"And when I am done answering questions, you will tell me where the place called Oz is located, and why my daughter wishes to see this man named wizard."

"I promise."

⋮

It was another hour after the failed bombing of Sorrow Falls before someone developed sufficient nerve to raise the nuclear question.

This followed a great deal of analysis of the kind that only happens in emergencies: quick, contingent, back-of-envelope calculations made by very smart people in many rooms around the world. These were the same scientists charged by their governments and the science community at large with understanding the spaceship as well as they could with whatever tools they had. There were solid reasons to think these men and women would have, if not complete answers, some agreement on approximate answers.

What was apparent to anyone who listened to them argue for more than a few minutes was that this wasn't the case, and likely never would be. In three years, this team had measured everything they could, but the ship was so good at keeping its secrets, they were as surprised as anyone by its capabilities.

As an example, everyone knew perfectly well what happened if one attempted an open assault of the ship. Small objects like rocks were repelled gently. Small rapid objects, like bullets, were vaporized, and their kinetic energy absorbed via some unexplained physics.

(*Vaporized* was not a truly accurate observation, as the bullets weren't turned into vapor. Nor did they cease to exist, nor were they converted into energy—this would release a truly enormous amount of energy if they had been—or any of the other descriptions readily available to anyone with Internet access and about thirty seconds. What happened was that the protective barrier around the ship absorbed the impact of the bullet and then turned the small projectile into several million extremely small projectiles. The metallic dust remnants of the first bullets fired at the ship remained in the field three years after the Sorrow Falls sheriff fired them.)

Larger objects were dealt with in a range of ways that were similar only in that they each seemed to represent the least complicated solution. Flying drones had their altimeters confused and ground-based robots lost their understanding of left-right and back-forth. People lost the will to continue.

What had *not* been tried was a more overt assault.

Eighteen months after the ship landed there was a plan in place to hit it with a surface-to-air missile from forty yards away. The idea had a lot of supporters, but most of those supporters were people who were convinced it would have no effect and only wanted to take the measurements that would come out of such an experiment. Well, that and they wanted to be proven right about it. The detractors argued that deliberately and actively antagonizing an advanced race with advanced technology just to see what would happen was a really dumb idea. This counterargument was also used when someone suggested they just drive a Jeep straight ahead really fast, and when someone else suggested crashing a jet into it.

The counterarguments carried the day, which meant the upper limits of the protective shield around the spaceship had never been tested but it was assumed—unreasonably, as it turned out—that a sufficiently large non-nuclear weapon would be adequate.

But that was only part of the problem. Not one of the men and women with multiple degrees and Nobel Prizes and so on ever advanced the notion that this shield might be *expandable.*

There was no reason whatsoever to entertain this thought. Yes, they all knew about the munitions explosion, and the truck breakdowns, but half were convinced this was a case of the government giving up after coincidental setbacks and not actions initiated by the ship. Also, it was already assumed that the ship was using a tremendous amount of energy just doing what it did in a five-foot radius. The energy needed to turn the same shield into a dome covering the entire town?

Staggering.

When asked for a more precise calculation by none other than the president of the United States, the scientists offered other words that also meant "staggering," which was unhelpful.

After the shield — clearly not weakened by the expansion — dealt with the two thermobaric bombs they dropped on it in a manner similar to the way a windshield dealt with two mayflies, the first question was not *what do we have which is bigger that we can deploy instead? It was *what do we do if the shield keeps expanding?*

This was a very good question, because while nobody was going to say it — certainly none of the scientists with advanced degrees were going to — there was a thing going on inside that Sorrow Falls bubble, and that thing involved zombies.

This seemed like a really good reason to try to prevent the ship from doing anything else.

At a little after two in the morning, a three-star general in the Pentagon cracked open a top-secret action plan for the nuclear destruction of Sorrow Falls. Enclosed was a list of U.S. and world leaders who were expecting calls. Those leaders had been briefed on this outcome, and were expected to provide the kind of assent a sitting president needed to cover his butt when nuking his own people.

The missile would be fired by a nuclear sub that was patrolling the waters between Long Island and southern Connecticut, specifically for this contingency.

The plan included a token evacuation plan for Sorrow Falls and the surrounding towns, but that was mainly for show because there was no reasonable expectation that anyone would make it outside the blast radius in the time allotted, and the radioactive fallout could potentially reach New York and Washington anyway. It was going to be the most devastating and horrific event in the history of the country, and the only reason it was under serious consideration was that the president and his advisors had reason to believe they were preventing something that would have global consequences.

One thing the author of the nuclear option hadn't considered was what to do if there was reason to believe the ship could weather an attack from a thermonuclear weapon. As the men and women tasked with executing the plan took the necessary steps to hand the president all he needed to sign the order, someone decided to try to reach the plan's architect.

His name was Edgar Somerville, and he was unavailable.

⋮

"Why do you want her?" Annie asked.

"She is mine."

"That's a terrible answer."

"I do not see any reason for . . . elaboration. Are these all your questions?"

"What makes her yours?"

"I thought of her. She was my idea."

"Ideas can have ideas of their own?"

"It is not something that can be explained easily to someone so limited."

"How am I limited?"

"You are trapped in that body. That is a limitation. There are places you cannot go because your body cannot make the journey. I have no such limitations. I am an unbounded idea."

". . . that can have ideas of its own."

"Ideas can be simple, and ideas can be complex. Simple ideas do not often obtain sentience. They are too . . . inflexible. They cannot adapt. Ideas never die, but ideas can become useless, or irrational. Something over-specific would not thrive independent of where it was born. An aquatic creature riven from liquid media."

Annie laughed. It echoed through the ship. She wondered if anyone outside could hear them.

"A fish out of water, you mean."

"Your metaphors are new to this one. But such is a simple idea. There are many ideas in every civilization in every world, every-where. She is not a simple idea, which is why although she is *in* you, she is not *of* you. Your idea of her is a shadow of her entire conception. It is the version of her which casts that shadow I would like back."

"All right, so you're an idea and you *had* an idea, and that's who my friend is. What was the idea that became her?"

"This is difficult to explain."

"You keep saying that."

"It is . . . it's true. I didn't intend to create a new idea."

He hesitated.

"*I* was once a new idea. I remembered what it was like, and that remembrance became something other than myself. Then that something left me. I can remember what I lost, but I can no longer *feel* it. This is why I say she is mine. She took something from me and she *is* something from me."

"Don't take this the wrong way, but you're starting to sound kind of human."

"You've developed an idea of me. It's been a long time since that has been true."

"Apparently my idea of you uses contractions when he talks."

"This is humor."

"Hey, don't go nuts."

He went silent.

She tried to gauge how long she'd been in the ship, and wondered what was happening outside, and as soon as she wondered that, the images in front of her coalesced to show the field.

"Whoa, did I do that?"

The alien didn't answer. It was clearly a current image, though. The soldiers remained frozen in place, and Dougie and Dill were still at the car. They were arguing about what to do, pointing frequently right at Annie, which is to say right at the ship.

They were discussing whether to leave her, go in after her—if the ship would let them in—or stay where they were.

Higher, she thought. The view became a bird's-eye view of the field and the surrounding area, and it was quite literally a bird's-eye view. The ship was borrowing the eyes of a bird.

Zombie birds.

"Yep, I'm definitely doing this," she decided.

"Annie."

"Oh, there you are."

"I have located Oz."

"Oh? Okay?" She crossed her fingers and hoped the next sentence would have to do with Australia. It didn't.

"You have lied to me."

"That's totally unfair. I may have misled you, but only a little."

"This Dorothy, this place called Oz, they are fictions. There is no wizard. These are lies."

"It's a movie, and a movie is an idea, and ideas are real."

"You no longer amuse me. Reveal where I can find her, or I will cease the atmospheric intake of all the drones in this place you call Sorrow Falls."

⋮

Ed had this notion that the spaceship hidden in the root cellar was going to be at least the size of the more familiar one on the other side of town. It was considerably smaller: roughly the size of a coffin for a child, and shaped like a vitamin capsule.

"Did that come from the ship?" he asked Dobbs, who had gone down with Violet, Todd, and Susan. (Ed didn't know what to call Todd and Susan. He knew they weren't people and he knew they weren't aliens, and they didn't behave like zombies. Faced with such a quandary, he continued to refer to them as Todd and Susan.)

"That's it," Dobbs said. "That's the whole thing."

"Is it at least heavy?" The aforementioned non-human Todd and Susan were carrying it in a blanket.

"It's heavy," Violet said. "But not so heavy as to represent a risk to the camper."

Ed hadn't actually thought of that, but was glad someone had.

They slid it into the back of the camper on the floor next to the toilet and under a rack of leather clothing. The device was the same matte black as the ship, and when Ed put his hand on it he found the kind of friction-free material Annie described. This explained the blanket, as surely it would slip right out of anyone's hands, even the undead kind.

While that was happening, Laura and Sam siphoned gas from the car. There wasn't a whole lot to add, but it was better than nothing.

Oona took the time to change out of her pajamas and into something more futuristic dystopian warlord. He imagined she'd been waiting for a long time for the opportunity to dress in a way she considered appropriate for the circumstance.

"What's the plan, Edgar?" she barked, while verifying that she had a full cartridge in one of her handguns. This was probably for Violet's benefit.

"Start driving, head for the ship, try not to kill anybody."

"Should I start the screamer?" Dobbs asked.

"May not be needed," Ed said. "Assuming it still works."

"We'll man the roof," Laura said, pulling Sam along, "and keep an eye out for Annie."

The camper got moving. Ed knelt down next to the alien device.

"I guess it doesn't make sense to call this a ship," he said.

"It's closer to a probe, or as you said before, an antenna array."

"Does it open?"

"Put your hand back on it."

He did, and after a second or two of nothing, his mind was flooded with images. It looked like a travelogue for a beam of light, only one that took detours outside of regular space.

"Wow," Ed said. "I'm not really sure what any of this means, am I supposed to?"

"The visuals are a form of communication, yes. It's going to figure out you're not an advanced being. The next step would be to activate its defenses, but I've disabled that feature."

"Oh good, thanks." The images stopped, and he removed his hand. "What defenses are we talking about?"

"Just a sonic alarm. Dobbs, would you like to try?"

Dobbs did want to try. He put his hand on and acted suitably impressed by the show going on in his mind.

"But it didn't open," Ed said.

"Oh, right. Wait until he's finished."

"Was that eighth-dimensional space?" Dobbs asked.

"Yes, very good. It's a short cut. The universe is incredibly large if you're stuck inside of it, but very reasonable otherwise. Dobbs, think about the capsule opening."

"Okay."

A horizontal line creased the center of the tablet, and then it popped open like an old-fashioned lunchbox. The interior was bathed in a baby-blue light.

The device was full of stacks of circular discs or coils. It appeared almost solid-state.

"This looks like a large radiator," Dobbs said. "Probably isn't, though, huh?"

"No, it's much more than that. You're familiar with quantum computing technology?"

"Oh, wow, really?"

"You're only seeing the portion of the machine that exists in this dimension. It's actually much larger, if size even means anything in this instance."

"What's the power source?" Ed asked. "Is that here, or is it hanging out in the extra dimension?"

"It's both. It uses a combination of zero-point energy resources and . . . there's no word for the secondary technology. Imagine a way to collect and store chaotic energies. Discharges from the corona of the sun, kinetic energy from a gravitational slingshot, and so on."

"That would violate the third law," Dobbs said.

Violet smiled. "Yes, it would, in a closed system. The waste product of this energy storage would be entropic, and it is, but the entropy isn't manifest in this dimension."

"Okay," Ed said. "But nothing nuclear?"

"Oh, yes, there's a nuclear core too. It's only a backup, though. Like a battery in an alarm clock if the house loses power. The core isn't active right now."

Ed stepped back instinctively, and nearly fell over. Dobbs decided he didn't want to touch the probe anymore.

"It's shielded," Violet said. "Don't worry. Radiation would do the same to me as to you."

"Sure, but you can go find another body," Ed said, "we're sort of stuck with these."

"Comin' up on zombie world, everyone," Oona announced from the driver's seat.

"Is this still extending the . . . I don't know what to call it . . . invisibility cloak?" Ed asked.

"It is."

Ed walked to the front to look out the windshield. "Stop at the turn, I want to see what we're facing."

"A lot of confused marionettes, Edgar," Oona said.

The zombies in the street looked like their equilibrium had been severely compromised: a hundred instant inner-ear infections and extreme vertigo.

"Perfect," Ed said. "Violet, can you shut it off?"

"Why would you do that?" Oona asked.

"I don't want to ruin the surprise."

"It's done," Violet called.

The zombies righted themselves.

"So now they're all in my way and you don't want me to kill anybody, so how do you plan to get there from here?" Oona asked.

"They're not moving."

"Yeah, I *know* they're not moving, that's my problem."

"No, I mean they're not moving toward us or away from us. Honk."

Oona honked. The zombies immediately in front of her got out of her way. Slowly, but successfully.

"What the hell."

"Annie made it to the ship," Ed said.

"How do you know?"

"They're not looking for her anymore. They're on standby, in some sort of basic self-defense mode."

"It's gonna take us a while to get to the ship, just honking and rolling."

"Do the best you can." Ed turned to the back of the camper. "Dobbs, maybe try the screamer again to get some of them moving. It might help."

"Okay."

"When we're close, I'm going to need you focused on finding that signal again."

Ed sat back down next to Violet, with her alien capsule at his feet. The zombie parents were standing across from them, holding their balance pretty well in the rocking trailer.

"Do you want to tell me what you're doing, now?" Violet asked.

"Not sure yet. But I have a few questions. First, how big can you make that invisibility cloak extend?"

"I've never tested its range, how far did you want it to go?"

"How about the same size as Sorrow Falls?"

She studied him carefully.

"Perhaps. But why?"

"Maybe question two will answer question one for you. What did Susan and Todd die of?"

"Susan perished from tuberculosis. Todd was crushed by a carriage wheel."

"Todd looks pretty good."

"Yes . . ." And then she understood. She smiled.

"How long would it take?" he asked.

"I don't know. But if it works, everyone is going to be extremely hungry afterwards."

⋮

Annie had no particular strategy in mind when climbing into the ship, or at any subsequent point in the conversation—possibly except for the part where she mingled Dorothy Gale of Kansas with Violet Jones of Sorrow Falls. She didn't expect that to actually work, but thought it would be funny if it did. It *was* funny, up until the part where she pissed off the super-powerful alien in the planet-ending spacecraft.

She'd been rolling with the *just keep him talking* rule that really only made sense in different contexts, like talking a jumper off a building, giving law enforcement time to trace a phone call, or keeping someone with a concussion awake. She was pretty sure it didn't make as much sense here, because if she was stalling, she didn't herself know what she was stalling *for*. There wasn't anyone coming to the rescue.

Except of course there was. Ed would come running. So would Sam. Dobbs, Oona, Laura . . . they probably would too. Maybe even Violet.

Violet was the only one who could *actually* rescue anybody, and only by surrendering. Likewise, Annie could rescue herself just fine by telling the alien where to look. But as angry as Annie was at Violet, it was the kind of angry she expected to get over eventually. When she did, she wanted Violet to still be around.

Besides, Violet's dad was turning out to be a scary combination of innocent and amoral.

"Drones, you mean all the zombies?"

"That word doesn't correspond to their function. I have heard it said many times tonight and reviewed the meaning."

Annie thought about mentioning the whole *undead* thing, which was definitely a zombie standard, but it seemed beside the point. He recognized that a lot of his drones were living people and was threatening to change that, so he understood alive versus dead.

"So you're an evil idea," she decided.

"No. Ideas are neither good nor evil. It's only in their application that they can be one or the other, and even then they can only be judged one or the other from a subjective viewpoint. If I tear apart this planet looking for my daughter, you would no doubt see these as evil actions, but I have seen a million such worlds and consider her of far greater value. I would call it a good thing. Now tell me where to find her or I'll begin with the drones and stop only after I've set the world on fire and picked her out of the remains."

"You sound like a movie villain."

"My speech is built upon your expectations. The intent is mine but the syntax is based on what you anticipate. The voice I'm using has been lowered by your expectations as well."

"So, but the threat's legit."

"Yes. You're running out of . . ."

"Why do you think she came here?"

". . . continuously changing the subject is not going to result in a solution."

"No, no, I understand that. Look, I'm sorry, you're the first alien I've talked to. Well, second, but the first one didn't tell me what she was, so I never had a chance to ask things. I get it, though, you're a really, really old idea. I'm not all that clear on how I'm talking to one, because we're not used to ideas with sentience, but okay."

"There are many ideas, but only a few are powerful enough to live forever."

"And, to live outside of whoever thought you up. That's the part there. Like, if you're ever in a situation where you have to explain yourself, in the future, I'd start there."

"You are not advanced enough, as a species, to understand."

"Yes, yes, I know, we're primitive, I get it. And my friend, your daughter — or offspring, or piece of you or . . . whatever — she's another super-advanced being, right? Then why do you think she'd come *here*, to hang out with a bunch of people who, so far as you're concerned, can't even understand what she is?"

". . . I don't know."

"She's your idea, and your idea had an idea and *that* idea was to come here and hang out for a few hundred years. If I ask her she'll say it was to hide from you, but she did a pretty crappy job of that. So why was she really here?"

The alien began showing a series of images. These were different from before, in that Annie didn't feel so much like she was experiencing them. They were purely visual, and none of them were moving. It was a photo album.

They were extraordinary. She wished they were more interactive, because the scale and scope were magnificent. Great cities of iron, of crystal, of frozen gases and sculptured lava. She saw platforms to slingshot a vessel from the surface into upper orbit, and humanoids with webbed clothing to help them to fly. There was an undersea kingdom beneath a sky of eternal permafrost, and vast libraries of knowledge preserved on stone and cloth, in jars of electrical impulses and three-dimensional models made of silk. She saw ships powered by starlight traveling through holes in the universe poked open by controlled singularities, and beings of radiation living on an artificial ring around a dying sun.

"To be an idea such as myself is to be a part of the greatest accomplishments in the history of all histories. I existed—I was born—as an idea inside of these beings. They were a part of what made me, as I was a part of who they became. But the great civilizations are all gone."

"Wait, I don't understand. Which one of them thought of you?"

"All did. It's equally reasonable to say I thought of them. I appeared in the minds of those who were ready. From their perspectives, I was something new, even as from mine I was older than their stars. But each of these civilizations had a different way of using me, for good or ill. There is a sense of connection, and belonging, and growth, and that's what your friend Violet took with her. The sense of being something new again. That's what I truly want back. And that is what I'm sure led her here. To belong. Even among beings unprepared to accept her, which was immature of her."

"I never told you her name."

"I know. I've found your true idea of her."

"But we aren't done talking yet!"

"I have no need of you, or this place, any longer."

She heard the hiss stop as the alien cut off Annie's air supply.

⋮

"*Edgar, we're here!*" Oona yelled through the ceiling. Ed was already on the roof with Sam, Laura, and Dobbs, who was perhaps the most important person in Sorrow Falls for the next few minutes.

Sam was marching up and down the right side of the camper, which faced the ship. He'd been misidentifying various members of the zombie class of the town as Annie for the entire journey, and now he was mostly just angry and looking for someone to shoot.

"Whole base is here," he said. "Look at 'em, lined up in a row. We're not gonna get through without running them down. I think they're operating on different orders."

"We don't need to get through," Ed said. He leaned over Dobbs at the computer. "Can you find the signal?"

"I don't know, I told you this isn't my equipment."

"Oh, get out of the way," Laura said. She pushed Dobbs aside and tapped a few commands. "You gotta at least bring up the array first."

The "array" was a series of microphones on a stanchion in the middle of the camper, with small parabolic dishes cupping each of the microphones. Dobbs spent the better half of the trip reassembling the array because it had been partly broken down earlier that evening to amplify the screamers. (That it took so long for anyone to point this out only underlined exactly how tired everyone was.) It also meant they made the trip without the one proven means to disable zombies.

"That's got it," Dobbs said.

Oona popped up through the trap door. "I'm just gonna leave us in the middle of the road. Don't think anyone's driving down here anytime soon. Did you screw up my computer, Dobbs?"

"Not yet."

"Why we looking for the signal, Edgar?"

"You'll see. Where's Violet?"

"The zombie queen's downstairs fiddling with her magic suppository."

"*I'll be right up,*" she shouted from below.

"I'll be damned. PICKLES?" Sam shouted the last part, and Ed for just a few seconds wondered if the soldier was now hallucinating gherkins. Then he remembered Dill Louboutin's nickname.

"Hey, Sam!" Dill shouted back.

Dill was standing next to a Humvee on the other side of a crashed-in fence, just at the edge of the ship's safety zone. He had a kid with him, but the kid wasn't Annie.

"The hell you doin' over there?"

"Waitin' for you. See you got a better ride. You want me to mow down these dead-eyes for you?"

"Better stay there. What were you thinking, did you try to run over the ship?"

"I was thinking maybe it was worth a shot. But then the girl went in, so we were just waiting on you. She said you'd be by."

Sam turned to Ed. "The girl . . . went in."

"How'd she do that?" Ed asked.

"How'd she do that, Dill?" Sam asked.

"She said she was here and the thing just opened. Someone should've tried that before we had zombies, you ask me."

"I've got it, I think," Dobbs said. "Just sounds like breathing. Did he say Annie was in there?"

"Yeah, can you hear her with that?"

"No, it's just the breathing."

Violet came up. "She went inside."

"Can you get her out?" Ed asked.

"Only by taking her place."

"It may come to that."

"I realize."

"Then go do it," Sam said. "Get her out of there."

"Not yet, Sam," Laura said.

Sam didn't like the plan, and had said as much more than once.

She can take care of herself, Ed thought. *For at least a little while longer.*

Violet extended a coaxial cable to Dobbs.

"Can you plug this into the output? I'm going to need to analyze the signal."

"S . . . sure. You had a jack for this? That thing doesn't even have an interface."

"It does now. I asked it for one."

"How long?" Ed asked.

"Five minutes, at most. I need to piggyback the signal, but I already know what I'm sending."

"Ed?" It was Laura. She was looking over the side of the camper. "Don't think we have five minutes."

"Here comes the army," Sam said. "Looks like they've decided we're a threat."

"Hot damn, I *do* get to shoot somebody," Oona said.

⋮

"Hey!" Annie shouted. The tinny echo came back on her as if to underline how alone she was inside the ship. She was *always* alone, in a sense, because the alien was only as *there* as a computer program or a TV show. He was an idea of a thing instead of a thing, which should have made him less real but somehow didn't. Somehow it felt like he was much more real than she or anything on the planet was.

Perhaps he was rubbing off on her as much as she was clearly affecting him. His voice had gotten deeper, he started using contractions, and it felt like she was talking to an actual person, right up until he decided he was done with her.

Not that that wasn't also a very human quality.

"You still need my help," she said. It probably wasn't true, and she didn't even sound convincing to her own ears, but it was worth trying. The only other option was to suffocate.

Unless that's not the only option, she thought.

The ship responded to her before. She got a glimpse of the outside, and maybe the alien didn't even realize that had happened. She was also still carrying the entire operating manual in her head.

Annie started thinking of an idea. It was a simple idea, of a ship with an aperture that pumped air in, and a filter that scrubbed CO_2. There wasn't a lot to it; if she wanted to take the ship into space she'd have to come up with a better idea, but this one would keep her alive for a while.

It worked. There was no telltale hiss and the air quality hadn't devolved sufficiently for a change to be notable immediately, but she could sense the handoff. The idea had been uploaded in some kind of invisible exchange, and the ship acted. She was going to be okay for a little bit longer.

"Annie."

"Oh, hi. Where've you been?"

"Did you do that?"

"What, turn the air on? Yeah, I didn't want to die."

"Not that. The drones are missing."

"Uh . . . I don't really know what that means. You lost contact with them?"

"Based on their feedback, each of them was bodily relocated outside of Sorrow Falls at the speed of light. This is possible for one such as myself, but not for one such as you. They also can't leave through the shield I've placed over the town, so it's impossible for them to be where I'm told they are. Therefore, they weren't relocated at all and something else has happened. Did you do this somehow?"

Violet is here.

"No, but that sounds like a cool trick."

⋮

"I think it worked," Sam said.

The fact of this was self-evident, because the camper stopped rocking and Oona, Sam, and Laura weren't shooting anymore. That they had to take any shots at all became necessary once the soldiers tried scaling the sides, something the townsfolk reportedly never tried during an earlier siege.

They were shooting to wound, in theory, but ultimately the goal was to get the zombies off the side of the camper by any means necessary. If an arm or a leg could be disabled, great. More than a couple of times, it was a head or a heart, though, and there wasn't anyone to blame for that, aside from whatever being was inside the ship with Annie.

"They're just wandering around," Laura said.

"This is funny as hell," Oona said. "Like they all got drunk at the same time."

Their movements reminded Ed of what someone might look like when missing the bottom step on a staircase. Their feet weren't finding land where they were expecting to.

"Looks like phase one worked, Violet," Ed said through the open trap door. "Ready for phase two anytime you are."

⋮

Annie decided she wanted to see outside again, so she asked the ship and the ship showed the outside to her. The zombies were still there, but they were acting less zombie-like and more staggeringly drunk-like. She also saw Oona and Laura's camper and understood exactly what had happened.

For some reason, the alien hadn't figured out his daughter was the only one with the technology to do what they just did, and had been using his zombie network for information for long enough that he forgot he could just look out the proverbial window.

"So what'cha doing?" Annie asked.

"I'm performing a diagnostic of the ship's systems. They're clearly malfunctioning."

"Okay. Hey, can I ask you a really dumb question?"

"Yes."

"Why don't you just go out and be a new idea for some other civilization? If what you're missing is that sense, like you said, of being something new, just go out and be that for someone else. I mean, if you're right and that's why Violet came here—and I think you probably are—what do you even need her for? Make your own memories and all that."

"I am the greatest idea that ever was. There is no civilization prepared to fully grasp all that I am."

"What happened to the ones that were?"

"They're gone."

"But why?"

"Great ideas have many uses."

"So you're saying they all destroyed themselves."

"I'm saying *some* did. Some grew out of a need for me. I'm still a part of them, but a historical part. I continue to exist in the minds of others, but as an idea that no longer provides value and doesn't change."

"So you're kind of a snob, basically."

"I'm sure I don't understand."

"You could involve yourself just like Violet did, but you don't think we're worthy of your big, total ideaness."

"My offspring didn't involve herself in the way you describe. She isn't an idea that exists within this civilization. If she were, I'd have found her immediately instead of having to engage in this puppet show. She remains a self-contained idea, engaging ones such as yourself for reasons I won't fully appreciate until I have her back and can ask."

"I don't know."

The alien sighed. The emotion of exasperation was a new one for him. Annie was definitely having an impact, because she heard this tone from every adult in her life at one time or another.

"What is it you don't know, Annie?"

"I don't know how great an idea you actually are."

". . . I would cause your mind to explode."

"I think you're exaggerating."

"I'm not."

"Look, you already dropped the ship's entire design into my head, and that included a ton of things nobody with my kind of brain ever experienced. That didn't wreck me."

"You didn't understand what you were shown."

"Dim the lights."

The blue lights dimmed slightly.

"That is unremarkable."

"Fine. Give me a second."

Mariachi music began to play inside the ship.

"What is that sound?" the alien asked.

"When I was ten my dad took me to a Mexican restaurant in Athol for my birthday. This is the song they played for me. It's kind of repetitive; I don't remember the whole thing, so it's on a loop. I can also turn off the defensive shield from here, I'm pretty sure. And a few minutes ago I thought about what the government archives for this machine must look like, and the ship dropped a bunch of emails into my head. So maybe it's just that I carried Violet around, or maybe the human mind is a little more advanced than you think."

"... All right. But why would I do this?"

"I don't know, you seem lonely. I mean, we've only just met, but if I were an idea too and I were hanging out wherever ideas hang out, I'd say you need to get out there and introduce yourself to new species. Change things up."

"This is a preposterous conversation."

"I have a lot of those."

"... Even assuming you survived, you wouldn't know what to do with me."

"Why would I have to *do* anything? Ideas can just be ideas sometimes, right? Look, you don't have anything to lose. In a couple of minutes you're going to go back to the whole *kill all the people* thing you've got going on, so I'll end up dead either way. I'd rather go by way of the greatest idea ever. I mean, if you aren't exaggerating."

He fell silent, which she took to mean he was thinking but could also have meant his ship diagnostic was finished and he'd managed to overcome the distractions Annie kept throwing at him for long enough to notice that Violet was sitting in a camper fifty yards away.

"All right," he said.

The gentle blue of the interior brightened, and then crawled inside of her, or so it seemed. She was being pulled away from reality, down Alice's rabbit hole, up the tornado spout, and into Oz.

Ideas already in her head connected with other ideas already in her head, establishing relationships with one another she couldn't believe she'd never seen before. These weren't strictly her own ideas. They were things she'd picked up from books, and movies, and school, and Violet. They were ideas other people had that she'd taken and made a part of her. They fit perfectly, and then started to connect to other things: things she'd never known before, that nobody on the planet had ever known before.

There was a vast network of interconnected ideas in her mind,

Einstein's grand theory of everything multiplied by ten, laid out across extra dimensions. It was beautiful, and very nearly too much to bear.

Then came the idea.

He was right. It was the greatest idea she could have imagined.

She thought maybe her mind really was going to explode.

23
DEUS EX MACHINA

*T*he president of the United States was in the second year of his first term when an extraterrestrial vehicle landed in Massachusetts and changed the world.

It made for pretty good politics.

There were a lot of complications, certainly. The riots were bad. International politics got about ten times weirder. Suicide rates were alarmingly high. But at the same time, a smart politician could capitalize on the upside of being in charge when the world changed, while suffering from almost none of the customary downside.

There was no alien invasion, no need to develop some kind of space armada — as if that was even an option — and no cities were destroyed. No ultimatums were issued or negotiations brokered with alien generals. Essentially none of the options from any work of fiction on the subject ever came up.

Instead, strategies were debated and official plans drawn up within the government, while outside, in the declassified world, the president ran for re-election with the pedigree of a wartime commander-in-chief, only without the body count.

The whole time he was busy being a Leader, effectively Handling the Situation just like his campaign strategists said, there was the nagging thought in the back of his mind: *what if I actually have to make a decision here?*

He knew the doomsday scenarios. He signed off on them. But by the third year, with the ship still showing no signal of intent, he figured he was in the clear. Maybe the worst-outcome plans they'd drawn up would get used one day, but it would be a day long after he left office, and a decision made by someone else.

The ship was not so kind.

In front of him was an executive order. It had been drafted over a year ago and left unsigned in a folder kept in a locked safe somewhere in the White House. He didn't even know precisely where that safe was, and made a note to ask his chief of staff later. (It was a strange thing to think, but it had been a strange night.)

He was at the head of a table in the harshly labeled "war room" of the building. It was a surprisingly pedestrian room: no polished oak tables or any of that. Half the chairs were of the folding variety. It was not a room meant to impress like the Oval Office was, because nobody who required impressing was allowed into the war room.

About the only cool thing about it was the monitors on one wall, which carried all kinds of interesting satellite feeds depending on the crisis.

At this moment, the screens were dark, and the president was alone. He'd already received the formal briefing, which included a long list of the world and national leaders who signed off on the decision he would be making as soon as he put his signature on the bottom of the order. He wished some of those leaders were in the room and literally standing behind him, telling him that what he was about to do was the correct decision.

He picked up the pen, and hoped to God it was.

The phone began to ring.

It was a conference room speakerphone. It sat in the middle of the table, looking somewhat flying-saucer-like. There was only one button on it. Hitting the button opened a line to the switchboard, and the White House switchboard could place a call from there to anyplace in the world.

It wasn't the sort of phone line people called into.

He pushed the button.

"Um . . . hello?"

"Mr. President! Hi, I'm glad I caught you."

It was a woman's voice, but he didn't recognize it.

"Is this the switchboard? Whom am I talking to?"

"It's Annie. Annie Collins. We met once, but I'm sure you don't remember. I'm calling from Sorrow Falls."

"Miss, I don't know how you got this number, but you're going to be in a great deal of trouble."

"I *know*, it was tough! The ship was already jacked into the White House Wi-Fi, but it took, like, *forever* to find a port to a video feed, and then it turns out you're in a room without security cameras. Figures. Anyway, had to try a few numbers."

"What *ship* are you talking about, Ms. Collins?"

It was a prank. Clearly. The worst-timed prank in the world.

"Look, I don't have a lot of time. After I hang up with you I want to call my mom, I know she's probably flipping out, but I figured I'd better get you first. Before you nuke the town."

"How could you . . . Who are you again?"

"Annie. Like I said, the ship was already hooked up to the White House. It has the Pentagon too. Has everywhere, actually. It's how it was learning about us. Advance probe and all that."

"The spaceship, you mean."

"Yeah, that ship. So the nuke isn't a big secret. But look, it's not going to work."

"I've heard a lot of expert opinion that thinks otherwise."

"Sure. Okay, so, first problem. You guys use GPS satellite targeting, right?"

"I think we do. Ms. Collins, how old are you?"

"I'm sixteen, but I don't think that's relevant right now. Hang on, I'm gonna conference in Steve from the Pentagon."

Steven Prentiss was a three-star general. Exactly two people in the world called him Steve: the president, and Mrs. Prentiss.

One of the screens on the wall blinked to life. It was a wide-angle shot of Massachusetts. *Wide* meaning it was far enough up that it was difficult to tell where the state was except for the Cape Cod hook on the right. A pinpoint dot generated by the satellite delivering the image identified Sorrow Falls, in the northwestern part of the state.

"Mr. President, you asked for the satellite imaging?" Steve said. It was definitely Steve's voice. "Did you wish to watch?"

"I haven't signed the order yet, Steve. Stand by. Ms. Collins, can you tell me why I'm looking at this?"

"Can you zoom in?" she asked.

"I'm sorry, who is this?" Steve asked. "I thought . . ."

"Humor me, Steve," the president said. "Go ahead and zoom."

The world on the screen got bigger. The president had seen satellites zoom in for close-ups a hundred times and it never failed to disorient him. He always felt like he was falling.

"How long shall we do this, Ms. Collins?" he asked.

"Keep on going . . . okay, stop. See that light?"

In the dead center of the image was a bright light, but the focus was insufficient to identify the source.

"I do."

"All right, try and get a closer look at that."

"Mr. President?" the general on the phone asked.

"Go ahead."

The image zoomed some more. It was—of course—a shot from directly overhead. He wished he could get side angles, but there was only so much a sub-orbital satellite could do. As it got closer, the light split into dozens of smaller lights. It was a parking lot shaped like a digital zero.

"Gentlemen, that is the Oakdale Mall. Your precise GPS coordinates are targeting the wrong town."

"Steve?"

"Mr. President, I don't know what to say . . . We're comparing this to still images of the area . . . I think she's right."

"Are you doing this, Ms. Collins?"

"Me? No, not me personally."

"Seems you've hacked the war room *and* the Pentagon in the past few minutes. It strikes me as a reasonable question."

"Mr. President, who is this person? Is she not in the room with you?"

"According to her, she's a sixteen-year-old calling us from Sorrow Falls. So Ms. Collins, the targeting package is off, we can adjust that."

"It'll miss in every direction. Right now, Sorrow Falls doesn't exist according to any of your satellites. You'll keep hitting the wrong town. But that's only the first problem."

"Did you say she's sixteen?" Steve asked.

"Go on, tell me what the second problem is."

"So you're probably thinking, well, Annie, it's a nuclear bomb. We can miss left or right and still take out the target."

"That's exactly what I'm thinking, yes."

"The bomb won't work on the ship. Now, it's true the amount of energy coming out of one of those is too much for the shield to straight-up absorb like it did with the other things you dropped earlier, but whatever it can't absorb it'll just reflect outward. Basically, you hit it with a bomb and you'll destroy New England. And the ship will still be here."

"Miss, how could you possibly know this?" Steve asked.

"I'm in the ship, General. It's a really super-long story, and I don't have time to tell you the whole thing right now. I'd like to call my mother, then I'm going to take down the shield, but I'd appreciate it if you didn't destroy the entire East Coast while I was doing that. Everything'll be okay, guys, I promise. You can stand down. What *would* be great is if you guys can figure out how to feed about five thousand ex-zombies who are gonna wake up super hungry. No brains, just pizza or something."

"I'm sorry," the president said, "did you say zombies?"

⋮

The invisible shield over Sorrow Falls came down at oh-three-thirty, but the army didn't realize this until oh-four-hundred, as the problem with invisible shields is that it's difficult to tell when they aren't there anymore.

There were multiple entry points to the town, but only a few that could accommodate heavy artillery. After an aerial review—via helicopter, at a distance—of the bridges leading to Main, it was determined that the best route to take was from the west, down Spaceship Road. This plan also satisfied members of the Army Corps of Engineers involved in the planning and execution of the project that widened and paved Spaceship Road specifically for the purpose of supporting an invading force.

The reason the bridges were considered bad options was the traffic clogging them, and the assumption that there were people in those cars. In a worst-case-scenario sort of situation, the army might still consider pushing the cars off one of the bridges or simply driving over them with tanks, but this was a less-than-ideal solution, for a number of reasons. One was that commuter bridges were more or less designed to prevent cars from simply tipping over the sides. Another was that as much as tanks were designed to climb over cars, that sort of thing could take forever, and leave a crushed obstacle in its wake, rendering the bridge even less passable for all the non-tank vehicles.

Spaceship Road also had a lot of cars on it, but there was no precipitous drop on either side, and not even a shoulder to bar cars from drifting off. This opened up a range of possibilities for clearing the road. The choice the army went with was to ask the occupants of the cars to kindly get the hell out of the way immediately.

It was an effective approach, involving the least amount of property damage, but it also took a terribly long time, because the line of cars was thirty deep, taking up both travel lanes, and everyone was facing outbound.

At oh-four-thirty, the general in charge of the invading force tasked Major Sharon Price with the responsibility of entering town ahead of the rest of the army in order to scout the terrain.

Major Price grabbed the nearest Jeep and a driver for that Jeep, took it off-road around the traffic jam, and became the first non-resident to enter Sorrow Falls since the ship self-activated.

She and her driver—a corporal named Wentz—headed straight for the spaceship, past what looked like an utterly ruined army base. A number of observations were reported up the chain-of-command immediately, including the discovery that everyone in the town was either dead on the side of the road or sleeping on the side of the road. This was not strictly an either/or, although it was interpreted as such by the higher-ups initially, which was why the first news reports that morning announced incorrectly that the entire town was dead.

Travel past the very edge of the town was slow, because not all of the people dead/sleeping were on the *side* of the road. Quite a few were in the middle of it. Since a couple were actively snoring, Price and Wentz agreed that the best recourse was to evade them as much as was possible, and try to figure out later why so many were napping on the median strip.

The only place Price discovered people both alive and conscious was around the ship. There, she met Corporals Corning and Louboutin, the only two unaffected army soldiers from the base, and a handful of civilians, all of whom later became famous in their own way for having survived the night.

None of them was Annie Collins.

When the military was ordered to the scene, it was with two mandates: secure the ship, and take Annie Collins into custody. Sharon Price had no idea who Ms. Collins was or why she might warrant such particular concern, but orders were orders.

By oh-five-fifteen, Price had notified the trailing force that the town of Sorrow Falls was no longer in immediate danger, and urged the general to exercise caution, as there were private citizens and army officers sleeping out in the open.

This point had to be repeated several times.

Price also declared the ship to be secured, or at least as secured as it had been the day before it came to life.

At oh-five-twenty-two, the side of the ship opened, and a sixteen-year-old girl in muddy clothing emerged from a blue-tinted interior. Price and Wentz drew their weapons and ordered the survivors to step back. This order was roundly ignored.

The girl was Annie Collins, and Price finally understood her orders.

According to most accounts, the first thing Annie said — after the hugs she received from essentially everyone in the clearing who wasn't Price or Wentz — was:

"Step back."

This was excellent advice, because at oh-five-twenty-nine, the Sorrow Falls spaceship roared to life, lifted off the ground, and after hovering seven feet above the earth for several seconds, shot straight up and into space.

Step back was not actually the first thing Annie said, however. The first thing she said was addressed specifically to Major Price and Corporal Wentz. It was: "I thought I ordered pizza."

24
A GOOD IDEA IS HARD TO FIND

*A*nnie had never been to Washington, D.C., before.

The only other time the opportunity presented itself was a class trip to the capital that was canceled last-minute because half the grade came down with the flu at the same time. It was the same year the ship landed anyway, so there was a lot less interest locally in going to see the White House and the Smithsonian when a much more interesting thing was happening on the town's front lawn.

She remembered that year pretty well, not just because of the ship. That was the year everyone on the planet—it seemed—passed through town, and when she learned that being famous didn't preclude anybody from being a total nutbar. The cancellation of the annual D.C. class trip seemed like a formality.

So far, she hadn't had a chance to see anything up close. It was easy enough to spot important landmarks from the back of the SUV—the Washington Monument, Congress's gold dome, the Lincoln Memorial—but it was all in passing, and largely ignored by everyone else in the car. She wondered what it must be like to live around things other people considered extraordinary. Then she remembered she was from Sorrow Falls.

She could see the tip of the monument from the window. She was in a corner room on the top floor of an unassuming, square building that looked a lot like several other such buildings in the district. She had no idea what the name of the building was—if it even had one—or which government agency it belonged to.

It was a little alarming. Nobody would tell her precisely where she was going from day to day, only that they would *like it very much* if she came with them. It had been like this since the morning after. That was four days prior, but felt like it was months ago.

Incredibly, since her initial interview, conducted in the field in front of the ship by an army officer and consisting of only five questions—*are you all right, are you sure, can you step over here, please, can we ask you a few questions,* and *are you Annie Collins*—nobody questioned her. Once she answered the fifth question with an affirmation she was politely escorted to the back of a Jeep and had been on the move ever since. She guessed this was standard protocol for sixteen-year-olds who call the president in the war room.

Only one other question was asked since. That was, *can you write down everything that happened to you on the night of the ship, in your own words?* She'd done that. Nothing was sent back with notes or feedback, or even a smiley face sticker like the one Mrs. Winston in English put on the essays she liked.

It probably should have been a little intimidating. She didn't feel intimidated, though. She'd had no contact with anyone from the media, but they hadn't taken television away from her—that would probably, at some point, require that they decide to call her a prisoner instead of a guest—so she was well aware that her name came up quite a lot in the national discussion. Her friends from the trailer, plus Dill and Dougie, had clearly already been spoken to and released back into the wild, as they were all over the news. All except for two of them.

The door on the other end of the room opened.

"Ed!" Annie shouted. She stepped around the table and gave him a long hug. Then she punched him in the shoulder. "Where the *hell* have you been?"

"Sorry, I'm sorry, it's been crazy." He released her, stepped back, and took a good look. "They're treating you all right? Looks like they took you shopping."

"Yes! I can't go to the Smithsonian, but the mall? That they can do for me. I think the girls in the Gap thought I was some head-of-state's daughter. It was awesome. The hotel, too. But look at you, you look more tired than the last time I saw you."

"Fewer bruises, though, I hope."

"Yes."

"Like I said, it's been crazy. Look, has anyone talked to you about . . ."

He stopped himself when the door reopened, admitting an army officer in full dress.

"Ms. Collins? Hello, I'm Major Corcoran." His introduction came with a firm handshake. He had a cold hand and a dry grip.

He dropped a shoulder bag onto the table and took a seat on one side of it, then extracted a tape recorder and a stack of folders. These he arranged on the table in a way that implied there was an exactly correct place for them. Then he took out a new pad of paper—white, standard size, lined—and a pen. They had places as well. Finally, he looked up at the two other people in the room, as if they'd only just arrived and he'd been there the whole time.

"Please, sit."

He turned the tape recorder on as they took his suggestion.

"This is Major Donald Corcoran, in an interview with Ms. Annette Collins. Also in attendance is Mr. Edgar Somerville, who has already provided independent testimony."

Ed looked at her. "Annette?"

"Literally my first words were, 'Never call me Annette.' They must have looked at the first draft of my birth certificate."

"Mr. Somerville, for the record, I have an objection to your presence in this interview."

"I'm aware of that, Major. I'm also Annie's legal guardian, and she's a minor. I believe we had this argument already."

"So we did; I wanted it on record."

"You guys have been fighting over me?" Annie asked.

"Ms. Collins, in the past four days you have been the subject of very nearly every conversation Mr. Somerville and I have been a part of, as have a significant number of other people."

Major Corcoran spoke as if his words were as starched and ironed as his shirt.

"Well, that's cool. Every girl's dream."

"Yes." He cleared his throat. She noted a lack of comfort on his part with informality. "I'm going to walk through the events as we understand them, and ask that you fill in details whenever you can."

"All right."

He opened the first folder, and examined the top page for several seconds before speaking, as if what was on there were a prepared speech.

"According to statements made by Corporal Louboutin and a Mr. Douglas Kozinsky . . . private citizen . . . at some time around two in the morning on the night in question, you approached the anomaly, asked to be admitted, and went inside."

"Can't you just call it the spaceship?"

"The spaceship, then. Is that right?"

"Yeah, but you knew that. The major on the scene, in the Jeep . . ."

"We'll get to that."

"Okay." She rolled her eyes at Ed, who smiled.

"You asked to be admitted," Corcoran repeated. "Is that accurate?"

"More or less."

"What did you say?"

"Open sesame. I'm surprised you guys never tried that."

"Ms. Collins, these are important questions. What exactly did you say?"

"I said, 'I am her.'"

Corcoran leaned forward and made a lengthy note on one of his clean pads of paper.

"That was in my statement too," Annie said.

He held up a finger to indicate he was still writing, and evidently couldn't do more than one thing at a time.

"Yes, it was," he agreed, putting his pen down. "All right. You went inside. According to your own statement it was . . ." He searched for the right folder, opened it, and read, ". . . blue."

"Yep. Very blue."

"Could you provide any more detail?"

"Um . . . baby blue, I guess. Not quite a cerulean. Almost a pastel."

Ed put his hand on her arm.

"One second, Major," he said. He nodded his head, and they turned their chairs around, away from the recorder. A good one would still pick up most of their conversation, but Ed didn't appear to have the kind of authority necessary to insist it be shut off.

"Look," he said, "I don't want to scare you, but if you want to go home again, you need to start taking this seriously."

"Home again *at all?*"

"Like I said, I don't want to scare you."

"Despite which, you're going to say something terrifying, sure. Ed, you worry too much. I have this covered."

"Annie . . ."

"Trust me."

She turned her chair back around.

"Sorry," she said to the major. "Ed thinks I need to give you a better answer, so I'll try. It was blue and fuzzy. There wasn't any visible technology, and as much as I was sitting in a chair inside a chamber, the spaceship was an unmanned probe that wasn't built to carry and sustain biological life forms. It created the chamber to accommodate me. So, blue, fuzzy, and comfortable, I guess. Especially once the ship added air conditioning."

"According to your statement, you spoke to an alien, explained to him he was in the wrong place, and suggested he look elsewhere. He was . . ." Again he quoted verbatim: ". . . really cool about the whole thing."

"Yeah, he just needed directions."

"You were in the ship for over three hours."

"He needed a *lot* of directions."

"And those directions required him to enter lower orbit?"

"I don't know what you mean."

"I think you do, Ms. Collins. That's where the ship is now."

Annie wanted to add that *so much more* happened in those three hours, beyond even the parts she wasn't telling Major Corcoran. There was the part where Ed and Violet hijacked the zombie network and made everyone go to sleep, and the part where everyone who wasn't dead already woke up at sunrise fully healed of whatever wounds they'd incurred overnight.

That was easily the coolest trick anyone pulled, but nobody was talking about it because the rest of the story was that over two hundred people died over the course of the evening, and when the survivors awoke there was a literal scramble to get everyone protein before they collapsed or began *actually* eating brains or whatever else they could get their hands on.

Annie told the president to send pizza, but on that he didn't listen. Fortunately, he paid attention to everything else she told him.

"I understand," Annie said. "You're a little confused, see, the alien isn't on the ship anymore. The ship is just a probe, he showed up later. Like, what, a month ago?"

"I can pinpoint the date," Ed said. "If you need it, Major."

"I'm not confused, Ms. Collins. I'm dubious. A non-corporeal super-intelligent electrical space ghost inhabited a weapon with world-destroying capabilities until you knocked on the door and told him to go away, and then he did. This is what I'm dealing with. You can imagine how unhappy that story has people on my side of the table."

She gasped.

"*Space ghost?* That's an awesome description! Ed, did you think of that?"

"Annie . . ."

"I know, take it seriously."

"It's *very* serious," the major said. "All we have to go on is your word that there's no alien intelligence remaining in the ship. It manifested as a hostile, and now it's in low orbit."

"Right, but I don't know how else to help you, Major. I mean, if you want to try nuking it *now*, I guess you can. It won't do anything, and I have no idea what that would do to the upper atmosphere, but sure. Ed, what would happen if a nuclear blast, like, *bounced* off an object in low orbit? Wouldn't all that force directed back toward the planet kind of suck for the planet?"

"If there's a hostile entity in that ship," Corcoran said, "we need to know."

"There isn't. Can I go home now?"

"We need more than your word."

"I don't really think you do."

Major Corcoran was the kind of person who needed glasses, Annie decided. He needed them for moments like this, so he could remove them dramatically and rub the bridge of his nose, or throw them on the pile of papers and sigh deeply. He could even chew one of the earpieces and point across the table with them. The possibilities were endless.

He didn't have glasses, though, so his expressions of impatient exasperation were so much less than they could have been. He could sigh, and rub his chin, but that was about all. Perhaps the military had drummed the more interesting displays out of him already.

"Ms. Collins," he said, "if this statement and these answers are all you have to offer, it may be a *long* time before you get to go home. I'm speaking now for the people above me, not myself. I would be happy to let you get on with your life, but if you think the government isn't going to find a way to detain you solely because of your age or your current celebrity status, you're mistaken. Right now there's an entire team of scientists waiting to perform medical tests on you, and that's not even to satisfy a security concern. I'm the only thing standing between you and a long, uncomfortable existence as a de facto prisoner of the state. I need you to stop treating me like an enemy and start being more cooperative."

Annie laughed.

"Oh, come on."

"Annie, he's serious," Ed said. He looked pale and worried. It was cute.

"Look, Ed, he's either bluffing or he's an idiot, and I don't think he's an idiot."

"Well, this interview is over," Corcoran said, addressing Ed. He reached for the tape recorder.

"Hold on, hold on," Annie said. "Keep that running. Ed, here's what the major isn't telling you . . . unless he doesn't know either and the people pulling his chain sent him in here without all the information he needed. Doesn't matter. I'm guessing someone who listens to this tape knows, anyway. Two days ago, a message showed up in a place where a message shouldn't show up, on a computer nobody is supposed to know about. I'm going to keep on giving the major the benefit of the doubt and assume he's bluffing and knows about that message."

At that point, the major did turn off the tape recorder.

"Yes, I know about the message."

"Go on. For Ed: what did it say?"

"It said . . ." He cleared his throat, as if these were perhaps the most difficult words ever. "It said 'Annie Collins was here.'"

"Which is *funny* because I wasn't *there* when that happened, I was in a hotel a few blocks from here, having all my standard electronic communications monitored. I mean, I'm assuming that's true, you guys aren't that stupid."

"She was being monitored closely," Corcoran said, to Ed.

"So here's your problem, Major. You've got a spaceship in an established orbit carrying sensitive data from every government database in the world. You think since the ship took off after I climbed out, and the message appeared in that secret computer while I was in custody, therefore an alien is still on board, planning something terrible. If that's the case, I must be lying to you. But that's only one possibility. The other possibility is I'm telling you the truth."

"Then how did the message . . ." Corcoran stopped in midsentence, because that was when it came to him. "Oh."

"C'mon, I even signed it for you guys. But look, it doesn't matter. Either there's an alien presence controlling the indestructible spaceship, or the sixteen-year-old you've been trying to intimidate for the past half hour is. One way or another, we'd both like it very much if you arranged for me to go home now."

⋮

"So are you going to tell me what really happened?" Ed asked.

It took about a week to convince the necessary members of the government that Annie, a sarcastic but otherwise seemingly harmless young woman from a tiny Massachusetts town, could exert control—somehow—over an extra-terrestrial warship. This was undoubtedly how long Ed had been holding on to this question. It might even have been why he insisted on being the one to return her to her home.

They were crossing the southern bridge to Main Street when he asked. At that point they were already seeing some of the impact on the town from the last time they were in Sorrow Falls. The bridge they were going over had scuffmarks on the side railings, there was still broken glass and debris in the margins, and the traffic was about double what it should have been. Up ahead, right near the library, there were several mobile satellite towers.

The media had returned.

Two days ago, Annie spoke to the most positive-sounding, enthusiastic woman on the planet. Her name was Nita, and she was a publicist. Nita was arranging a modest media blitz. This was something of an unfortunate inevitability. Annie needed the media to make sure everybody knew who she was. She was still the little girl who touched the spaceship when nobody else could and didn't particularly want people to know that, but she appreciated celebrity as a form of protection in this case.

The ship in orbit holding international secrets was a better form of protection, but one couldn't be too careful.

Soon, Annie would be appearing on national television in a variety of controlled settings and telling *her side of the story*. She hadn't decided yet what that story was going to be, but there was still some time.

For the short term, she could ignore all the mobile TV units who would no doubt fall over themselves to talk to her.

"You didn't like the story I gave to the army?"

Ed laughed.

"That was barely a story at all."

"Where do you want me to start?"

"How about with *so I met an alien.*"

"Okay. So, I met an alien. He was pretty much as Violet described."

"Terrifying, vengeful, willing to destroy the planet?"

"Maybe not terrifying. Confused. But that isn't what I mean. He was a sentient idea. So I treated him like one."

"I'm not sure I understand how one treats a sentient idea."

They made it off the bridge and hung a left, up the hill to Spaceship Road. The whole area was an unfortunate combination of wrecked vehicles and roadside memorials. There were entirely too many memorials. Even more than when the ship first landed, Sorrow Falls was never going to be the same.

"Ideas aren't meant to be alone," Annie said. "They're supposed to be shared. I asked him to share himself."

"To . . . is there a non-creepy way to phrase that?"

"Probably."

"So, um, was he a good idea?"

"Not a clue. He was right when he said he was too advanced for me to really understand. But that didn't matter. As soon as I had him in my head I started thinking of a nicer version of him."

Ed didn't have a response to this. He just looked at her with a raised eyebrow.

On their left, they were coming up on the field where the ship had been until recently. The army still had the place cordoned off, and a state policeman was directing traffic. The campers were all gone. This made Annie sad.

"You gotta understand, everything worked different in that ship. It responded to thoughts. Actually, no, that's not really right, it responded to ideas. I had to formulate a complete idea and . . . push it to the ship, I guess is the only way to describe it. The alien was kind of the same way, only more . . . pure. I couldn't *think* the ship into being something other than what it was. But I could *think* him into being a slightly less malevolent idea."

"Even if you didn't understand it?"

"Apparently, yeah. Because I took his idea and imagined a version of him that wanted to leave the planet and go find another one."

"And that worked."

"He left, didn't he?"

Ed smiled.

"Annie, honestly, I'm in the same position as everyone else. You tell me he left and I have no way to prove that's true or untrue. I'll take your word for it."

"C'mon, Ed, after all we've been through, would I lie to you?"

⋮

It was another twenty minutes of traffic and wreckage before they arrived at their destination, which was not Annie's house. They went *past* the house, but her mother wouldn't be back from Boston for another four days, so technically Annie still couldn't stay there alone. That was sort of okay, because her address wasn't a secret and there were two news trucks parked on her lawn already.

The destination was Violet's house.

They'd called ahead; Violet was sitting on the porch waiting. As a courtesy, her "parents" weren't around. There was no point in maintaining that illusion any longer.

"Meant to say, thanks for keeping her out of this," Annie said.

"You're welcome. I didn't have a lot of choice, though. Nobody else remembered she was even there. I would have come off as crazy, talking about the dead kid with the anti-zombie baby coffin space capsule. I have about a million more questions for her, though, so I'm planning on coming back. Unless she makes me forget her too."

"I think it's too late. You've got an idea of her now."

"I'm not going to get used to that."

"I don't expect to either."

She leaned over in the car seat and gave him a long hug.

"Thanks for everything," she said. "And hey, we saved the world or something."

"I think we did," he said. "Thanks for being the best translator I could have asked for."

She kissed him on the cheek, and then climbed out.

Ed waved to Violet, and drove off.

Annie stood at the base of the steps for a time, just listening to her own breathing and appreciating the silence and isolation of the woods. Violet's cabin was a whole lot more appealing to her this time around. After the past couple of weeks, it was exactly what she needed.

"So," Violet said.

"So."

"I'm glad you came back."

"Yeah. Me too. I didn't really know where else to go, anyway. You're the only one who can understand. Plus, you're my best friend."

Violet came down the steps and hugged Annie, then leaned back and looked her in the eye for several seconds.

"He's still in there, isn't he?" she asked.

"I think I'm gonna burst. I need a chalkboard and a computer and a ton of paper and then you have to explain to me what all of it means, because I don't get half of it. But it's beautiful."

She smiled.

"I'll do my best. Are you hungry? I still have some of your food here."

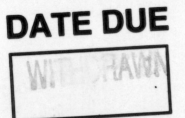